Dzogchen Teachings

on Mahayana and Vajrayana

by

Khenpo Sangpo Rinpoche

Translated by

Lama Changchub

Dzogchen Teachings
on Mahayana and Varjayana

By Khenpo Sangpo Rinpoche
Translated by Lama Changchub
Edited by Christian A. Stewart
Produced by Aksel Sogstad

First edition

ISBN 9798668679058

Foreword

The teachings in this book were given by Khenpo Sangpo Rinpoche during his visits to Karma Tashi Ling Buddhist Center in Norway from 2000 until 2018. Lama Changchub, resident lama of Karma Tashi Ling, served as translator.

Khenpo Sangpo belongs to one of the closest Dzogchen Longchen Nyingthig-lineages in the world, consisting of 1) All-knowing Jigme Lingpa, 2) Jigme Gyalwe Nyugu, 3) Migyur Namkhar Dorje (teacher of Patrul Rinpoche), 4) Orgyen Tenzin Norbu, 5) Shenpen Choki Nunwa, 6) Great Khenpo Yonten Gonpo, 7) Dzogchen Pema Kalsang Rinpoche, and 8) Khenpo Sangpo Rinpoche.

From childhood he has felt a special connection with Chenrezig (Skt. Avalokiteshvara, the Buddha of compassion) and Guru Rinpoche (Skt. Padmasambhava). As a young boy, he was recognized by Dilgo Khyentse Rinpoche as the fifth reincarnation of Gonzi Rinpoche. From the age of seven, Khenpo Sangpo started studying a wide range of Buddhist treatises. He then entered Dzogchen Shirasing Buddhist College to receive the supreme lineage of Nyingma teachings and traditions under the supervision of many accomplished and renowned masters, such as his root master Dzogchen Pema Kalsang Rinpoche, Padma Tsewang Rinpoche and Khenpo Dhazer. He obtained the honorable Khenpo degree with the very highest possible result in the short time of eight years, completing his studies with four years in retreat.

He started teaching at Dzogchen Shirasing Buddhist College before serving as abbot at the famous Samye Monastery for three years. This monastery was constructed by King Trisong Detsen and Guru Rinpoche in the 8th century and was Tibet's first Buddhist monastery.

Today, Rinpoche is a compassionate and accomplished Dzogchen master. He has established many centers in Taiwan,

Malaysia, and China, and has been invited to teach regularly in several countries, including Singapore, Japan, Nepal, Germany, the UK, Denmark, Spain, Sweden, and Norway. Rinpoche is tireless in his efforts to benefit people all over the world.

Part One of the book contains shorter teachings on various topics. They may serve as a good introduction to central topics in Tibetan Buddhism and Buddhism in general.

Part Two of the book contains three longer teachings. The first, Rinpoche's commentary on Lama Mipham's *The Gateway to Knowledge* is an essential part of the curriculum at Buddhist colleges in Tibet. This text presents ten topics for realizing ultimate reality. Some of us might have found it difficult to read the root text alone, as one can get lost in the long lists of scholastic classifications. Reading a commentary by an accomplished master such as Rinpoche may facilitate understanding.

The second teaching is a commentary on the second book of *The Trilogy of Rest* by Longchen Rabjam. Longchen Rabjam is regarded as the king of Dzogchen practice. His poetic expressions of realization are exceptional. He renounced worldly life completely and exerted a tremendous effort to attain the realization of Dzogchen and purify his mind through spiritual practice.

The last text in this collection, *View, Meditation, and Action in Mahayana and Vajrayana*, were given by Rinpoche in 2018. This teaching is spoken directly from Rinpoche's own experience and heart. The first part of the text explains the view of emptiness in the Madhyamika, as taught in the Buddha's Abidharma. Rinpoche recommends reading his commentary on *The Gateway to Knowledge*, pointing out that a good understanding of emptiness according to the Abidharma is a necessary foundation for understanding the higher tantric view expounded in his commentary on Patrul Rinpoche's commentary on Garab Dorje's *Hitting the Essence in Three Words*.

4

Rinpoche often states the importance of understanding the skandhas, our psychophysical aggregates, as he believes that this is the one thing that will help a practitioner the most. The skandhas are treated in various places in this book, for example, *The Four Logical Arguments*, the commentary on *The Gateway to Knowledge* as well as in the last teaching, *View, Meditation and Action in Mahayana and Vajrayana*.

Boyce Teoh assisted Lama Changchub with translating *View, Meditation and Action*. My wife, Berit Seem, also helped with proofreading this text. Christian A. Stewart, who has translated several books by Dzogchen Pema Kalsang Rinpoche, has served as editor. Any errors or misunderstanding are of course entirely my own.

Meeting Rinpoche and compiling these teachings has been a journey for which I am very grateful. I hope the efforts of this book will help transmit some of Rinpoche's clear insight, good humor and compassion, and that it will be an inspiration and benefit to everybody who reads it. The revenue from the book sales goes directly to Rinpoche's foundations.

Oslo, 22nd of July 2020
Aksel Sogstad

Content

Foreword 3

Part One: Shorter Teachings 9

Mindfulness of Mind 10

Shamatha Meditation 14

The Four Seals 21

The Six Disturbing Emotions 37

The Eleven Virtuous Factors 55

The Four Logical Arguments 64

The Four Foundations of Mindfulness 93

The Two Truths 111

The Great Perfection 122

Cho Practice 135

Part Two: Longer Teachings 147

Commentary on Lama Mipham's Gateway to Knowledge 148

Introduction 148

The Five Psychophysical Aggregates 149

The Eighteen Elements 165

The Twelve Sense Sources, the Ayatanas 172

Dependent Origination 172

The Correct and the Incorrect 188

The Faculties, Indriyas 195

Time 199

The Four Noble Truths 202

The Vehicles of Spiritual Paths 210

The Composite and Non-Composite 221

Final Words of the Teaching 229

Commentary on Longchen Rabjams's Finding Rest in Meditation...........230

   Introduction 230

   The Preliminary Practices...235

   The Actual Practices 247

   Questions and Answers 255

View, Meditation and Action in Mahayana and Vajrayana......................266

   View, Meditation and Action in Mahayana 266

   Commentary on Patrul Rinpoche's teaching on Hitting the Essence in Three Words...329

   Guru Yoga..378

   Conclusion...384

Part One: Shorter Teachings

Mindfulness of Mind

When we talk about mind or consciousness, we usually mean something unified, autonomous, permanent and eternal. But when we cultivate mindfulness of the mind, it turns out that we cannot find any basis for our usual interpretation of the mind. Instead, we are led to a totally different insight: the understanding of the impermanence and the interdependence of the mind — the fact that the mind is without a permanent self — that it is selfless.

Still, the mind is not a single unit, some kind of big lump. It can be classified into different collections of consciousnesses and the different mental events that spring from these. Therefore, when we talk about the mind, the term "mind" is simply a label, and the mind does not exist as a single unified entity at all.

The nature of mind is clarity and intelligence as a cognitive capacity. Because of the mind's selflessness, we can make it evolve to reach the culmination of enlightenment, or we can cause it to deteriorate. The mind is not stuck but can be made to change direction and go the other way. If we cultivate positive qualities, it can begin to move upwards; by growing negative attributes, it may start to move downwards.

Being mindful of the mind also allows us to understand and experience the interdependence of the mind. For instance, visual perception takes place when specific causes and conditions come together: the sense consciousness, sensory organs, and sensory objects. Three elements are needed to have visual perception. From a conventional point of view, consciousness comes into existence because of the assembly of these kinds of causes and conditions. But from the point of view of the true spiritual nature of phenomena, the ultimate nature, mind has never experienced birth, dwelling or cessation.

Ordinarily, most of us regard nirvana as something to be

pursued and samsara as something to be abandoned, and we see a person as an individual self that takes the journey from samsaric existence to nirvanic peace. But the fact is that there is no distance to cover between samsaric misery and the peace of nirvana because there is no place to go. The difference between samsara and nirvana is as simple as awareness and unawareness. Cultivating mindfulness of our phenomenal experience will produce insight into the selflessness of samsara as well as nirvana.

If we want to create a dream appearance, we do not need to travel somewhere else. Even if we think we are flying in our dream we are not going anywhere. In the same manner, from the perspective of samsara, there exists no other place we must reach. The term "peace of nirvana" or "enlightened state" is designated to an individual who has recognized the true nature of his or her mind. Samsaric misery occurs when the individual fails to acknowledge the true nature of the mind. So, the difference between samsara and nirvana is the difference between being awake and being asleep, or in other words, being aware and being unaware.

The individual meditator should also cultivate mindfulness of nirvanic peace, although the true nature of nirvanic peace is also empty of self. Grasping onto the reality of nirvana causes suffering in the same way as gripping onto the reality of samsara, just as falling off the right side of a horse causes the same kind of pain as falling off the left side. Only by cultivating mindfulness of the phenomenal existence of both samsara and nirvana will we realize the true nature of phenomenal life, which is that both samsara and nirvana are empty of self. Therefore, there can be no nirvana to pursue and no samsara to abandon, and there can be no individual who, as a permanent entity of self, needs to cover the distance from samsara to nirvana.

Kumbum Monastery is one of the most significant Gelugpa monasteries in eastern Tibet. As the story goes, there was a strict "disciplinarian monk" in this monastery who discovered some monks trying to smoke a pipe. The next day, during the usual gathering in the main hall, he stood up and spoke about the disadvantages of smoking. He then made the monks who were caught smoking stand up to humiliate them. But while he was doing this, a small pipe fell out of his own pocket. When he saw this, he started laughing and said, "It is not allowed to smoke a big pipe like yours, but it is allowed to smoke a small pipe like mine."

Of course, it is the same whether we smoke a small pipe or a big pipe. Whether we cultivate attachment to the reality of samsara or nirvana, it is the same. Do you have any questions?

Question: So, is not having a self like staying on the horse?

Answer: Having insight into the selflessness of the person is like being able to sit on the horse without falling into the extremes of nihilism, which is the left side, or eternalism, which is the right side. (Laughter.) But if we remain on the horse, and grasps onto the reality of the horse itself, this will also cause difficulties related to falling into the extreme of nirvanic peace. If we develop an attachment to the horse, the rider will suffer pain in his or her backside. I have experienced this myself in Tibet! (Laughter.)

Question: If you do something that you enjoy, and it is not harmful or positive — it is just something you like to do — how does this relate to selflessness?

Answer: The sensory object of our enjoyment, whatever it is, is not a valid criterion for whether it is something we should pursue or not. The actual test that determines whether an action will be positive or negative lies in the individual's mind as the mental motivation for acting. If we involve ourselves with sensory objects with a spirit free from the emotional reaction of attachment, then it does not matter. But if we end up cultivating the emotional response of attachment for the things we like, and aversion towards the things we do not like, we will become a victim of the experience.

The external world, with its sensory objects and grosser

forms of reality, does not possess the right criteria for something to be positive or negative. It is the state of the mind that is the exact criteria. It is a little bit like the gentle movement of a cat: it does not create any noise, but its mental state can be that of an aggressive predator.

Shamatha Meditation

Our compassionate teacher, the fully and perfectly enlightened Buddha, has revealed an infinite number of teachings so that we can overcome the limitations and afflictions of our minds. Two such essential teachings are tranquility meditation (Tib. shine, Skt. shamatha) and deep insight meditation (Tib. lhukthong, Skt. vipassana). Today I would like to give a talk on tranquility, or shamatha meditation.

All sentient beings naturally long for happiness and peace of mind. To be able to experience genuine peace of mind we should involve ourselves with true tranquility meditation. This has been proved over the centuries by many spiritual seekers and meditators. We need to prevent our minds from being distracted by the past or wandering to the future and instead set our mind single-pointedly on the object of meditation — the moment of here and now.

To be able to give rise to a genuine experience of tranquility meditation we must acquire many favorable causes and conditions. We do this by performing three preliminaries. The first preliminary is to find a suitable environment. A beginner meditator should choose a place with an atmosphere that will not be stressful and prevent him or her from accomplishing the practice of tranquility meditation. The outer atmosphere makes a lot of difference for the beginner meditator. For instance, I now live in a bustling city in Taiwan, but some time ago I went to visit Tibet, and because of the quiet atmosphere of Tibet I could at once experience the feeling of shamatha meditation. The calmness of the external atmosphere causes calmness of the inner mind. The second preliminary is to cultivate a sense of contentment, a sense of satisfaction, which is followed by less involvement in complex activities. Creating simplicity in our life causes calmness and simplicity in our mind as well. The third preliminary is to cultivate moral ethics. Pure behavior creates a pure mind.

To prepare for meditation, we should try to distance ourselves from mental, as well as external, busyness. Mental busyness is the inner noises and distractions that hinder us from cultivating meditation. Such distractions give rise to a lot of emotional complexities that disturb the mind. If we expect to be able to give rise to the genuine experience of meditation without having gone through the initial preparations, then we expect too much.

When we have fulfilled the requirements of the preliminaries, we should proceed with the actual meditation. The famous meditation teacher Kamalashila suggested that we should adopt an eight-point posture. This posture corresponds very much to the seven-point posture of Buddha Vairochana. First, we should straighten our back. Second, assume a fully cross-legged position, or if this is not possible, use the half-crossed posture. Third, calm the consciousness by gazing at the space in front along the angle of the nose. Fourth, place the shoulders evenly. Fifth, relax the jaw with only a small gap between the teeth. Sixth, let the tip of the tongue touch the pallet. This last point will prevent excessive production of saliva, and quiet the consciousness that relates to the tongue. Seventh, breathe as naturally as possible. And last, eighth, direct the gaze at the object of meditation, for example, a Buddha statue or a small stone.

We then proceed to visualize all enlightened beings, including our masters, in front of ourselves and offers a supplication prayer to experience favorable causes and conditions and become free of difficulties by performing the tranquility meditation. The supplication to the invoked energies of the buddhas and bodhisattvas is called the seven-branch prayer.

We then try to simplify our body and consciousness as much as possible and to look directly into the non-fabricated state of our mind. We then discover complex emotional states such as anger, attachment, desire, dullness, jealousy, pride and so on. The predominance of these emotional afflictions will vary according to the individual. One person may be afflicted by anger, another by jealousy, some are more attached and so on. This is due to the infinite number of past lives that have conditioned our minds in various ways. When we look directly at the mind and discover one of these predominant complexities, we should seize that complexity with meditative awareness. It is essential to instantly recognize the significant "troublemaker" that hinders us from meditation.

If we investigate the state of our mind and discovers that our predominant emotional complexity is desire, the Buddha has described three methods that can be used to deal with this emotional complexity. The first method consists of contemplating on impurity, the second method is contemplating on ugliness, and the third method consists of contemplating on the skeleton.

Reflection on impurity is done by reflecting on our body. By contemplating, we will discover many essentially impure substances within our body, for example, bones, puss and so on. Buddha said that there exist thirty-six of such substances altogether. By going through all of these, we contemplate on the physical substances that relate to our physical existence. This will lessen the attachment of desire that was identified as the predominant complexity.

Contemplation on ugliness is done by contemplating on a corpse. This can be done by approaching an actual physical corpse, or it can be done by visualizing a corpse within our mind. The point is to develop some renunciation. Altogether, the Buddha has prescribed nine different ways of contemplating on ugliness, for example the meditation on a rotten corpse, but we do not need to go into detail about these meditations here.

The contemplation on impurity and ugliness is followed by contemplation on the skeleton, beginning with our own. We start by imagining a bare area of bone between the eyebrows. This area then expands all over the body to reveal the skeleton, which then grows to fill the entire universe, and the whole world becomes made of bone. The visualized skeleton is then withdrawn and contracts into itself, disappearing at the level of the feet. At this point, it stands itself up and then becomes a normal skeleton, which then gradually becomes covered with flesh again, and everything returns to normal. This contemplation can be done in the same way as the movement of the sun causes the shadows to move.

Meditation upon these three aspects will temporarily prevent attachment to the desire for physical sensations of color, shape, and touch. The method will not uproot desire completely but offers a favorable ground for cultivating the genuine experience of shamatha and insight meditation. The cause of the desire will only be uprooted entirely when the meditator is genuinely able to give rise to the simultaneous meditation experience of shamatha and deep insight meditation.

If by looking directly at the state of our mind, we discover that the main affliction is the emotional complexity of anger or aversion, we should try to cultivate love and compassion as an antidote to temporarily suppress this anger.

If we discover that our mind is preoccupied with dullness or indifference, the Buddha suggested meditating on the twelve links of interdependent origination one after another, as well as backwards, from the last to the first.

If our mind is predominantly occupied by the emotional complexity of pride, the Buddha suggested meditating on the classifications on the eighteen elements of the phenomena, in order to temporarily suppress this.

If our mind is predominated by discursive thoughts, the Buddha suggested using meditation techniques that utilize awareness on the breath. The mind is said to be the primary existence compared to other phenomena. Directing our mind toward the breath is therefore important because it makes the mind more flexible. One method of breath meditation is, to begin with breathing naturally through the nose, counting one inhalation and exhalation as one cycle, going up to ten cycles without forgetting to count and being mindful of the breath.

Another method is, as we breath out, to let our consciousness ride on the horse of the exhalation and likewise when we breathe in.

A third meditation method connected with the breath is to visualize a thread of light uncoiling from the nostrils while we exhale. The light thread uncoils all the way down to our feet. As we inhale, the light thread goes back up into our nose. We should also visualize the entire body being filled with the energy of the breath, all the way from the nose, through the interior part of the body down to the feet. As we exhale from the nose, conceive that the breath comes all the way from the feet up through the body and then out of the nose. When we breathe in and the breath descends within the body, we should conceive that our consciousness becomes more grounded as the air energy falls toward the feet. We should develop a sense of steadfastness—feeling wholly pacified. Inhaling, we should conceive that we inhale all the pure energies of the air. By involving ourselves with these meditations, we have a good chance of calming a disturbed mind and making it into a peaceful ocean free from agitated waves.

Question: Can you say some more on the meditation on the corpse?

Answer: I talked about nine of the contemplations as antidotes to temporarily suppress the emotional complexity of attachment to desire. This teaching is from the general vehicle of the Buddha's teachings. From the perspective of the tantric approach, there is a different way of dealing with such complexities. Instead of suppressing the emotional complexities just temporarily, we can liberate them in their own place from the very beginning. We must bear in mind that this was taught from the perspective of the general vehicle. From the perspective of tantra, we do not involve ourselves with ideas such as the impurity of the body of ourselves or others. The tantric teaching of Buddhism suggests that we should regard our body as the mandala of the fully enlightened Buddha and all enlightened beings. So, there is no mention of impurities, dirt and so on.

The Buddha taught this specific meditation to help ordinary people distance themselves temporarily from attachments. When he explained this for the first time, many of his followers, among many of whom were monks, nuns and serious, intense practitioners who did not have a particular problem with desire, practiced so much on revulsion for the body that they became suicidal. So, the Buddha had to give new teaching to counteract this mistake.

These specific contemplations, the thirty-six impure substances of the body and the nine disgusting states of the corpse, are associated with the first turning of the wheel of the Dharma, and more particularly with the first of the four noble truths that the Buddha taught—the truth of suffering. The contemplation that we went through is closely related to this suffering.

Question: Is it necessary to start with this form of practice or is it a matter of choice?

Answer: Generally, it is excellent and skillful to follow the gradual path, rather than trying to jump directly to shamatha meditation. If we try this without going through the preliminaries, it is not likely that we will manage to do a proper meditation. Attachment to the emotional complexities acts as a stumbling block for meditation on calm meditation.

Question: The antidotes for pride and arrogance are to meditate on the eighteen classifications of the different elements. What are they and how does meditating on them reduce ego?

Answer: In Buddhism, the elements are classified into the six sense organs, the six consciousnesses of these, and the six types of objects that are identified by the consciousnesses—making eighteen altogether. With all the subclasses, this is a complex subject, and trying to grasp the sheer complexity of it all will temporarily suppress our arrogance.

The Four Seals

First, I would like to express my greetings and regards to all of you present here today. I am delighted you are able to be here, especially those of you who arranged this course and those who have prepared your spiritual path with a certain amount of study, listening, and reflection that has given rise to faith. Not blind faith, but faith based on analysis and investigation of Buddha's teachings.

All sentient beings, and particularly human beings, long and search for happiness and joy. From the perspective of Buddhism and the teachings of Buddha, joy is twofold, mental joy and physical joy. Of these two, mental joy is more important since it can give rise to physical joy.

The enlightened being known as Buddha has revealed numerous enlightened teachings to grant us happiness and inner peace. Whether these teachings are a cause for experiencing more profound levels of inner peace depends on our ability as individual seekers and practitioners to scrutinize and analyze the teachings and validate them in our own life.

The teachings given by Buddha are infinite in number but can be summarized in what is called The Four Seals. Since some of you attending this talk seem to be new to the teachings of the Buddha, I would like to present a summary of these teachings in the context of the seals.

Generally, all experiences can be classified into external phenomenal experiences and internal phenomenal experiences. What do we mean by internal phenomenal experience? All the phenomenal experiences that are experienced by our mind are referred to as internal phenomenal experience. And what do we mean by external phenomenal experience? External phenomena are defined as inanimate objects or matter not embraced by a stream of consciousness as opposed to internal phenomena which are embraced by consciousness. This is the original definition.

Whether we experience internal or external phenomenal existence or experience, all phenomenal experiences or existences come into being through the aggregation or the composition of many causes and conditions. If phenomena are produced by these combinations of causes and conditions, Buddhism asserts that these phenomena are also subject to change and impermanence, precisely because the phenomena are only collections.

The impermanence that pertains to both internal and external experiences is twofold: subtle impermanence and gross impermanence. Most of us understand the changes caused by the gross aspects of impermanence. Such changes are changes of weather during the four seasons, changes in material objects, and changes in physical existence when experiencing illness and pain, and so forth. All these substantial changes that take place are regarded as the gross aspect of impermanence. Why is it important to understand the gross form of impermanence as it relates to all kinds of phenomenal experience? Let us say, for example, that we possess some gross material property. If that possession is embraced by the understanding of impermanence applied to the property itself, we can enjoy and utilize our property without becoming a victim of that property or possession if it is separated from us. On the contrary, if we try to indulge ourselves with our physical possessions without an understanding of the impermanence of these passions, then grasping at the permanence of these objects will create a contradiction between our state of mind and the object, whose basic nature is impermanence. When the object becomes broken or lost, we will become victims.

If we understand the teachings of the Buddha on impermanence, then clinging onto the self will not develop, no matter what kind of social status we have, even if we are very wealthy and have good looks, because we understand the law of impermanence also applies to these things as well. In the same manner, we will not develop a sense of contempt for other sentient beings. On the contrary, an individual who has contemplated the teachings of the Buddha on the law of impermanence will begin to develop a sense of closeness, concern and respect for all forms of living creatures.

Additionally, if we have a partner, and if we bring the understanding of impermanence into that romantic relationship, the relationship will be enhanced by understanding the law of impermanence rather than letting the relationship deteriorate. So, the understanding of impermanence enhances a relationship even on that level. Why? Because if we cultivate the understanding of impermanence within our mind while having a relationship with a romantic partner, we will value the other person and respect the relationship itself, and we will try to contribute to that relationship to the best of our ability. We are aware that impermanence can occur at any moment and interrupt that relationship. So, before the law of impermanence shatters the relationship, we can decide to live life to the full in that relationship. One of the Buddhist mystics has said that "The law of impermanence also embraces family members. They will all experience the law of impermanence, the law of change. The gathering of family members and relatives is like a gathering of a crowd in the marketplace. The crowd can disperse and part at any moment."

Thus, if we familiarize ourselves with the understanding of the law of impermanence, as the Buddha taught, we will attain a transformation that will give us the experience of inner peace. This is also my personal experience.

The second aspect of impermanence, subtle impermanence, is as the name suggests, difficult to detect and understand. Take, for example, my body. When you observe me talking to you, you are not able to observe the minute changes occurring within my body. These minute changes constantly occur moment to moment and are referred to as subtle changes or subtle impermanence. Our perceptions delude us because we are not able to detect these changes, and our observations do not correspond with the subtle changes that are continually occurring on the physical level. The body is just an example. The concept could also be applied to every inner and outer phenomenal experience an individual undergoes.

No exceptional phenomenal experiences exist that are not subject to the minute changes that occur moment by moment. The first moment cannot last and is superseded by the second moment, and the second moment by the third, and so on. There seems to be no entity that can remain fixed and unaffected by subtle changes.

Ordinary individuals will usually be unable to understand or detect these subtle changes intuitively. However, those who are spiritually developed can detect and understand the subtle changes that are occurring within and without. In addition, it seems that scientists can observe parts of these subtle changes. Maybe they are not able to detect the overall nature or totality of the subtle changes, but when it comes to grasping minute changes, they can do so.

We can draw upon the examples of a flame and a river to understand this concept. A flame seems to the conventional eye to be a singular phenomenon, as does a river. But the fact is that neither a flame nor a river is a singular phenomenon. There is a constant change occurring within a flame as well as within a river. The flame that is produced in one instant is exhausted in the next. Similarly, for the individual, the flow of a river seems singular and independent, but the truth is that lasts year's river has gone far, far away, replaced now by so many new streams. We are not able to see the minute changes that are occurring within a river or a flame because the gaps between the instants of different flames and the instants of different rivers or any other phenomenon are so minute and ongoing.

To illustrate the difference between the wisdom of ordinary beings, and the superior wisdom of highly evolved spiritual beings like bodhisattvas, we can use two examples. To illustrate ordinary wisdom, we can use the analogy of our hands. To illustrate superior wisdom, we use the example of our eyes. The difference between ordinary and superior wisdom is like the difference between our eyes and our hands. If we place a single hair in the palm of our hand, we will not be able to feel the sensation. But if we place that single hair into our eye, we will immediately feel the sensation — and it will be an intense sensation. The wisdom of highly evolved spiritual beings is sensitive like an eye. They can perceive and detect not only the grosser level of impermanence or change but also the subtle level of impermanence or change. Somebody who has attained such sensitive intelligence, such vulnerable wisdom, can enjoy every possession without falling victim to any of them, whereas an individual with ordinary wisdom will at some point become a victim of their property.

Suffering comes about because our state of mind, or our attitude or perspective, does not correspond to the actual situation, external object, or phenomenon. The true nature of the appearance is that of change, but our attitude is only one of clinging to permanence and static phenomena. Because of our misinterpretation, our attitude toward any phenomenal experience will not correspond to the true nature of that experience, and that non-correspondence becomes the cause of pain and suffering.

Up to this point we have talked about the first seal, impermanence. The first teaching that Buddha gave in The Four Seals was that all phenomenal existence or phenomenal experiences are impermanent and subject to change. The second seal that Buddha explained was that all contaminated phenomenal experiences are subject to pain. Whatever defiled phenomena, polluted, or contaminated phenomenal experiences that occupy our minds becomes an occupation of conceptual and superstitious thoughts that will prevent us from further spiritual development. We can say that these experiences "pull us down." The exact definition of the expression "defiled phenomena" is the experience when our mind is occupied with thoughts and emotions and then starts to deteriorate.

The various kinds of defiled phenomena are numerous,

but here we can draw on just the one example of the defiled phenomena of anger or aggression. For example, if we as Buddhist practitioners give rise to an emotion of intense violence and aggression, then we should view the emergence of such a complex of emotional anger and aggression as negative and destructive for our self and others. Because of the negative consequences, it is a mistake to allow ourselves to give rise to such destructive emotional complications.

We can be someone who possesses good looks, but the very moment we give rise to very intense emotional anger or aggression, we do no longer look like a beautiful person. A mind in an ugly state of being will affect the appearance of the body as well. Not only is the physical appearance of such a person changed, but also the speech is affected, and communication with others will be unfruitful, or even very destructive and negative. So, whenever we give rise to the emotional thought of intense anger or aggression, we should try to utilize the mental factor known as "mindfulness" or "awareness" and catch hold of the emotion of anger. We should also work to understand that the true nature of this emotion as not useful. It is destructive. This knowledge alone will inspire us to do away with negative emotions, such as anger and aggression. This is precisely the reason why the second seal states that all defiled phenomenal experiences bring pain and suffering.

The Buddha expressed the third seal as "All phenomenal existence and experience is empty, as well as empty of self." All phenomenal experiences are summarized by the five psychophysical aggregates: Form, feelings, perceptions, mental formations, and consciousness. These five psychophysical aggregates are empty of personal self. No personal self can be found within the five psychophysical constituents. By grasping onto the notion of a self, a person will support defiled phenomenal experiences.

In Tibet, there is an expression that says if you hear a loud noise created by falling water, you can be sure that the water must have hit something hard. Similarly, if there are a lot of psychological and emotional complications in our minds, there must be some substance from which all this inner noise is produced. This substance is called grasping onto the notion of the existence of a self. If there is a big gathering and we hear a shout, we can assume that there must be somebody doing the shouting. Similarly, there must be a fundamental force behind all psychological complications. This force is the belief in the notion of a self.

If we have given rise to the emotional complication of anger, we should immediately scrutinize and question this anger. Who is the one experiencing this anger? Who is producing this anger? Toward whom is the anger directed? Look into yourself as someone who has given rise to the thought of anger and try to find out if you exist independently as a self, as the individual who has given rise to this thought. Similarly, inquire also into the objects at which the anger is directed. Does this object or person exist naturally as an independent entity? If we reflect in this manner when we give rise to the thought of anger, the impact of the thought of anger will be lessened immediately. The reason is that there does not exist an entity known as the self of the person that gives rise to the anger.

We are familiar with the concept of a self. Usually, when we say "I" this is like establishing the existence of a self, but we must inquire into the efficacy of this concept. Where does this self exist? Does it exist in our body or in connection with our body? Or does it exist in our mind or in connection with our mind? Try to analyze further whether the self of the person is the same as the body or separate from the body. If the self of the person is posited based on our physical existence, then our physical existence is manifold in the same way as we have several limbs. So, there arises a difficulty when we posit the existence of a self based on physical existence. We may then assert that the self is not identical to our body but is something completely different from the body. This conclusion also creates difficulties because we cannot pinpoint a separate existence of the self of a person other than the physical appearance of the person itself. Similarly, we can apply the same reasoning not only to our body but also to our consciousness.

This form of reasoning is called the reasoning of identity and non-identity. Applying the same reasoning to our mind, we will discover that there neither exists a self which is the same as our consciousness nor a self that is different from our consciousness. In this manner, we can prove that the self of the person does not exist in connection with our body or in connection with our mind. There still exists a conventional self which experiences joy and happiness, and pain and suffering. So, the concept is somewhat like saying the self does not exist, but there exists something else which experiences happiness and suffering.

Dream experiences obviously do not exist other than as mental projections of the person dreaming. So, while we are dreaming and experiencing, all kinds of dream appearances occur. If we can recognize our dream at that moment, we are having a lucid dream, and we will not take the dream as a reality. So therefore, we can be liberated from nightmarish dreams. So, if we gain insight into the emptiness of the self and base our activities on this idea, then none of our activities will cause any form of suffering, but instead produce pure joy and peace.

The fourth seal as spoken by the Buddha is "nirvana is peace." The term nirvana in Tibetan can be translated as "transcending suffering." The difference between Buddha Shakyamuni, who transcended beyond the suffering, and those who have not done likewise and are still submerged in the suffering of cyclic existence, samsara, is small. The difference is that of mistakenness and non-mistakenness. One of the famous teachers of Tibetan Buddhism, Longchen Rabjam, has given an example of this difference in one of his essential writings. He asks us to imagine an incredibly beautiful mansion occupied by two persons — one possessing supernatural perception, the other completely asleep. The person sleeping is experiencing a complicated dream, and because of this dream, the person suffers. On the other hand, the person who sits next to him, who is not dreaming and is completely awake, is able to see everything that unfolds in the mind of the sleeping person. So, the person who is not sleeping is in a very favorable situation; he is residing in a magnificent mansion and surrounded by many beautiful objects. The person who is awake and possesses supernatural perception is a spiritually awakened being. The person who is fast asleep is a person who is unenlightened and residing in the wilderness of samsara.

This story illustrates that the mind of every being, whether we are enlightened or not, awake or completely asleep, inherent possesses what is known as the Buddha potential. At any moment we can actualize this inherent nature. From the perspective of Buddhism, there is not a big difference between somebody who is enlightened and someone who is unenlightened. Unenlightened beings are those which are taken care of in Buddhism. They are looked upon as those to be cherished and taken care of, beings to be looked after and be concerned about. A person who is awake will try his best to wake up the person who is asleep and going through all kinds of nightmarish dreams. The activity of the Buddha is nothing other than simply counteracting the sleep, so we can wake up completely. Still, it is difficult for an enlightened being to awaken us or shatter our dreams because we are so deeply asleep.

For the person asleep in the beautiful mansion, everything seems to be impure because of their inner turmoil. But for the person who is completely awake, there is no room for impure appearances because the person sees the suchness of reality free from ignorance.

The first and second seals state that all composite phenomena are subject to change and that all defiled phenomena cause pain. These two seals establish relative or conventional truth. The last two seals — that all phenomenal existence is empty and empty of self and that nirvana is peace — establish ultimate truth. Here ends the presentation of the four seals. If you have any questions, please ask them now.

Question: If the mind is the instrument of our investigation, and our mind is constantly changing, how can we trust what we find?

Answer: The true nature of our mind is not disturbing emotions. The mind can be occupied with such emotions, but these emotions are not its true nature. And our mind is not always occupied with disturbing emotions. The fundamental quality of our mind becomes more dominant when our mind is not subject to disturbing emotions. The fundamental quality of our mind is clarity and intelligence. These qualities can be utilized to look at the mind itself.

Question: Will an enlightened person view a natural catastrophe and a human catastrophe as being empty?

Answer: An enlightened being experiences a natural catastrophe in exactly the way I described earlier. Enlightened beings view the natural catastrophe to be empty of self. But to the human beings who are the victim of this catastrophe, the disaster is real. This sense of reality is because the person is still spiritually asleep. However, the enlightened being will develop a tremendous sense of loving-kindness and compassion toward the people who are experiencing such catastrophes.

Question: Do you mean that the enlightened being does not experience all the pain of a natural catastrophe?

Answer: The enlightened person can see, feel and sense the suffering of each living sentient being. As in the previous example we looked at the person who was sleeping and experiencing nightmares, the person who is awake will try to help the person who is asleep—help him or her to wake up. Here we can talk about the unity of compassion and emptiness. The enlightened person sees the selflessness of the person and the tragedy. At the same time, his or her mind is full of compassion and concern.

Question: Is an enlightened person at the same time compassionate and detached?

Answer: In Buddhism, we can strive for personal liberation, or we can strive for what is known as universal liberation. Mahayana Buddhism is the pursuit of universal liberation. The intent is to liberate every being from their limitations. So, if we are someone who follows the first approach, we will become enlightened according to that tradition. But we will not be capable of helping others very much. As for helping ourselves, we have already been helped by gaining individual liberation. With the second approach, not only are we able to help ourselves, we are also able to help many other beings in terms of liberating them from their conditions, weaknesses, and so forth by revealing spiritual insight to them. There is a technical term that describes this state of universal liberation. It is called abiding neither in the extreme of nirvana or in the extreme of samsara. It refers to a complete and perfect state in which there is neither the extreme of pain nor the extreme of peace.

Insight into the selflessness of the person or phenomena enables us to attain nirvana. When we then practice loving-kindness and compassion, we achieve an altruistic state of mind that prevents us from remaining in the extreme of nirvana for sole benefit to the self. The enlightened being is drawn into helping the sentient beings and society.

Question: The Dharma says that a belief in a self is the root of our suffering and that this belief forms the basis of all the emotions. Can you explain how this belief comes about?

Answer: Grasping onto the concept of a self comes about because of basic ignorance. Ignorance is not able to understand the selfless state of mind and phenomena. This fundamental ignorance will give rise to the defiled emotions that arise because of a distorted view of reality. We cannot dream if we cannot sleep, right? Similarly, if there is no basic ignorance, there will be no grasping of the self.

Question: So, it is as you said in the beginning, that the way in which we see things and the way things are do not correspond. Is that where the trouble starts?
Answer: There is the appearance, and there is the nature of things. We know the presumed appearance. As for the essence of the appearance, we do not know it. The mind that is ignorant of the true nature of the essence of the appearance grasps onto the existence of a self.

Question: How do we come to this understanding?
Answer: To liberate ourselves from samsaric pain, we should meditate on the selflessness of persons and phenomena. However, in order to liberate ourselves from falling into the extreme of nirvanic peace, we should meditate on loving-kindness and compassion. By practicing these two approaches of meditation, we will be prevented from falling into either extreme.

Question: I am a psychologist, and I work with people in my everyday life. One of my main tasks is to try to make people think in another way — another way of perceiving themselves and situations. One of the practices of psychology is to get to know ourselves. I have seen how difficult it is to do so. Many people are very frightened by getting to know themselves. So, in a way, they choose to be in a samsaric state and suffer, rather than taking a different approach where they would be better equipped to deal with their suffering. If you have some good ideas about this concept, I would like to hear them. Can you also comment on this aspect concerning what you said about the third seal?
Answer: The third seal states that phenomena are empty and void of a self. The emptiness of phenomenal existence should be understood as meaning the psychophysical aggregates are empty of a self. There is no self to be found anywhere in or among these aggregates. If we want to

effectively employ the selflessness of persons, then we should apply the seven stages of reasoning found in the Buddhist Middle Way School. The seven-point logical reasoning is quite difficult to grasp because it is very subtle. It can be summarized into what I just talked about — the reasoning of identity and non-identity.

When we say, "my head," the immediate concept we get from the statement is the picture of a simple head. But if we analyze further, we cannot find such a single head. We are not able to discover, by such analysis, a single unitary autonomous independent head. The head is empty! (Laughter.)

Question: How does this example apply to the example you gave on aggression?

Answer: It is quite easy to apply this example to the emotional complication of anger. If somebody says, "You are terrible!" our immediate reaction will be aversion and dislike for that person. The reason is because we still grasp onto the notion of self. So instead of reacting with anger to this person, the person deserves compassion. This person has no understanding of the emptiness of the self of the person. The person is therefore completely ignorant of the reality, and based on that ignorance, is saying something which is abusive to us. But if we understand emptiness ourselves, we will see that the person deserves loving kindness and compassion.

Buddha said that since everything is empty, everything is interdependent. When we understand the emptiness of self, we can easily understand the interdependency of every phenomenon. Then we naturally appreciate others because a human being depends on others and the environment to survive. This is how the understanding of interdependency occurs. That understanding comes from the understanding of selflessness and gives rise to the altruistic mind, which will then take care of fellow human beings and the environment.

Question: Does this explanation mean that anger will

disappear because I have this interdependence and altruistic feeling?

Answer: If we understand Buddha's teaching on interdependence than we will naturally be able to liberate ourselves from emotional anger. If we give rise to anger and react to this anger, it will create consequences, and the effects of violence are not necessarily pleasant, but usually rather destructive. Since our basic longing is to avoid pain and to experience peace, such an action is contradictory to achieving this fundamental goal. We will not then contribute toward something that will fulfill our basic longing. By reasoning and understanding in this way, anger will liberate by itself.

Question: You said that the Buddha is constantly trying to wake us up. How can we help?

Answer: We can help an enlightened being by being receptive. Another way of helping the enlightened being when the enlightened being tries to wake us up is to help other sentient beings. Still another way is not to resist when an enlightened being tries to disturb our sleep.

Question: Can you understand "empty of self" as "empty of consciousness"?

Answer: There is a vast difference between emptiness of consciousness and emptiness of self. By asserting emptiness of self, we do not mean emptiness of consciousness. But a person can wrongly perceive the piece of rope as a snake. This misperception came from the sense of self.

Question: I have difficulty understanding. On the one hand, you say that we should try to do away with all negative emotions, polluted states of mind and all that. But on the other side, in meditation, are you not supposed to be open to these things?

Answer: To suit the different needs of different beings, Buddha presented many different techniques such as sutra and tantra. The different way of relating to our emotions is the difference between the presentation of the teachings according to the sutra and the tantra tradition. According to the sutra tradition, Buddha states that we need to renounce disturbing emotions. However, according to the tantra tradition, Buddha says that we do not need to abandon such feelings, that we can utilize their presence and transform them onto our spiritual path. If the wisdom of the path embraces disturbing emotions or afflictive states of mind, all disturbing emotions will be changed and used as a benefit to our spiritual practice, according to the tantric presentation.

Question: Would you say that one of these approaches is easier than the other? It seems very tiresome to spend the entire time trying to push such emotions away, like trying to be somebody I am not. It seems easier when I can relax sometimes with the negative emotions.

Answer: There is no general answer to your question. I cannot say that this approach is suitable for you, or that another approach is not suitable. The different techniques were presented by the Buddha to suit the different mental dispositions, spiritual inclinations and diverse interests of all sentient beings. So, we cannot generalize.

Generally, we regard something impure as something which is no good. By something impure I mean, for example, human or animal excrement. We do not like it. But if it is utilized skillfully and intelligently, this waste can be used as fertilizer to produce a good harvest. So, within the tantric approach, if our disturbing emotion is embraced by intelligence, the disturbing emotions will act as useful manure and give rise to inner spiritual blossoming.

As an analogy, to defeat or subdue an external enemy, there are two methods we can use. We can kill the enemy, or we can win the enemy over. In the tantric teaching, we try to win the enemy over.

Question: Is perhaps one reason that we have difficulty in realizing nirvana is that we are afraid, or we do not believe that it exists?

Answer: The reason why nirvana seems to be rare is due to how we approach nirvana. Obtaining nirvana is not impossible; it is our approach that is inadequate. Usually, when we approach a spiritual path, we are not very honest in our approach. Even when we enter meditation, we want to experience some mental pacification, so we can overcome our tension and become active in competing at work or school or in relationships. These are small goals, and such meditation will not bring us closer to enlightenment or the attainment of nirvana. Many people are interested in meditation because they experience a lot of tension in society. They want to escape the confrontation of society. Such an attitude will not bring us closer to nirvana.

It is essential to precede meditation with contemplation of Buddha's teachings. The contemplation of the teachings should be preceded by proper study and listening to provide a basis for our reflection. People who are young should emphasize the approach of listening and studying, and then later reflect and meditate. If our spiritual practice is conducted in this manner, it will create wellbeing for our mind and the minds of others, and we will become able to perform beneficial activities. We should have a broad scope of mind and try to embrace every living sentient being with loving-kindness and compassion. We should not just aim to attain individual liberation and only think about ourselves.

If there are no more questions, I will now conclude this session. I would like to thank every one of you who have made an effort to develop spiritually. Thank you for being here today. Tashi delek!

The Six Disturbing Emotions

Day One

As spiritual aspirants, our main spiritual goal is to generate a compassionate and intelligent mind. Therefore, it is crucial to precede the teaching by creating the altruistic mind of bodhicitta.

Every individual has the goal of attaining happiness. Whatever action we pursue, whether spiritual or worldly, we do so by hoping to achieve happiness. According to the Buddha, the sources of joy are the generation of a loving and compassionate attitude and a wise mind. The purpose of engaging in Dharma practice is to attain a more profound level of peace and happiness.

The obstructions to a mind of love and compassion in union with wisdom are a discursive mind and disturbing emotions. Disturbing emotions are infinite. Forget about the disturbing emotions that we have been generating since time immemorial. The disturbing emotions we have been experiencing since this morning are enough.

The Buddha expounded the eighty-four thousand tenets with the intention to work with the eighty-four thousand varieties of conflicting discursive thoughts and emotions that we generate. In order to subdue the mind that entertains the disturbing emotions of attachment and desire, the Buddha expounded the twenty-one thousand tenets of the Vinaya teachings that deal with moral ethics. The essence of these teachings is to subdue our mind. In order to subdue hatred, the Buddha expounded twenty-one thousand tenets of Sutra teachings. In order to subdue indifference, the Buddha expounded twenty-one thousand teachings related to the Abhidharma (the wisdom teachings of the Buddha). These are the three baskets of the Buddhas teaching (Skt. Tripitaka). So, the teachings of the Buddha consist of Sutra, Vinaya and Abhidharma. These entail training in moral ethics, concentration and wisdom.

For a morally ethical person, the experience of meditation of samadhi will dawn spontaneously. A person with a mind blessed by samadhi will naturally experience wisdom. The most important practice in the beginning is therefore the Vinaya, moral ethics. In the middle of the practice, concentration is crucial. Then finally, the practice of wisdom is essential. The practices of moral ethics and meditative concentration can be compared to the rungs of a ladder. Without the first rung we cannot climb to the second or third.

Moral ethics relate to the body, the speech, and the mind. The moral ethics associated with the body and speech are practiced so that the mind can also practice moral ethics. For example, the purpose of building a house is to reside inside that house. When we observe moral ethics with our body and speech, we do so primarily in order to attain peace and harmony within our mind. The person residing within a properly constructed house will not suffer from extreme cold or heat.

To observe the practice of moral ethics regarding our body, speech, and mind, we must understand what should be abandoned and what should be cultivated. The Buddha has explained that as soon as we generate discursive thoughts or conflicting emotions, we will experience misery. In contrast, as soon as we create harmonious thoughts and attitudes, we will experience peace and harmony.

The Buddha described discursive thoughts and disturbing emotions. If there is a variety of dishes on a table, and some of those dishes are poisoned, it is important to know which dishes are poisoned.

Prior to our enlightenment, we possess mind (Tib. sem). As long as we possess mind, it will be filled with discursive thoughts. As an example, our mind is like our stomach. When we feel hunger, we need to eat. If we consume food tainted with poison, the poison will affect the stomach, but if we chose the right food, our stomach will be comfortable. Given the choice of negative or positive emotions, we should choose positive. If we pursue spirituality in terms of cultivating pure thoughts or pure emotions, meditative concentration will follow. But if we entertain disturbing thoughts and emotions, the possibility of meditative concentration is remote.

In the following example, our mind is compared to a guesthouse and the discursive thoughts, positive or negative, are its guests. When we receive good guests, everything will be in order. But if a bad guest arrives, then everything will be a mess. Nevertheless, none of the visitors are the guesthouse. They are the guests. If positive emotions and thoughts arise in our mind, would you say that these are our mind? Most people would say no. In the same way, if negative thoughts and emotions arise, then these are also not our mind.

The real mind is free from fabrication. The practice of moral ethics is crucial for beginners, to shut the door to negative thoughts and emotions and to open it to positive thoughts and emotions. But finally, if we practice moral ethics, there will be nothing to cultivate and nothing to abandon. If we only allow our mind to rest in this original purity, this is the highest form of moral ethics.

According to the previous example where our mind is compared to a guest house and the positive and negative thoughts are compared to good and bad visitors, then as the host of the guest house, we should be very mindful about what kind of guest we invite. If we allow disreputable visitors, then those guests will probably steal from our house. Therefore, we must be vigilant. Without controlling negative thoughts and emotions, they will become stronger with time. But if we do not invite these negative emotions to our guesthouse, then their power will weaken and fade away. To be able to recognize these bad guests, we need to know the six root disturbing emotions. They are termed "root" because they are a source of all other negative emotions.

The first root disturbing emotion is ignorance. When our mind does not correspond with reality but holds a distorted notion, our mind is ignorant.

For example, the suffering that we undergo is initiated by ignorance. The disturbing emotion of attachment or desire acts out the intention of the disturbing emotion of ignorance. For example, ignorance can be compared to Adolf Hitler who instigated the Second World War. Hitler's ministers can be compared to the disturbing emotion of desire and attachment.

Ignorance should be understood in terms of not understanding reality. The ignorant mind entertains the notion of a true independent existence. The actual meaning of the ultimate truth is empty of self, but our ignorant mind does not comprehend this. We should attain a decisive conclusion that holding onto the notion of true independent existence is the source of all the misery of samsara and strive towards cutting that notion as much as possible. If we doubt this, we should study and contemplate the teaching of the Buddha further to arrive at the conclusion of emptiness of the true independent existence. If we then still believe in the existence of the self, then consult the great Indian masters such as Nagarjuna and Chandrakirti who presented an analytical method of discovering the selflessness of the "I".

Many of us believe in the existence of a solid separate independent ego or "I". Based on this if we superficially pursue the path of emptiness and try to convince our mind that nothing exists as far as the "I" is concerned, this will not have any impact. For example, if we are sitting directly in front of a fire with our eyes closed and try to convince ourselves that this fire is not hot, we will never manage to do so because we know that the fire is hot. If we mediate without having attained certainty about the emptiness of the self, this would be like the Tibetan proverb of a fox trying to leap like a lion — the fox will end up breaking its back. When bodhisattvas meditate on the selflessness of the ego, they do this because of having understood the emptiness of the self. But if we meditate on emptiness without having understood the meaning of the emptiness of self, it can be compared with the proverb of the fox. To overcome the root disturbing emotion of ignorance, we need to meditate on its antidote, meditation on the emptiness of self.

If we pursue meditation by having correctly understood suchness, reality as it is, then such meditation can be compared to the Dzogchen trekcho ("cutting through"). Lama Mipham stated that to be able to meditate on the trekcho of the Dzogchen tradition, we should obtain a certain understanding of the view of the Prasangika Madhyamika.

The second root disturbing emotion is desirous attachment. Desirous attachment should not be understood as affection or compassion. The source of desirous attachment is holding onto the true self. For example, many people claim to do virtuous acts for the benefit of others, but in fact some of these acts spring from desirous attachment. If such a person receives praise, they appreciate it, but if they are criticized, they resent it. In the same way people enjoy obtaining something and dislike not obtaining something. The enjoyment of the praise and resentment of criticism can be traced to the holding on to the notion of true existence of the self.

Desirous attachment can be easily mistaken for compassion, so we should be careful. Desirous attachment is unlike love and compassion, which do not divide people. With the practice of love and compassion that knows no division, we can bring joy and happiness to others and ourselves. This will not be transient and fleeting joy, but a very profound joy, which we will be able to shower upon everyone, because loving compassion does not discriminate. Because desirous attachment does discriminate, the person who has attachments lives with fear and misery.

The failure to accomplish our intentions also comes from desirous attachment. The misery of having to experience something unpleasant comes from desirous attachment. The suffering of separation from our beloved stems from the same source, as does suffering of having to encounter a feared enemy.

If we feel love and compassion towards our friends and family, and hatred towards our enemies, these emotions separate friends and enemies, and do not constitute loving compassion. The desirous attachment also knows only a little compassion. Genuine compassion and love do not discriminate. But it is possible to transform that tinge of compassion into the loving compassion that knows no discrimination.

It is difficult to do away with desirous attachment as long as we remain within the realm of desire, the human world. This is because we are so easily exposed to temptations and seductions. Therefore, many meditators prefer to go to an isolated retreat where they will not be tempted by desirable objects.

The meditation practice of loving-kindness and compassion, in addition to meditation on ugliness, nullify desirous attachment. But we should not meditate on the ugliness of our enemy, because instead of generating loving compassion, we will then create aggression and hatred.

The third disturbing emotion is hatred. Many of us often feel hatred. The Buddhist texts use the terms "demonic forces" and "evil spirits" to describe this. Hatred is the enemy of our own person. When we encounter a person with a mind filled with hatred, no matter how beautiful that person might be, we will not appreciate their beauty.

Nine rationalizations generate hatred. For example, someone who has injured me in the past is likely to injure me again. Because of these nine rationalizations, I hate that person. Another such rationalization is the thought that someone who has harmed the person that I love continues to do so. Other people who have helped my enemy in the past will probably help my enemy now and in the future.

In English, what is the difference between terms "hatred" and "aggression"?

Respondent: Aggression is an action. Hatred is an emotion.

In Tibetan we also have these two terms. Hatred has the potential to become aggression. If we pour oil onto a small fire, we will have a conflagration. Aggression is full-blown hatred. We need to abandon hatred and aggression. To do this we need to see hatred as harmful. Giving in to hatred changes the chemical balance of the body and creates negative physiological processes.

Someone who generates the disturbing emotion of hatred cannot experience happiness and peace. Even if we have a beautiful spouse, friends, and colleagues, if our mind is filled with hatred, the people that we love will still desert us.

The primary cause of having to be reborn in the hellish realm is to generate the disturbing emotions of hatred and aggression in this life. A person whose mind is filled with hatred and aggression creates mental swords, spears, and arrows that become manifest when the person dies.

Mindfulness is very crucial when we are feeling hatred and aggression. For example, when we encounter our enemy, we feel hatred at first, but with the help of mindfulness, we can control the hatred. Therefore, recognition is important.

If we generate hatred, then all the money we spend on cosmetics and makeup will be wasted, because no matter how hard we try to be beautiful, it will not work. (Laughter.)

While our mind is filled with hatred and aggression, it is crucial for us to practice mindfulness and awareness and see that there is no difference between our enemies and our friends. We can understand this by reading the teachings of the ancient masters, and from learning from our day-to-day experiences.

Meditating on the four immeasurable thoughts, particularly the meditation on equanimity, will counteract hatred. We cannot practice loving kindness and compassion in the context of the four immeasurable thoughts until we cultivate immeasurable equanimity. With immeasurable equanimity we can easily cultivate immeasurable love, immeasurable compassion, and immeasurable joy. The reason the Buddha suggested cultivating immeasurable equanimity is because there is a tremendous amount of hatred within people's minds.

Do you have any questions?

Question: Equanimity is quite difficult to practice on a deep level. Can you give us a further explanation?

Answer: Equanimity or equality should be understood in terms of there being no difference between our friend and our enemy. For example, we may see somebody as an enemy, but if this were true, then every human being on earth should see this person as their enemy. The truth is that some people hold the same person to be their friend. Therefore, this person is neither a friend nor an enemy. The same applies to a person we hold to be our friend. The friend that we had last year could be our enemy today, and vice versa. Everything is uncertain. If we believe a superficial reality, then we become miserable. Our mind will be filled with fear and paranoia because of our belief in something that is not real.

Question: Isn't the promise of Dharma that you will have more harmonious relationships, meet people who are friendly and create a better life? Doesn't this mean that there is a difference between enemies and friends?

Answer: If we must hold onto the notion that some people are our friends, and other people are our enemies, it is more important to treat everyone as a friend. But if we want to experience ultimate joy and happiness, we must transcend the notion of friendship.

Everything is interdependent. If we have an enemy, we will also have a friend, and without an enemy, there is no friend; friends and enemies are interdependent.

Question: Isn't it possible to have only friends, and no enemies?

Answer: I do not think so. It is karma. If we have friends, we will have enemies. Friendship is an antidote for enmity but clinging to the notion of friendship is not transcendental wisdom. However, it acts as a steppingstone towards attaining this wisdom. This is how friendship can counteract enmity.

Who decides who is our enemy and who is our friend? We do, of course. Our mind does. But if our mind is deluded, how does it know a real enemy from a real friend? Therefore, the Buddha said that the three realms are nothing but mind.

Question: "Enemy" in English has a strong connotation. Could you say, "someone that you dislike," instead?

Answer: Yes, or we could name the disturbing emotion of hatred to be the enemy. If we want to kill an enemy, then this name can be attributed to hatred, which is what needs to be killed. If we dislike certain people, the mind attributes the word "enemy" to this person, although the English word "enemy" may be stronger than the Tibetan word. What is the opposite of "friend" in English?

Respondent: There is a Norwegian word that means "not-friend."

Question: Sometimes disturbing emotions are strong. Still, if we are aware of them and try to apply antidotes, we still must live with them for a few hours. Is there a way to get rid of them more quickly?

Answer: If we suffer for one or two hours after having practiced mindfulness and applied the antidotal powers to subdue the disturbing emotion, for example hatred, this subsequent suffering arises because the hatred lingers. If we believe that aggression has an extremely negative effect, then we will not entertain it any longer. It depends on how intensely we believe that these negative emotions are harmful. So, we should not harbor disturbing emotions. These emotions cause misery and suffering, but nevertheless we persist in harboring them. It is like the thorns on the plants eaten by a camel; the thorns sting its mouth, but the camel still eats them. Therefore, the bodhisattvas develop great compassion.

Question: What if you are afraid of somebody?

Answer: There is a reason for fear. If we can find the root

of the fear, we can uproot it. When some people contract incurable illnesses, they consult hypnotists or regression therapists to overcome their fear. When we gain insight into our thoughts and emotions, we can conquer them.

Day Two

Please listen to the following teaching by generating the altruistic mind of bodhicitta.

The teachings of the complete and perfect enlightened one, the Buddha, stress the importance of the mind. Virtuous and non-virtuous acts are classified primarily by our intentions. The consequence of performing noble acts is happiness. The result of performing destructive actions is misery. Therefore, the Buddha stated in the Dhammapada that the mind precedes all phenomenal experiences. This is the reason the mind is given such importance.

If our thinking is initially wrong, many other mistakes follow, whereas if we think in a pure way, good things follow. Hence, we should understand that our mind is the master, and the body and speech are its servants. If we use our mind in a very pure way, then our body and speech will follow this course of purity as well. Conversely, if we hold our mind in an impure way, our speech and body will follow, and misery will ensue.

Today we are talking about the six root disturbing emotions. We have already covered the first three: ignorance, desirous attachment, and hatred. Afflictive emotions stir up and create conflict. Afflictive emotions create disturbances within our mind. If our mind is disturbed by conflicting emotions, this state of mind is samsara. Conversely, if our mind becomes liberated from these conflicting emotions, this is nirvana. Nirvana is the purity of our own mind.

The mind can be compared to water. Water can be either clear or muddy, but the nature of the water is neither clear nor muddy. In the same way, our mind can experience samsara or nirvana, and this implies that our mind is neither samsaric nor nirvanic. This is why our mind is capable of experiencing the content of both samsara and nirvana. If we were to speak from a very elevated view, this would be called "the union of samsara and nirvana."

The fourth root disturbing emotion is arrogance. The root of the arrogant mind can be traced to the mind that holds onto the existence of the self. A person with a proud mind will not have any good qualities. The arrogant mind prevents the cultivation of the wise mind and is incapable of seeing other people. When we say "I," we refer to only one person, but when we say "others" we refer to an infinite number of sentient beings. From the perspective of the Dharma, an arrogant person is very narrow-minded. There are several kinds of arrogant mind: one comes from youth, another comes from our possessions, and a third comes from power.

Enlightened masters of the past have said that the arrogant mind cannot learn. It is crucial for spiritual aspirants to understand the mistaken nature of the arrogant mind. We should strive to abandon arrogance. The best way to eliminate arrogance is to meditate on the six or eighteen dhatus.

Let us consider the six dhatus. The six dhatus are the five elements: earth, water, fire, air, space, as well as the mind. The six dhatus do not generate arrogance, because our psychophysical structure is made up of the six dhatus. My psychophysical structure is not superior to yours, and yours is not inferior to mine. We have the same building blocks. Another way of saying this is that your body is made of flesh and bone just as mine. You love and cherish yourself, and others also love and cherish themselves.

Our body is made of the four elements, and we should use the sword of wisdom to cut the tangible form down to the smallest particle to arrive at the partless particle. Subsequently, by also cutting this with the sword of wisdom we will arrive at the complete realization of emptiness. At this point, the arrogant mind will disappear.

Previous, present and future moments of consciousness are like a stream. Consciousness is not composed of building blocks such as particles or atoms; therefore, we cannot talk of a past consciousness meeting a present consciousness, or a present consciousness meeting a future consciousness. The meeting of past, present, and future consciousness does not happen in a tangible manner. It is helpful for our mind to know this. We should own our minds, but now this is not so. From the moment we achieve true ownership of our minds we will strive to benefit others, and we will indeed be able to do so.

The birth of one instant of consciousness is followed by a subsequent moment of consciousness. Between these two instances, there is a gap. Whether we at this moment are experiencing discursive or non-discursive thoughts, we will be capable of realizing the transcendental wisdom of this gap.

The mind experiences appearances and emptiness at the same time. This is the inseparability of appearances and emptiness. We can meditate on this as it is taught in the Heart Sutra, by meditating on fourfold emptiness. First, the mind is empty. Second, emptiness is mind. Third, there is no emptiness other than this mind, and fourth, there is no mind other than this emptiness. Therefore, the true nature of mind is the union of emptiness and appearance.

The Buddha stated that sentient beings are enlightened and that the only difference between a sentient being and an enlightened being is understanding. If we were to consider dharmakaya, the authentic body of the Buddha, which also exists within the mind of ordinary sentient beings, there is not the slightest difference. We should not aim to arrive at the enlightened state in the distant future. Enlightenment and happiness can be attained right now.

Most people identify the arrogant mind with the self or the ego. The antidote for the arrogant mind is to meditate on the classifications of the six or eighteen dhatus. Whatever spiritual study we do, it should subdue our arrogant mind. The spiritual work that is done through the Madhyamika ("middle way") philosophy or Dzogchen ("the philosophy of the inseparability of samsara and nirvana") has the same purpose — to work with the egoistic mind. If we take out the essence of all the different aspects of Dharma practice and blend them together, we will have a tremendous ability to work with the egoistic mind. It can be compared to hundreds of small creeks that converge and become a big river, which finally flows into the ocean. All the smaller rivers can only flow into the sea because of their collective force.

Doubt is the fifth root disturbing emotion. The doubtful mind is said to have two directions; it is like a person with a single body having two heads. Such a person is not able to work properly on his or her path. But this does not mean that we should not analyze and investigate. We are welcome to analyze, doubt and examine. Even the Buddha said this when he expounded on transcendental wisdom: "Even if you were to generate doubt on my teachings on emptiness, you will be capable of actually shredding the world of samsara." To overcome doubt, we need to attain decisive certainty regarding the Dharma. To do this we need to study, reflect and meditate.

Many people question the existence of past and future lives and karmic cause. These questions fall into the category of doubt. We need to make a distinction between negative doubt and positive doubt. Negative doubt leads to a negative conclusion about something that is positive. Positive doubt invites further investigation. Doubting our friend prevents us from accomplishing anything. We should not go to sleep with the doubt; instead we should use the doubting mind to come out of the doubt. If the doubting mind leads us to a conclusion, then the doubt has served its purpose.

The sixth root disturbing emotion is wrong view. When we think about all living beings, or all human beings, we decide everything by ourselves. Therefore, there are so many spiritual traditions. Many groups regard their spiritual traditions as pure. When sentient beings look upon an objective reality such as water, they all see it in different ways. Also, followers of different religious traditions like Hinduism, Buddhism, Christianity, and Islam believe that a particular path is right, and that everybody should follow that path.

The sixth root disturbing emotion has five wrong views. The first wrong view is singularity. The five aggregates are subject to impermanence, but the individual wrongly perceives the five aggregates to be permanent and unchanging; this depends on other factors. The five aggregates of the person are not a single entity. Also, the five aggregates are held to be clean, whereas they are unclean. Through these erroneous views, beings hold onto the existence of a self. It does not matter if we are religious or not.

The second wrong view is extremism. Regarding the first view, sentient beings hold that there is only one reality concerning the five aggregates. The second wrong view is an elaboration of the first wrong view. Some sentient beings perceive reality to be impermanent, some perceive reality to be nihilistic, and some perceive reality to be eternal. For example, some non-Buddhist traditions assert that the creator of this world is permanent. Some ancient non-Buddhist Indian philosophies assert that there is no law of karma of cause and effect, that there is no rebirth, no previous birth, and no future incarnations. Such statements correspond with the view of nihilism. Based on extreme views, sentient beings quarrel and create turmoil.

The third view is the perverted view. The perverted view does not understand reality and so perceives reality in a perverted manner. The perverted view applies to conventional reality. The conventional truth or reality is understood in a perverted way. All dharmas manifest based on causes and conditions. The manifestation of inner or outer phenomenal experiences comes about because of the law of interdependency, and the belief that there is no such law is perverted.

The fourth view is attachment to ethics. People in one religious tradition claim that their moral ethics are superior to those practiced by other religious traditions. Believing that our ethics are superior to others' ethics, that our technique is superior to others' techniques is the fourth wrong view because it creates trouble. If we praise our own moral ethics and condemn those of other spiritual traditions, our view is the opposite of the Buddha's.

The fifth view is the view that holds our view to be superior. The fourth view is connected to behavior, but the fifth view is connected to attitudes. For example, some non-Buddhist traditions claim that God, the Creator, is the Supreme Being. Buddhism claims that the creator of the world is not some kind of Supreme Being; the creator of the world is the law of interdependence.

The Buddha has stated that not everybody must adopt the Buddhist view, and that it is wrong to assume that our view is better than all others. For example, if we hold ourselves as superior, this is arrogance. People with an arrogant mind cannot respect and revere anyone else. It is quite easy for that arrogant mind to criticize, condemn and bully others. The practice is to overcome discursive thoughts, but the practice of such a view will increase the discursive thoughts. We should strive towards recognizing the six root disturbing emotions and try to eliminate them. Otherwise, they will cause our mind to undergo confusion and misery.

When the Buddha turned the first wheel of the Dharma and gave the sermon of the Four Noble Truths, he said that we should understand suffering. Similarly, following the statement of the Buddha, we should understand the root of the disturbing emotions; and we should attempt to overcome these disturbing emotions.

Question: Rinpoche, would you say that it would be possible to be free from wrong views by practicing other disciplines than Buddhism?

Answer: This question should be asked of the teacher of the other discipline. (Laughter.) I am not knowledgeable in that particular tradition, so I will not know if that spiritual tradition has the capacity to liberate you from wrong views. Only people who have delved deeply into that tradition can know this. During my travels in China, I met several older Chinese men who said that Tibetan Buddhism is awfully bad.

When I asked them what Tibetan Buddhism was, they did not know. If we do not know what a religion is, then how can we know if it is bad?

Question: In some way, I can understand cause and conditions, but when I come to this concept of time immemorial it is easy to have doubt because in many ways it easier to understand that somebody started it.

Answer: The teachings state that we are the creator of the world. But, we may question whether it is relevant to trace back to the creation of the world, because we can go back ad infinitum. There seem to be enough problems to deal with in this life, and many people even commit suicide due to this unbearable suffering, so if we remembered all our past existences, our pain would only be multiplied.

Samsara has existed since time immemorial; this accords with reality as it is. If we were to posit a point of origin, this raises contradictions. It does not correspond to reality. Would you like to have a samsara with or without beginning?

Respondent: I am not sure if it is so important, but I do not know why you are so sure that there is no beginning.

For example, we cannot even find the beginning of one grain of sand. We have our parents, and they have their parents. Can we find the original parents? If we can find our original parents, then these parents will be our creator. However, they are impossible to find. Or take the example of the chicken and egg. Which comes first?

Respondent: That is why I do not understand how you can be so sure why there is no start.

Answer: Based on the teachings I have tried to find the origin of the world. I could not find it, and therefore I am sure about this. Since I explored and could not find a point of beginning, maybe there is no point for you to explore, maybe it is merely a waste of energy. Perhaps it is more important to look at the endpoint.

Question: You talk about disturbing thoughts and

emotions. Do you distinguish between thoughts and emotions?

Answer: A thought is general; an emotion is specific. For example, the conceptual mind has pure and impure thoughts. Impure thoughts generate impure emotions. It is difficult to classify tangible particles like atoms because they are so small. But now we are talking about the intangible phenomena of our mind, which are even more difficult to talk about. If we do not understand precisely, but understand in a general way, this is sufficient.

If we recognize disturbing emotions the moment they appear in our mind, they will be liberated immediately. If we detect impure thoughts and conceptual mind, we will be able to understand what pure thought is and what pure conceptual mind is. When we experience suffering, we appreciate times when we are free from suffering.

Question: There are different ways of dealing with disturbing emotions. We just let them play themselves out and try to learn from them. Then you have the method of applying an antidote, and then you have the Dzogchen view of self-liberation. How do you know which one to choose?

Answer: It depends on the practitioner. If we have cloudy water, we can filter out the mud to restore the clarity, or we can just allow the water to rest and become clear by itself. The first method is a fabrication; the other method is non-fabricated and can be compared to the Dzogchen method.

Respondent: It seems to me that I have a couple of seconds to apply the self-liberating approach, and then if I can spot it soon enough, it may just dissolve on its own. If that does not work, I can use the antidote, and if that does not work, I can just let it affect me in a negative way.

Answer: It is appropriate to alternate techniques. The main thing is to make sure that applying all the techniques will reduce the discursive thoughts. If this happens, any technique can be applied. Whether we take regular medicine or homeopathic medicine, it does not make any difference if it cures our disease.

I have explained the six root disturbing emotions with a few subclasses. This subject comes from the fifty-one mental factors. What is, for example, the difference between hatred and aggression? You see, usually we use these terms, but we do not know the subtle differences. Things become overly complicated. Although it is difficult for me to work with a computer, understanding the fifty-one mental events and so on is rather easy. It would be beneficial for you to study a little Madhyamika and then enter Dzogchen or Mahamudra practice.

The Eleven Virtuous Factors

Please listen to the following teaching by generating the altruistic state of mind, bodhicitta.

Sentient beings long for happiness but are ignorant of its cause. To create the cause of happiness, we need to know precisely what needs to be abandoned and what needs to be cultivated.

The cultivation of virtue comes from the mind. The distinction between what is and is not virtuous is made in our mind, thoughts and attitudes. Therefore, we talk about the six root disturbing emotions. Whenever these six root disturbing emotions arise, we should immediately try to lessen or eliminate them. The Buddha spoke about the virtuous thoughts and acts that should be cultivated, among them, the eleven virtuous mental factors.

It is difficult for someone who is new to meditation to meditate on a view without grasping existence or non-existence. Of the two realities, existence and non-existence, it is better to meditate on the reality of non-existence. By relying on such meditation, we can avert our clinging to existence, which is strongly rooted in our mind. Meditation on non-existence, that is, meditation on emptiness to counteract the view that holds onto true existence, will gradually lead us to attain the transcendental unfabricated state. For example, fire can be used to burn garbage. As soon as the garbage has been burned, the fire goes out.

It is not recommended for beginners of meditation to meditate on togal meditation, the transcendental state that transcends existence and non-existence. We should meditate on non-existence. If the beginner jumps into togal, it is questionable whether the practitioner is meditating on the actual transcendental state. Most probably the practitioner is fabricating the transcendental state. We can relate this to the story about a flock of swans flying in the sky. The king of the swans instructed that when they reached a certain region, they should not make any noise. The swans passed the message to each other and every swan ended up squawking, and as a result many swans were caught and killed. If we were to attempt to meditate on the transcendental state, then our very attempt would create more fabrications and conceptual thoughts.

The actual transcendental state is neither existent, non-existent, both existent and non-existent, and neither existent nor non-existent. It is beyond these four extremes. Conceiving of this transcendental state is difficult for beginners because they have so many discursive thoughts. Beginners should study, recognize and understand what discursive thoughts are. Then they should strive to lessen or abandon them. Next, they should try to recognize and understand the eleven virtuous factors. Having recognized them, they should try cultivating them. Usually, this is done with a certain amount of attachment, but gradually this practice will lead us to a state free from attachment. For example, a baby prefers milk. The baby will not enjoy solid food. If a baby is fed solid food, there is risk. In the same way, if we misperceive what emptiness is, the Buddha said that we will be harmed, not benefited.

The first of the eleven virtuous factors is faith based on trust. Real trust is based on understanding or wisdom. If our trust is based on examination and analysis, such trust cannot be lost. Trust that lacks wisdom is not reliable, because it can be easily changed or lost. The object of our belief should allow us to lessen or overcome the disturbing emotions, and the mastery of techniques that will enable us to cultivate virtuous thoughts and positive feelings.

It is important to understand what we mean by trust or faith, because some forms of trust or faith can be deceptive. We should try to attain the trust that is accompanied by wisdom and understanding. When we have attained such trust, this can be interpreted as finding refuge. Refuge is a very firm state of mind that is experienced when irreversible trust dawns. Trust is therefore the ground. Based on this firm ground of trust, we are able to harvest all kinds of plants. When we experience a profound sense of trust, it will be quite easy for us to have meditative experiences of samadhi.

The second virtuous factor is caution. It is like mindfulness or carefulness. Caution can be compared to eyesight. A person with good vision is capable of walking without stumbling. Whenever our mind is blessed with the virtuous mental factor of caution, we will be able to avoid discursive thoughts, and our mind will not stumble on these emotions.

All beings long for freedom, but it is unwise to give freedom to our discursive thoughts and emotions. Freedom gives rise to peace and serenity. But if we give freedom to our rambling thoughts and emotions, our mind will not experience peace and tranquility. We should, therefore, be very conscious of what needs to be abandoned and what needs to be adopted. When we talk about caution, we do not talk about being careful about objective reality; we talk about being careful concerning discursive thoughts and emotions.

By practicing caution, we attain the third virtuous factor, which is mental flexibility. Mental flexibility comes with a certain amount of freedom. A literal translation of the Tibetan term is "extremely purified of disturbing emotions." If the discursive thoughts and emotions are thoroughly purified and pacified, then the meditator will attain a certain amount of mental power and freedom. If the meditator wants to release his or her mind, he or she will be able to do so. Likewise, the meditator will be able to control his or her mind if he or she wants to do this. It means the power to have thoughts or not to have thoughts.

Sometimes we do not like to think, but thoughts keep intruding. Because of this, the first virtuous factors have a causal relationship. The attainment of the third mental factor of flexibility is accompanied by supernatural mental powers, like being able to read people's minds or perform miracles. The first mental factor comes from wisdom. The second virtuous factor, caution, comes from meditation. Meditation enables us to stop disturbing emotions and cultivate virtuous and non-discursive thoughts and emotions. This experience of non-discursiveness can be the experience of meditation. The third virtuous factor comes from the two preceding virtuous factors.

The fourth virtuous factor is equanimity. Equanimity should be understood as bridging the gap between things being superior or inferior, for example equalizing our enemies and friends, existence and non-existence, permanence and impermanence, singularity and plurality, self and others, or purity and impurity. A mind that bridges all these polarities experiences equanimity. This realization is not fabricated. Because we recognize how things are, we recognize the suchness of things. The actual reality is equanimity or equality; we are merely uncovering the reality as it is.

Our minds create divisions, but the nature of objective reality is boundless equanimity. On one earth there are many countries. This is not how the reality is, but we have created divisions, countries and based on these divisions there are disputes and wars. Ultimately, the world is one, and if our mind were to interpret the objective reality of the world as such, then world peace would be the outcome.

But erasing all the divisions would be a difficult task. It seems impossible to equalize all objective phenomena, but at least the perceiving mind can be made whole. For this reason the Buddhist master Shantideva says that if you want to protect your feet from being hurt by stones and thorns, it would be an impossible task to cover the whole earth with leather, simply a waste of energy, but if you were to cover your feet with leather soles, the effect would be the same. If we try to defeat objective enemies, we will strengthen them. If we instead turn within ourselves and try to defeat the enemies within our own mind, then the inner enemies will be weakened. In this way the mind that entertains polarities, contradictions and divisions should be trained to be made whole and experience the great equanimity.

The fifth virtuous factor is shame. Shame is not generated in external phenomena. It is produced within our own being; for example, when we create discursive thoughts and emotions. The natural state of our mind is excellent purity, but now our mind does not correspond with that actual nature. When we acknowledge this, we feel shame because we are not in accord with our nature.

If we experience self-hate, we should be ashamed when we recognize this. It is also evident that we upset ourselves when we hate and create pain for others. Whatever creates pain for us or others is shameful. The thought that recognizes the unstable nature of the mind is the shame. If we have a nightmare, it is possible to realize this and to be aware that we are dreaming. It becomes a lucid dream, and we will be liberated.

The sixth virtuous factor is embarrassment. Embarrassment is cultivated because of encountering certain people. If we refrain from some actions or discursive thoughts out of embarrassment, then this is the sixth virtuous factor. To practice the sixth virtuous factor, we practice veneration, humility and modesty. The mind that knows embarrassment is not an individualistic mind. It is not only concerned about itself but is concerned with the benefit of others.

The seventh virtuous factor is non-attachment. According to the Hinayana vehicle, non-attachment is a quality of the noble family, somebody who is completely content. To understand the wholeness of non-attachment, we need to understand what attachment is. Attachment is clinging to the objects of this world. But non-attachment should not be understood in terms of not needing our house, our car, our children, or our family. If we practice non-attachment in this way, we are forsaking sentient beings. This is not non-attachment; rather, it is non-compassion.

Our compassion should be directed towards external phenomena and reality, and toward other living beings. Without compassion, sentient beings will simply vanish. Without sentient beings there will be no bodhisattvas or enlightened beings. Therefore, the compassionate mind is tremendously powerful. If we do not care for an object, the value of that object, regardless of its original value, will be diminished. Even inanimate objects require our love, which creates the value of objects. As for sentient beings they need our love and compassion. So, the seventh virtuous factor of non-attachment has a very intimate connection with love and compassion.

Non-attachment should be understood in terms of profound contentment. Attachment should be understood as discontentment. If we do not possess a sense of satisfaction, then we will become miserable. For this reason, attachment is bad. Whereas when contentment takes root in our mind, such a sense of satisfaction is accompanied by happiness. For example, we may have a strong attachment to food, but we only have one stomach, and we cannot stuff it with more than it can hold. Gluttony can lead to misery. Similarly, we cannot wear more than one hat. And if we were to put on every hat that we own, we would be uncomfortable and look ridiculous. Non-attachment should be understood as having the sufficient means for survival and being satisfied with this without craving more.

Attachment prevents us from practicing generosity. Attachment is symbolized by the preta, the hungry ghosts that are unable to share with others. It is important not to allow the preta to influence our mind.

The eighth virtuous factor is non-hate. To stop violence, we must practice non-hatred. To understand non-hatred, we need to understand hatred. Hatred leads to the desire to harm other living beings. When people harbor a tremendous amount of hatred, then everything in front of them seems disgusting. Due to strong hatred, people have difficulty in associating with others. If they see two persons whispering, immediately they think that they are talking about them. All this comes about because of hatred. We should eliminate hatred and cultivate the virtuous mental factor of non-hatred.

Non-ignorance is the ninth virtuous factor. To

understand non-ignorance correctly, we need to understand ignorance. Ignorance is the first root disturbing emotion. Ignorance is the lack of knowledge of what needs to be cultivated and what needs to be abandoned.

When our mind becomes free from ignorance, it becomes filled with wisdom. The Buddha stressed the importance of generating the wise mind and said that the five paramitas without the sixth paramita of wisdom, is like a person without eyes. If the five paramitas are supplemented by wisdom, it becomes a complete practice. The first paramita is the practice of giving. If giving is not accompanied by the practice of wisdom it is not true giving. For example, if we share our ammunition and weapons, we are not being generous. In brief, whatever gift we make to benefit ourselves is not a pure act of giving. For example, if we practice the paramita of giving in order to encourage our religious ideology or dogma to flourish, this is not a pure act of giving. We could give to another country with the intention of acquiring benefit for our own country. Or we could practice the act of giving for the benefit of our family or give money in order to gain power. All these seeming acts of giving are not pure acts of giving, but what then is a pure act of giving? A pure act of giving is to give without any expectation, just for the benefit of the recipients. So non-ignorance facilitates wisdom, and wisdom is especially important in the act of giving.

The tenth mental factor is non-violence. If we have taken refuge in the Dharma, this commitment involves non-violence. The root of all Dharma practice is non-violence. The practice of non-violence is as follows: when people inflict violence upon us, we do not retaliate with force. If somebody insults, criticizes or strikes us, and we do not retaliate in kind, such a practice is non-violence. The practitioner who can do this is a spiritual warrior.

It is easy to practice non-violence with somebody that treats us kindly, but it is difficult to practice non-violence with somebody who is violent towards us. It is also easy to practice non-violence with strangers.

The eleventh virtuous factor is joyous effort. This relates to the practice of patience in the six paramitas. Joyous effort assists in the cultivation of all the preceding virtuous factors. A joyous effort focuses on virtuous acts, it does not involve consuming alcoholic beverages or illegal drugs. Joyous effort encourages virtuous acts. If we make perverted effort instead of a joyous effort, then such effort will not be conducive to virtuous thoughts and actions. In Taiwan there is one very unpopular teacher. One day, the teacher had parked his car in front of the school and his students poured water into the fuel tank. However, if you do not like what I have been saying and attempt to put water on the tank of my car, you can't because I don't have a car here! (Laughter.)

It is not necessary to know a lot about the Dharma. It is enough to know the six root disturbing emotions and the eleven virtuous factors. Reducing the six root disturbing emotions and developing the virtuous factors, constitutes the whole practice.

All Buddhist practice can be summed up in three good pieces of training: training in moral ethics, training in meditation, and training in wisdom. All of these comprise the practice of abandoning the root disturbing emotions and developing the virtuous factors.

For example, shravakas and solitary buddhas only meditate on the twelve interdependent links to attain the state of arhathood. If we practice the eleven virtuous factors and abandon the six root disturbing emotions, this surpasses the twelve interdependent links, and the impact will be even more powerful.

Life is a highway of impermanence. If we understand the nature of the world as it is, then, even if we must live within impermanence, that impermanence will not shatter us. We will be able to generate integrity within ourselves.

Consider the following story: The Lord of Death and his henchmen were holding a meeting because the population of hell was decreasing. One tiger-headed henchman said he had a method to bring more people into hell. If the god realm were emptied, then naturally many of the beings from the god realm would be reborn in the hell realm. He said, "If we tell the human beings on earth that the god realm does not exist, then the human beings will not practice the ethics that will lead them to rebirth in the higher realms, and they will fall into the lower realm of hell." The Lord of Death said, "This seems to be a very good suggestion, but I don't think it is powerful enough." Then the ox-headed henchman suggested, "If we say that there is no hell realm, then naturally many will do bad things, which will cause them to fall into hell." Many similar suggestions and proposals followed, and the Lord of Death agreed with all of them, even though he did not think that any of them were good enough. Then came a low-ranking henchman who claimed to have a special method. The Lord of Death said, "I don't think a low-ranking henchman like you can have a big idea, but nevertheless, tell us." The small henchman said, "You should proclaim to the human beings that tomorrow exists." Upon hearing this suggestion, the Lord of Death was delighted and said, "This is the most powerful suggestion; it will truly work!" Subsequently, all human beings were told that tomorrow exists, and consequently people kept on postponing their practice, procrastinating, and when death came, they fell into hell.

The Four Logical Arguments

Day One

It is said that there are sentient beings as far as space extends, and wherever there are sentient beings, karmic formations and conflicting emotions also exist. But the nature of these does not transcend misery. In order to establish sentient beings, which have such natures, in a state of happiness and to eliminate suffering, we should engage ourselves in the practice of Dharma.

If the motivation is highly extensive and intensive, then also the result will be comprehensive and exhaustive. The practice and reflection of Dharma should, therefore, be preceded by an altruistic mind or, in other words, the attitude of bodhicitta.

Generally, sentient beings possess what is known as a conceptual mind that fixates on the existence or non-existence of things. From our fixation on the notion of existence evolves many different views and conceptual elaborations. For example, certain spiritual traditions claim that God created the earth, and certain non-Buddhist traditions claim that the Supreme Self created the world. But the Buddha says that the world was not created by a Supreme Self or a Supreme Being, but by interdependency.

Therefore, the Lord Buddha gave his first sermon on the Four Noble Truths. Most of his audience, like most sentient beings, have a strong tendency to fixate on the notion of existence. The Four Noble Truths, therefore, reveal the law of karmic causation, which shows that there exists a cause and there exists a result. Causations can be samsaric, or nirvanic. In samsaric causations, the Buddha presented the cause and result of samsara. In nirvanic causations, the Buddha presented the cause and result of nirvana.

To avert the notion that fixates on existence — the existence or non-existence of everything — the Buddha gave the second sermon, which was an extensive teaching on emptiness. His third sermon, on the tathagatagarba, also rejected the idea of fixating on existence and revealed that the creator of everything is the sugatagarbha or Buddha-nature. In this third sermon, he said that the root of all phenomenal appearances and experience can be traced back to our mind.

If the mind thinks in the right manner, then everything seems to unfold in a good way. Conversely, if the mind thinks mistakenly, it appears that many things go wrong. Good and bad things, or negative or positive, therefore, cannot be established merely concerning external existence. Similarly, positive and negative cannot be found, as far as the Buddha-nature is concerned.

If good and bad cannot be established regarding external phenomena or the internal existence of our mind or Buddha-nature, then where do good and bad exist? The root of all these things can be traced back to a lack of knowledge. In the teaching of Dzogchen, it is stated that the nature of mind itself is Buddha-nature, that the mind itself is Buddha. Whether it is the smaller vehicle or the large vehicle of Mahayana or the Vajrayana, in all the teachings the Buddha gave during the presentations of these various vehicles, the main force was stated to be our own mind. Because of this, we can say that Buddhism is the science of mind. As Buddhist practitioners, then, we should try to attain certainty that the mind is the creator of both samsaric and nirvanic experience.

Now, sentient beings experience four confused, or wrong, views and, because of this, are said to experience the miseries of samsara. The first wrong view is to fixate on something being clean. The second is to fixate on the notion of happiness. The third is to fixate on permanence. The fourth is to fixate on self. In these ways, we tend to fixate onto our own physical existence as being clean, permanent, and happy and with an existing self.

As far as the truth is concerned, the skandhas ("aggregates"), the collection of our psychophysical existence, form, feeling, perceptions, will and consciousness, are impermanent. When sentient beings are not able to perceive the impermanent nature of their psychophysical existence, they will fail to realize their impermanent nature. But if they utilize the sword of wisdom and dissect the psychophysical life, they would be able to reveal the truth, which is that the skandhas are impermanent. When we investigate our psychophysical aggregates, it will be shown that this body and mind, the spirit and matter of our existence, is a composition of many particles and sub-particles, atoms and sub-atoms; it is not some solid lump.

From the perspective of gross appearance, we say that a person exists if all five limbs are present. But if we remove some of the limbs from a person—the arms, for example—and place them somewhere else, then those separate limbs will not be called a person. Therefore, the body is only a collection of parts.

From the perspective of the base of the composition, this base is said to be a conglomeration of atoms and sub-atoms. Preceding this base of atomic particles is the level of the atomic energy that gives rise to the subsequent unfolding of the particles. Therefore, even the subtlest level of atomic particles cannot be said to be the creator of the world, and the atomic particles cannot be claimed to be permanent. As soon as the subtlest particles appear, they vanish or transform into something else and so are not permanent.

Therefore, from the perspective of our psychophysical existence, we can understand that our skandhas do not remain constant; they go through constant changes because the building blocks of the skandhas go through constant changes.

If we analyze the skandhas by applying our wisdom and intelligence in this way, and if we further investigate this gross body in terms of the subtle body, this subtle body will be understood in terms of subtle impermanence. This understanding of impermanence will evolve into knowledge of emptiness. If we meditate in this manner, this is said to be a true meditation as mindfulness of our own body.

What is the significance of understanding

impermanence? Understanding the impermanent nature of things will allow us to avert our attachment to our experiences, and we will be able to enjoy a non-attached state of mind. Realizing impermanence will also allow us to develop further our practice of wholesome deeds and to stop indulging in negative actions. In the same way, the understanding of impermanence can give rise to certainty of and a longing for liberation. When we genuinely long for the attainment of liberation, it will be possible to attain ultimate happiness.

In many of the sutras, the Buddha said that, among all the footprints, the elephant's is the biggest. Similarly, among all meditations, the meditation on impermanence is the greatest. It is therefore initially essential to exert ourselves in meditation on impermanence. External phenomenal appearance undergoes constant change; in the same way, our own body also goes through continuous evolution. If our minds are not able to move in parallel with the external movement and changes of our body, we will experience misery.

Realization of impermanence will remove the fear we usually experience. For example, it will remove the exhaustion we may experience in spiritual practice, the suffering that occurs when we encounter something unexpected, and the pain that comes from seeking something and not finding it. Thus, meditation on impermanence has the power to lessen the impact of all these different miseries.

Suffering will occur, either momentarily or for a period, but then it will go away again. In the same way, happiness comes, remains for a while, and then vanishes — all because of the law of impermanence. Therefore, there is not much point in worrying about the beginning of suffering or the end of happiness because the law of impermanence will touch both experiences.

The Buddha said that, if we do not understand the fourfold knowledge of the impermanent nature of our skandhas, suffering, emptiness, and selflessness, then we will experience misery; if we do understand this, we will experience happiness.

Buddha formulated many rules, not merely to restrict us from doing certain things, but to protect us from certain things. For example, the restriction against monks living with women was not given because women are evil natured, but to protect the mind of the practitioner from disturbing emotions. The same applies to intake of alcohol: Alcohol is not wrong in itself, but the restriction is formulated to stop our addictions.

In some instances, however, it might be useful to perform seemingly negative actions. If we perform one of the seven negative activities through our body or speech, and the activity is associated with the Dharma, and there is a compassionate motivation for performing it, then we are not entirely restricted from doing it.

The Buddha did not state that all external and internal phenomena are suffering. But when we do not understand the nature of these phenomena, such a lack of knowledge will be a cause of misery. Hence, we should understand that the root of the teaching of the Buddha lies in understanding the law of interdependent origination. We should equally understand impermanence; that is, the fact that everything is empty and without self. When these things are understood in their proper context, then all outer and inner experiences become nirvanic experience, the experience of happiness. But when we fail to understand their nature, they become the suffering of samsara. It is therefore essential for a practitioner to become well versed and learned in the law of interdependency, emptiness, selflessness, and so forth.

Now I would like to discuss the four wrong views: the fixations on cleanliness, happiness, permanence, and self. The antidote to these four wrong views or attitudes is meditation on dirtiness, suffering, impermanence, and selflessness and emptiness.

When we fixate on our skandhas as something immaculate and blissful, or as permanent or having a self, we generate a tremendous amount of attachment which can lead to the development of many complications. To realize the impermanent and suffering nature of our skandhas, we must meditate on the meaning of emptiness and selflessness.

Let us explain the nature of suffering. Everything is not suffering, but when we do not understand the impermanence, the emptiness, and the lack of self of outer and inner phenomenal experiences, then everything becomes suffering. So, if we were to explain that everything is misery, that everything — all outer and inner phenomenal experience — has a suffering nature, then we are making a false statement. Such statements are traditionally said to be criticism and fabrication.

By now, the impermanence and suffering nature should be properly understood as the nature of the relative truth, so the nature of the relative truth should be understood. On the other hand, emptiness and selflessness are the law of the ultimate truth and, when we enter the practice of the Dharma, it is important to acquire certainty about such views, primarily through studying and reflecting on the Dharma. The practice of Dharma is, therefore, not something that should be studied outwardly, but something that should penetrate our heart and mind. There is a saying that, if Dharma is not practiced as it should be, instead of lifting us to further heights of wisdom, we will descend. According to the legend, it is said that Devadatta, the nephew of the Buddha, was extremely learned in the Dharma, but the knowledge had not penetrated his heart. Therefore, he was reborn as a preta, a hungry ghost.

In contrast, the Tibetan yogi, Milarepa, was not very learned in academic Buddhism, but he became completely enlightened. His teacher, Marpa, gave instructions as pith instructions ("concise instructions"), and Milarepa meditated very enthusiastically on these and attained enlightenment. So, even if we are not very well versed in the whole spectrum of Buddhism, we can familiarize ourselves with the four antidotes that will avert the wrong view: the meditations on dirtiness, emptiness and selflessness, impermanence, and suffering. That will be enough.

We live within the world of impermanence, experiencing it constantly, so failing to realize the impermanent nature of ourselves and others will cause suffering. As an example, if we are in very deep water and we do not know how to swim, we will be in trouble. Impermanence can be compared to a body of water, and the knowledge of impermanence can be compared to swimming. Swimming in impermanence, as we all do, is dangerous if we do not have the knowledge of impermanence. Today, the weather is very warm and nice; therefore, this example of swimming came to mind! (Laughter.)

We are still talking about the suffering nature, and while we are talking about this nature, I would like to mention two equal terms, subtle impermanence and all-pervasive suffering. These two terms mean the same thing because they point towards the same experience. You might have heard the term "all-pervasive suffering" mentioned.

If we genuinely understand the meaning of impermanence in this life, we will realize that there is not anything significant that we can acquire or lose. We will become free from the hope of both acquiring and losing things.

Understanding the nature of the relative truth requires understanding of impermanence. An understanding of impermanence is also said to be very essential to understand the nature of the ultimate truth, emptiness, and selflessness. Understanding of relative truth in terms of impermanence and suffering is a steppingstone that will allow us to understand the nature of ultimate truth. Because of this, the Indian master, Chandrakirti, said, "Relative truth is the method, whereas ultimate truth is the result of that method." He said that, if we do not understand these two things, we will be entering a wrong path. Just as a bird that jumps from a cliff without two wings will fall to earth and die. Due to the lack of knowledge about the nature of the relative and the ultimate truth, an individual will go through the turmoil of samsara, whereas individuals possessing the knowledge of both relative and ultimate truth can be compared to a bird having two wings capable of flying wherever it wishes, up and down, because it has complete freedom in the totality of space. From this example, we understand that we should try to equip ourselves with the two wings of understanding of both relative and ultimate truth. With such skills, we will be capable of flying through space.

By acquiring certainty of the relative and ultimate truth, it is possible to meditate on emptiness, which is said to be like the vast expanse of space. But if we lack this certainty, even if we were to meditate, and our meditation generates pain in our backside and knees, it would be no more than self-torture. Therefore, attaining certainty with regards to these views is essential.

What do we mean when we say "view"? The view is something that is decided by our thoughts or concepts. The Buddha taught the teachings on impermanence, emptiness, suffering nature, and selflessness from his certainty. Buddha based his teachings on the confidence he gained, and we should also examine whether meditation on such lessons will bring about a spiritual benefit or not.

The fourth antidote is said to be the understanding of emptiness. Generally, when we talk about emptiness in this context, it should be understood as the emptiness of phenomena. It implies that a phenomenal appearance is not a singular entity; it means there is no singular phenomenal experience. Also, the term "emptiness" implies that phenomenal appearance or experience relies on other factors, meaning that they are interdependent. The term "emptiness" also implies an assembly of many causes and conditions.

To recapture and establish a line of argument; phenomena are not found to be singular, because they depend on a multitude of other factors. Because the phenomenal appearances or experiences depend on other factors, they are interdependently originated, and because of the law of interdependent origination, phenomena are said to be empty. The emptiness of phenomena implies the interdependency of phenomena.

For example, the emptiness of space accommodates mountains — the external environment — as well as the sentient beings within that environment. Space functions to accommodate all these things. Therefore, emptiness accommodates the possibility of interdependent origination. Because of emptiness, the phenomenon that occurs from interdependency comes about in the beginning, remains, and finally disappears. Many teachers have worked towards establishing emptiness, like Nagarjuna, Aryadeva, and others.

Since time without beginning, up to this present point, our mind has been habituated in terms of fixating onto the true existence of things. In order to avert such fixation, we need to exert effort in terms of meditating on emptiness. For example, our confusion has become so solid that even phenomenal experiences like dreams are taken to be true while we are dreaming. In order to lessen our clinging onto true existence, many logical arguments were developed by the ancient masters of India. And even though there are many logical arguments which should be studied and reflected upon, they can all be summed up in the Four Logical Arguments.

The first logical argument is examining the cause. It is called the vajra ("thunderbolt") argument. Of course, vajra is based on a mythology. The vajra argument can challenge all wrong views and concepts. The first argument is therefore called the vajra argument.

Question: You used the word "singularity." I do not think I understand what you imply by the word singularity. It seems that it means that they do not exist by themselves, but as a result of many causes and conditions coming together.

Answer: Yes, a phenomenon cannot be singular because many causes and conditions need to come together for the phenomena to appear, and if "one" does not exist then "many" will not exist either. So, the understanding of emptiness transcends singularity and plurality. According to the view, it is said that, while phenomena are empty, at the same time there are appearances. You see, sentient beings generally get attached to appearances, but in the Nyingma view, these appearances are established as emptiness on the spot.

Questioner: On the spot?

Lama Changchub: What Rinpoche was saying is that we tend to generate attachment to appearances, right? To avert the attachment to things, the emptiness of an appearance is established on the spot. Emptiness is revealed in the very moment something appears; we do not to establish emptiness separate from the appearance.

Rinpoche: Now, do you feel like realizing emptiness? You look like a great meditator!

Before we meditate, we should use our conceptual mind to think. The reason is simply because we possess this mind, and this mind is capable of thinking. When we think about these subjects and gain certainty, then the thinking mind will disappear on its own. Leaving behind the thinking mind and gaining certainty is termed "acquiring the wisdom mind."

Certain spiritual traditions say the Buddha experiences both purity and impurity. They say the Buddha is omniscient, and therefore the Buddha must experience impurity as well as purity. But such statements are wrong. The reason is because, when we abandon this physical human existence, we are not able to experience humanness. When we leave our present physical existence and acquire a new physical existence, for example that of an ant, our experience of possessing a human body is completely gone. In this new body of an ant, we will not have the slightest trace of the experience of the human body, because we are completely enveloped by the new experience of the ant. It is therefore said that the Buddha knows what impurity is and what is purity. But the Buddha does not experience these; they do not present themselves in front of him; they are only known to him. For example, in order to train sentient beings, the Buddha sometimes talks about many precious jewels and articles within the pure lands. But, in fact, there may be no such jewels in those pure lands. The point is that we are fond of precious jewels and we are attached to them, so Buddha uses our liking of the jewels and says that if we cultivate the ten virtues actions, we will be able to acquire these precious jewels and we will be born in certain pure lands. But it is questionable that when we are born there, whether we are truly able to acquire such jewels, but certainly we are able to acquire the precious jewel of Dharma. Do you have more questions?

Question: Can Rinpoche explain more about subtle impermanence?

Answer: Subtle impermanence is said to be difficult to realize and understand for common people. This is because it is very subtle. For example, the gross changes of a child becoming a youth, and a youth becoming a grown-up come about because of the subtle changes that occur within the mind stream of that individual. Subtle impermanence cannot be seen by our eyes. For example, as soon as a plant sprouts, it goes through change, but this is difficult to perceive with the gross sense organs of our eyes. But if we placed a video camera in front of the small sprout, then we would be able to see the changes. Or we can sit in front of the plant until it grows big; then we will see all the changes that occur. But it is easier to use a camera. (Laughter.)

The Buddha has said that the experience of common people is like the palm of the hand. The experience of noble people, of realized beings, is like the experience of the eye. He further said that, if we place a strand of hair in the palm of our hand, we are not able to feel anything. But if we place that single hair on our eye, then immediately we will feel uncomfortable. Because noble beings have realized subtle permanence in this manner, they do not develop attachment to their body, not to mention other phenomena. But ordinary sentient beings, not having realized subtle impermanence, develop attachments and find difficulty in letting go of things, and so forth. For example, you might fixate on the Khenpo Sangpo that came to Norway four years ago as the same one who is here today. I have gone through a tremendous change. But I also perceive Reidun (a person in the room) in the same way, but my perception could be wrong.

Question: Is the realization of emptiness one of the primary conditions for achieving wisdom mind?
Answer: The realization of emptiness is the attainment of the wisdom itself because the realization of emptiness corresponds to the reality of phenomena. We are realizing the truth of phenomena as it is.

Question: How should we realize emptiness?
Answer: One of the methods is to realize impermanence on its various levels, including the subtle level. Understanding of the gross form of impermanence is quite easy. We should use this understanding as a steppingstone to understand the subtle nature of impermanence. This will lead to the understanding of emptiness. It can be compared to the construction of an airplane. In the beginning, somebody discovered the knowledge of how to build a machine that could fly. At that time, the knowledge was rather crude, but using that as base, it has been refined and airplanes have become more and more sophisticated. In a similar way, using the understanding of gross impermanence as a base, we should move slowly to understand more and more of subtle reality.

Initially, our meditation should take into consideration the grosser aspect of reality, such as impermanence, and so forth. Then, gradually, we should try to enter more subtle levels of impermanence, and then finally into emptiness. It is a little bit like all numbers are based on zero. Zero can be said to be the mother of all numbers. But zero itself is nothing. So similarly, the base of all phenomenal experiences is emptiness, but emptiness itself is nothing.

Question: So, when we meditate, can we meditate on a table or a brick stone or some other object?

Answer: We can select one object and then try to establish the emptiness of that object. When we do this, the same emptiness can be applied to all other phenomenal appearances as well. It is said to be like when we cut one bamboo, and we realize the emptiness of the bamboo, we will understand that all other bamboo in the world also has this empty, hollow quality.

Buddhist texts talk about the sixteen different types of emptiness, but as far as the truth of emptiness itself is concerned, we cannot divide the truth of emptiness into sixteen types. This division is made based on objective phenomenal existence. Take, for example, sixteen different sizes of vases placed in the middle of space; we are talking about sixteen types of emptiness, not from the perspective of emptiness itself, but from the perspective of the different-sized vases. The main thing is to look within ourselves and then try to establish the emptiness of our skandhas, the psychophysical aggregates. This is most important.

Question: Is that what you sometimes call selflessness?

Answer: When we realize emptiness of the self, this is the realization of selflessness.

There is a term that says, "the body simply vanishes into atomic particles." In other words, it means disappearing into a rainbow body. This happens because the person realizes the emptiness of the skandhas.

Our mind has created a diversity of phenomenal appearances and experiences in terms of big, small, good, bad, and everything in between, and so forth. When we realize that the creator of all the diversity of these phenomena appearances and experiences is merely our own mind, then this single realization allows us to make everything vanish.

Day Two

The compassionate lord Buddha Shakyamuni has revealed to us many different levels of teachings. Among all the teachings that he has given, if we know how to take the essence of his teachings in terms of instructions and implement these, this would be best.

Whether we are involved in listening to teachings or reflecting and meditating upon what we have heard, it is essential to precede such phases of practice by the altruistic mind of bodhicitta. Having thus generated the altruistic mind of bodhicitta, the teachings that we are trying to study and meditate upon can be termed Dharma.

If we want to find the essence of the Buddha's teachings, we should understand the fourfold knowledge of impermanence, the suffering nature, emptiness, and selflessness. If we implement this knowledge in our practice, this will constitute the essential instruction for practice.

During the previous session, we finished talking about the subjects of impermanence and the suffering nature. The law of impermanence and the suffering nature are the characteristics of relative truth. We should also understand the division of impermanence in terms of the gross level of impermanence and the subtle level of impermanence. Then we will realize the subtle form of impermanence by understanding the grosser form of impermanence. For example, the very fact that there is smoke above a hill signifies that there must be fire somewhere behind that hill.

Mere understanding will not allow us to eradicate the root of misery ultimately. In the beginning, it is crucial to gain knowledge of the different levels of impermanence. Based on this knowledge, we should try to attain the actual realization of the grosser and subtle form of impermanence. Mere intellectual understanding of the various types of impermanence will allow us to suppress our conflicting emotions, whereas the actual realization of the various levels of impermanence will enable us to eradicate the very root of our conflicting emotions.

What we need to eliminate from our mind stream is our

fixation on the notion of the four wrong views: the fixation on the idea of purity, the fixation on the concept of happiness, and the fixating onto the idea of permanence and self. These four wrong views should be abandoned. But how do we generate these wrong views? We create them by our psychophysical aggregates, or the five skandhas. In brief, it can be said to be grasping onto our spirit and matter.

Most individuals claim that they are pure or that they are beautiful; very few will claim that they are impure, or ugly. And most individuals, while being submersed in suffering, will still feel that they are enjoying happiness. This is the reason these individuals are not willing to separate themselves from the worldly existence of samsara. Because of our grasping onto matter and spirit, we cultivate the notion of a truly existing self. In the same way, the notion of one, or singularity, and the notion of permanence without having to depend on others come about. And, yet again, in the same way, we develop the notion of self as the owner of the five aggregates and develop grasping onto these aggregates.

Based on these various causes, we hold onto the notion of ourselves as supreme while others are inferior, and from this polarity, we tend to generate the conflicting emotions of hatred, jealousy and other forms of negative emotions. Also, if we fixate onto the idea of not having to depend on others, then the motivation for generating love and compassion for others will not arise.

If we were to look at the reality of matter and spirit from the ultimate perspective, then the question of purity and impurity does not apply at all. In the same way, matter and spirit elude permanence and impermanence as well as self and others. In other words, they transcend permanence and impermanence, and are beyond self and others as well.

Nevertheless, beginners on the path should try to understand the reality of matter and spirit in terms of suffering and impermanence. Why should they do that? Because understanding of impermanence will gradually give rise to an understanding of emptiness. If you, for example, were to realize the impermanence of my hand, or your own hand for that matter, because the hand is composed of many atoms and sub atoms, and because on the atomic level the hand is going through constant change, you would be able to attain certainty about the emptiness of the hand. Also, the hand seems to be a singular object, but it eludes singleness because there are five fingers joined. Similarly, there does not exist a single finger, because the finger is also a composite of joints and many other particles, and if we were to further dissect the atoms, we would arrive at the partless particles. These particles are not static, but dynamic because they go through constant change. The most subtle level of an atomic particle is not static for even a moment.

The followers of the shravakayana can realize the emptiness of personal self because they can analyze down to the most subtle level of the partless particle, but they hold onto the notion that these partless particles are static, that they do not go through change. Even with such a partial understanding, they can attain the realization of the emptiness of the personal self. They are not able to understand the emptiness of the self of phenomena; they realize only the emptiness of the personal self. This is because their arguments bring them to the partless particles, that they hold as static. Whereas the followers of the Mahayana realize the impermanent nature of even these partless particles, and this understanding leads to the realization of the emptiness of the self of phenomena.

For example, to change the grosser aspect of reality, a scientist will delve into the level of the sub-particles that act as building blocks for gross reality, and will try to do something at this level to produce a measurable result on the gross level. Similarly, by relying on the sword of wisdom, we should try to dissect reality to arrive at the level of the most subtle particles, and then, at this level, understand that these particles are empty.

To understand emptiness, we need to understand the mode of emptiness, how emptiness exists. If we fail to understand the proper mode in which emptiness exists, and persists in meditating on emptiness, then such a meditation can be termed shamatha. It is not meditation of vipassana. Shamatha meditation will allow us to suppress conflicting emotions temporarily but will not eradicate them.

For example, when we undertake the samadhi, or practice that pertains to the four formless god realms, we begin by conceptualizing that all phenomenal appearances and experiences are equal to space. Similarly, all phenomenal experiences and appearances are thought of as equal to consciousness, without any tangible form. Furthermore, we meditate on the concepts that all phenomenal appearances and existence do not exist at all. We think in terms of neither existence nor non-existence. These are the four samadhis that are cultivated in connection with the four formless god realms. But these four types of meditation are worldly meditations that will not take the meditator beyond the worldly realm.

Instead, when we cultivate emptiness as a pure view, or the antidote to avert the four wrong views, we are not talking about the seeming emptiness of meditation, as it pertains to the four formless god realms. Here, when we talk about emptiness, phenomena are empty in themselves. Many logical arguments have been created to establish a genuine understanding of emptiness, but all these arguments can be summed up as the four logical arguments.

It is quite difficult to understand these logical arguments, and it comes down to the question as to whether we are familiar with this manner of analysis. If we are familiar, it will be easy to grasp their meaning; if not, it will be difficult. When we have understood the different levels of these logical arguments, we should apply this knowledge in our meditation practice. The purpose of meditation practice is to familiarize ourselves. But it is not necessary to meditate on permanence. Also, it is not necessary to meditate on self. This is because we are already familiar with the idea of something being permanent and something having a self.

Since I entered the Buddhist academic institutes in Tibet, I have heard many lectures on impermanence, selflessness and emptiness. Because of hearing this, as well as the practice that I put into it, occasionally there would arise a certain understanding. A mere understanding of the classification of reality is not effective in terms of equalizing suffering and happiness, or of equalizing self and others. Only by putting into practice what we have understood on the intellectual level will we attain the equalization of self and others, purity and impurity, and so forth. To start with, to be able to understand the empty nature of things, we should familiarize ourselves with the understanding of the four great arguments and attain certainty based on that. Then we put it into practice.

Most of us conceive that matter and spirit come into being at some beginning, remain for a while, and then disintegrate at the end. We should try to establish the reality of the unborn by relying on the practice and understanding of the four great logical arguments. If we can do so, we can remove suffering. So, we are trying to establish the unborn state.

The first logical argument is the vajra splinters that analyze the cause. Why are we required to meditate on the first argument? Because usually we believe that all phenomena arise because of certain causes. And from the perspective of the individual who has not undertaken the practice of analysis, it seems to be so: that certain phenomena come from certain causes. But if we were to profoundly scrutinize the reality, we would attain the realization of the unborn state.

If something is born as a result of a specific cause, then the birth of that phenomenon must occur from itself, or it must come from something else, "from other." The other options are that the birth of the phenomenon comes from both self and other, or that the birth comes from the absence of self and others. These are called the four extremes. We cannot find different manners of birth other than these four extremes.

When we talk about a certain phenomenon being born from itself, no individual will be ready to accept such a proposition. For example, we cannot claim that a father is born from the father himself. The example of the father is used in order to establish that self is not born from itself or that certain phenomena are born from that phenomena themselves. If a father is born from the father himself, then the initial birth of that father becomes meaningless, because the father is born twice.

Question: But the definition of a father is that somebody else is born so that the father is born as a father.
Answer: For example, we cannot say that I am born from myself. If it were so, the initial birth becomes meaningless. If the initial birth is meaningless, then the subsequent birth also becomes meaningless. This logical argument should be applied to all classifications of the reality. If self were to be born from itself, then there comes about two faults: The birth becomes meaningless and the birth becomes ceaseless. Not only one birth becomes meaningless, but hundreds of subsequent births become meaningless as well. This logical argument is rather sharp. If we are not able to grasp it, we should try to think about it, and we will grasp the meaning.
Meditating in this manner will allow us to refute the notion of fixating onto the self. Particularly, it refutes the notion of holding onto a self that is permanent, like some non-Buddhist schools propose. If the self would be permanent, then a static phenomenon could not perform any function, as opposed to a dynamic phenomenon. If a function is being carried out, then that very performance implies impermanence.

Now, we have refuted the first extreme, the birth of self from itself. We shall try to refute the birth that occurs from others, as for example, the birth of a son from a father. If something is born from other, then there comes the fault of the birth of light from darkness. Examples of these are the birth of misery from the performance of virtuous acts, and the birth of happiness from the performance of negative actions. Another example is a man giving birth to a child, as only women can do this. The main point is that all this fall into the category of birth from other.

If the phenomena are not born from self and neither are born from others, then it will be easy to deny the third extreme that proposes that phenomena are born from both self and others.

When we were investigating the first logical argument of the vajra splinters, we were primarily analyzing the cause of phenomena. During the second logical argument, we are primarily investigating the result of phenomena regarding existence and non-existence.

Question: What are the relationships between the logical arguments and the four extremes?

Answer: In the analysis of the first logical argument, we primarily analyze the first two extremes. When we understand the first two, it is easy to understand the third and fourth. The purpose of the logical argument is to prove that birth does not happen from any of the four extremes.

We shall now examine the second logical argument concerning existence and non-existence. We shall consider the characteristics of matter and spirit. Matter and mind will be either a cause, a result, or an essence. For example, the pear in my hand is either a cause, a result, or an essence.

By establishing the cause, the result or the essence of a phenomenon, we tend to fixate on these. Through the first argument that analyzes the cause, we established the emptiness of that cause or the non-characteristics of that cause.

Through the second logical argument, we try to establish that the result is free from desire. If there is a result, we usually aspire to attain that result. And by this argument, we try to cut through the hope that wants to achieve that result.

The third logical argument is the argument of being neither one nor many. The first three logical arguments are sometimes called the three doors of liberation. The fourth logical argument is said to be the king of all logical arguments and is the logical argument of interdependent origination.

Let us suppose that we vaguely understand what is meant by analyzing the cause through the first logical argument. Let us go back and delve a little deeper into the second logical argument of analyzing existence and non-existence, or production and cessation. If a result is born from a cause, does that result truly exist or does it not exist? If the newly formed result was said to exist prior to its birth, it becomes meaningless to give birth to a new existence. Conversely, the cause cannot give birth to something that does not exist, because then there would be nothing. It would not be very meaningful to say that something that is non-existent has been born. In that case a lotus flower could be born in the middle of space. It follows that all non-existent things would come into existence by following this line of reasoning. Do you understand?

Question: Is this where we talk about the hair of the tortoise?

Answer: Yes, and the horn of the rabbit. Both are examples of things that do not exist. If a result is born by relying on the cause, what kind of result is born? Is it non-existent or existent? Do you understand the question?

Question: Is this where we say neither, and you go on refuting this too?

Answer: If the answer is that the result is non-existent, then it follows that it will be possible to find hair on a tortoise and horns on a rabbit. Because through this kind of logic we would be able to make everything that is non-existent become existent. You are welcome to analyze it, examine it, and comment on it.

The main point is that we usually experience many discursive thoughts and conflicting emotions, and that we meditate on the logical arguments to lessen the impact of these thoughts and feelings. The meditation works by challenging our discursive thoughts and emotions.

Sometimes students will ask their teacher how they should proceed with their meditation. Should we meditate on analytical or concentration meditation? To answer, we must prepare with some analytical meditation; otherwise there is nothing to concentrate on. When we talk about performing analytical meditation, we are not talking about analyzing how to subdue our enemy, how to win a victory over the enemy, or how to accumulate wealth, and so forth. If we focus on these, it can seem like analytical meditation, but it lacks the true meaning of true meditation. For example, the leopard prowls very quietly when hunting. Its intention is to capture the prey and devour it. The real nature of the leopard can be very non-peaceful. A mere adoption of physical postures does not imply the peaceful nature of an individual.

We try to attack the enemy that holds onto the notion of a truly existing self, as well as the conflicting emotions, by using the arrow of the logical arguments. So, try to grasp and be mindful of the logical arguments.

The third logical argument is termed neither being one or many. Generally, we perceive the skandhas, matter, and spirit, as being truly existent. To avert such wrong views, we contemplate on the third argument. If such phenomena exist, they exist either as one or many.

Phenomena do not exist in terms of one single entity, and the body does not exist in terms of one single lump. In the same way, we can analyze the spirit or the mind. The mind does not exist in terms of one lump, because from birth up to this point, how many conceptual minds, thoughts and attitudes have we generated in our mind? All these patterns constitute our mind, and there is no single entity that exists within the mind or the body. Now, forget about the time from birth up to this point; just look from one month ago up to this present moment, or from one week ago up to now, or from yesterday up to this moment. The number of discursive thoughts and conflicting emotions that we have generated is limitless. All this constitutes our mind. If "one" cannot be established, then naturally "many" cannot be established as well.

The fourth logical argument is the argument of interdependent origination. According to this logical argument, all phenomena are shown to be interdependently originated; therefore, phenomena are said to not be truly existent. This presentation is unique to Buddhism and is not shared by other spiritual traditions. Hence, the logical argument of interdependent origination is said to be the king of all logical arguments, and there is no phenomenal experience that lies beyond the law of interdependent origination. The great logical argument of interdependent origination analyzes the cause of phenomena, the result of phenomena, and the essence of phenomena.

If we have not heard this before, it is rather difficult to comprehend. But if we grasp the meaning of these logical arguments, then it will be easy for us to meditate on the true meaning of emptiness. If we realize the view of these logical arguments, we will not find a more superior view than this, even within the presentation of Mahamudra or Dzogchen. Therefore, Lama Mipham said, "In order to truly realize the meaning of the primordial purity, we need to understand the meaning of the presentation of the Prasangika-Madhyamika."

You are welcome to ask questions concerning the four logical arguments.

Question: Can you please give an example of the fourth logical argument?

(Rinpoche strikes a bell sharply with a vajra.) Answer: The sound that is produced comes from striking this bell with this vajra. Therefore, the sound is interdependent on the vajra, so the sound is the result of many causes and conditions coming together. Its actual nature is emptiness. That is the reason the bell is rung quite often: to teach us interdependent origination! (Rinpoche jokes.)

Question: But does this not show that something can arise from something that is different from itself? Indeed, the sound is different from the vajra.

Answer: It seems like the sound is born from something else other than the sound, but that is just how it looks. If we delve deeper into this seeming reality, we will arrive at the fact that the sound is not born from other. For example, in that case, say, if the vajra were placed as it is, without being used to strike the bell, then the vajra is the other, right? Then the vajra should be able to produce the sound by itself.

Question: But cannot happiness be born from suffering?

Answer: Well, then, in the same way, we must conclude that suffering is born from happiness. In the process of trying to establish emptiness, there is a risk that we do away with karmic causations. This is serious. In his Entering the Middle Way, Chandrakirti objects to the meditator meditating on the emptiness of the karmic law of cause and result. When the meditator focuses his meditation on emptiness of the law of karmic causations itself, this form of meditation can cause the practitioner to disregard karmic law; therefore, the author objects to the meditator meditating on the emptiness of the law of causation.

In the beginning, we tried to establish emptiness through negatives, using such terms as "non-existence", and so forth. This negative emptiness can be further analyzed in togal, a state completely free from any form of elaboration. But if the negative emptiness remains, there is a risk that we fall into the pitfall of nihilism, where nothing exists, and there is no meaning. To prevent the meditator from falling into the nihilistic state, we should establish the negative emptiness by togal.

As Shantideva said, "When the meditator becomes familiar with emptiness, the meditator will cast away his familiarity with materialistic clinging to the solidity of phenomena." He further stated that he had "familiarized with nothing whatsoever," which means leaving even the familiarization of emptiness behind.

In the Uttaratantrashastra, the author says that even the Dharma or the Sangha are not the ultimate objects of refuge. In this treatise, the path is compared with a boat. When the path is traversed — when the boat has been used to cross the river, and we have arrived safely on the other shore — the boat can be left behind; we don't need it anymore. Having realized emptiness, there is no point in holding onto the idea of emptiness, because we merely go beyond the realization of emptiness. But to understand emptiness, we need to achieve the meaning of emptiness.

But if we claim that we are meditating on a state that is free from fixation, it actually becomes very difficult to meditate and sustain such a state, because even the claim that "I am meditating without fixations" is a subtle fixation in itself. In the beginning, we usually meditate with a certain amount of fixation, and then, gradually, we leave the fixations behind and enters a state free from obsession.

As long as we possess a belly, we need to eat because we get hungry. Similarly, we must think in terms of conceptual thoughts and fixations because we have a mind. But when we talk about cultivating fixations in meditation, we are not talking about cultivating negative fixations; we are talking about cultivating positive fixations in the initial state of our meditation. Positive conceptual thoughts or states of mind are compared with a very fertile ground, based on this fertile ground we can reap a very prosperous crop. However, cultivation of negative thoughts and emotions can be compared with an infertile ground, making it impossible to give rise to a prosperous crop. By basing the cultivation on wholesome or positive thoughts and emotions, there is a possibility to give rise to wisdom that knows the nature of the reality. On the other hand, the possibility of generating wisdom that knows the reality as it is by relying on negative thoughts and emotions is zero. Hence, it is important to attempt to cultivate a noble mind or heart.

Generally, when we understand emptiness, it becomes rather easy to understand what we mean by selflessness. The teachings on emptiness aim to establish the emptiness of the self of phenomena, whereas the teachings on selflessness try to establish the emptiness of the personal self. Therefore, selflessness should be understood in terms of cultivating the emptiness of the personal self. For example, if we mistake a statue for a real person at a distance, then as we get closer, we will realize the nature of the statue to be a statue, and the mistaken idea will disappear. If we, by examining the body and mind, understand the emptiness of the person, this is said to be the realizing selflessness, the realization of the emptiness of the personal self.

I will stop here. Maybe some of you need a toilet break. This is a common problem during the teaching sessions in Tibet. When I used to receive teachings, certain khenpos would be a little inconsiderate and continue their lessons for several hours, maybe even three!

Question: If you understand selflessness and the fact that things are not truly existent, as we have just discussed — if you have a good understanding of this, if you have a very full bladder and a lot of pain, how will that remove the suffering of the bladder? (Laughter.)

Answer: That means we have not understood the true meaning of emptiness and selflessness. (Everybody is laughing.) If we were truly able to understand the true meaning of emptiness, not only understanding it, but also realizing it, then the fullness of the bladder would not be a problem.

In East Tibet, in the early stage of the Chinese occupation, one Tibetan boastfully claimed that he had realized the profound meaning of emptiness. From now on, he would not be harmed by anything. When a Chinese leader heard of this, he had the man tied to a post and shot him in his hand. Of course, the bullet pierced the hand, and the man began to scream. Finally, the man was killed. He had not understood the meaning of emptiness; he had simply proclaimed it. During those days, the Communists were very hostile towards religious proclamations like this.

Question: The shravakas can realize the emptiness or the absence of self by reducing the self to partless particles, but why are they not able to use this argument to understand the inherent emptiness of the phenomena?

Answer: The fundamental reason is that the followers of the shravakayana are fearful of realizing the emptiness of the phenomenal self. This underlying fear prevents them from fully understanding the emptiness of the self of phenomena.

Question: What is the difference in realizing the emptiness of self and the emptiness of phenomena?

Answer: Mipham Rinpoche gave a perfect example of this; if there is a rope lying in a very dark room, and a person happens to enter the room, the rope can be mistaken for a snake. This is confusion. The mistake can be eliminated by lighting a lamp and realizing the absence of the snake in the rope. This liberates the person from the fear of encountering a snake. But the person has not understood the suchness of the rope itself. The rope is not realized to be empty of real existence.

Followers of the shravakayana analyze body-mind phenomena to its most subtle level and attain the realization of the emptiness of the personal self. The reason they can realize the emptiness of the self of phenomena is because they have arrived at the subtlest level of particles, that of the permanent partless particle. But they fixate onto their notion of this, and because of this, they are not able to move further forward. This is the reason they are not able to realize the emptiness of the self of phenomena.

Question: Why do they believe that these particles are permanent? Does it not say in the sutras that everything is impermanent?

Answer: This is because one single teaching of the Buddha is being interpreted on many different levels. Also, the speech from one single person can be heard in many ways. For example, what I have taught today could be understood in many ways by many different people.

Question: Does everything come from the mind? It must start somewhere, or we would not have to do all these things.

Answer: When you ask where all these things are coming from, do you mean all phenomenal existence or what I spoke about?

Questioner: I mean everything, it must start somewhere.

All things come from emptiness. Our thoughts also come from emptiness. Our very thought is emptiness.

Questioner: Is this Madhyamika?

Answer: Yes. All the explanations that I have given to you are based on my personal understanding of the scriptures.

Question: How would you meditate on selflessness?

Answer: To meditate on selflessness, first we must establish selflessness by analytical meditation. For example, if we want to meditate on the selflessness of phenomena, the emptiness of the self of phenomena, then we need to go through the different phases of these four great arguments. We must conduct analytical meditation, the medium of these four great arguments. And we should analyze the meaning of the selflessness of phenomena until we gain profound certainty regarding selflessness of phenomena. Once we gain profound certainty, we should stop further analysis and let our mind rest within that certainty.

The presentation of the four logical arguments is like a handle that we can hold onto while trying to establish the selflessness of phenomena, but this does not mean that we should not use our intelligent mind to analyze the selflessness of phenomena. If we can come up with our own version of logical arguments in order to establish and validate the selflessness of phenomena, we are welcome to do so.

We should also alternate our meditation between the sutra tradition of the Buddha and the tantric presentation of the Buddha. According to the sutra tradition of the Buddha, we analyze and experiment, but according to the tantric tradition, we primarily allow our mind to rest within the state of certainty.

Question: Can you recommend a book on the four logical arguments?

Answer: You will find the presentation of the four logical arguments in the books known as Entering into the Middle Way by Chandrakirti and The Root Verses of the Middle Way by Nagarjuna. Among many of the treatises on this subject, these two are considered most important.

So, we will stop here and conclude with the prayers.

The Four Foundations of Mindfulness

Day One

A practitioner who wishes to attain the state of omniscient Buddhahood must travel along five spiritual paths. The first of these five spiritual paths is "tsog lam" in Tibetan, which means "the path of accumulation." On this path is the practice of the four foundations of mindfulness. Most practitioners are on this path.

While we are still traveling on the path of accumulation, we must understand what the main practice is. If we do not understand the practice on the path of accumulation, it will be like trying to climb a rock without hands. This is tremendously risky, and it is obvious that such a person should not attempt to climb a mountain. If we do not properly understand the practice, do not do it.

The four wrong views and the four right views that we discussed yesterday have a close connection with the teaching on the four foundations of mindfulness. Based on our physical existence and our feelings, on our mind and the content of our mind, we develop discursive thoughts and conflicting emotions. During the practice of the four foundations of mindfulness, we utilize the intelligent mind, the sword of wisdom, to penetrate the reality of physical existence as well as the reality of feeling, mind, the content of mind, and phenomena to arrive at the actual nature of these realities.

The cultivation of the four foundations of mindfulness leans more towards the practice of vipassana rather than shamatha. These days, many Buddhist practitioners practice the four foundations of mindfulness, and as a result they experience the conflicting emotions have a reduced impact. If we grasp the meaning of the practice of the four foundations of mindfulness and implement them in our training, we will be transformed.

Living beings are tremendously attached to and possessive of their physical existence. But we are not able to cultivate that much love and compassion for others. Therefore, we do not refer to this attachment as compassionate and loving—it is an attachment towards our own physical existence without regard for others.

Attachment distinguishes us from others; compassion bridges the gap between ourselves and others. Peace and joy cannot arise in a mind that distinguishes itself from others. The mind that divides reality into self and others experiences misery and other sorts of turmoil. Therefore, it is essential to cultivate the compassion that does not distinguish between ourselves and others.

The first of the four foundations of mindfulness is mindfulness of our physical body. Here we need to realize that our own physical existence is impermanent. It is empty, without self, and has a suffering nature. We should not fixate on our own body as if it is permanent, with a self, and a happy nature.

In the beginning we should relax our body, and then we should try to turn our mind inwards and observe our physical existence with mindfulness. If we cannot observe our own physical existence because of discursive thoughts, try to release these disturbing emotions with the practice of awareness of the breath. We can practice breath awareness five or ten times. If the discursive thoughts persist, we should continue to practice breath awareness, and then if attachment is still strong, we can meditate on the aspect of ugliness.

If there is a strong disturbing emotion of hatred, we should mediate on equanimity. If there is a strong disturbing emotion of ignorance, we should mediate on interdependent origination. Our mind is not hidden from us; therefore, we should identify what kind of disturbing feeling is the strongest and apply the appropriate antidote.

It is hard to accept that we are victims of disturbing

emotions. We might deny this, and therefore it becomes difficult to feel remorse when we have done something wrong. If we do not undertake the practice of confession and develop a sense of regret, then purification of bad actions and disturbing emotions cannot take place. Human beings hide their bad qualities and display their admirable ones.

While we practice, whichever disturbing emotions become dominant, we should try to eliminate them. It is futile to wage a war without knowing who the enemy is. We will not be able to defeat an enemy in such a manner. In the beginning, it is important to recognize and accept the disturbing emotions when they arise, and on the basis on this, try to practice the antidotes to eliminate them.

During the practice of mindfulness of our body it is essential to look carefully at our body. We fixate on our body as something which is extremely clean. But if we do not take a bath for three days, we will come to know the state of our body. It will be smelly. From this perspective there is not much sense in generating attachment to our body.

We also assume that the nature of our body is healthy, but the body is suffering. The Buddha says that our body does not transcend the three levels of suffering: the suffering of suffering, the suffering of change, and all-pervasive suffering. Fixation on our body's cleanliness and healthiness is inconsistent with its fundamental nature.

Similarly, we insist that our body is permanent. It is strange that we regard our body as permanent, because it is impermanent, and even if we know this, we still latch onto it as if it will last. If our body is not permanent, it must be impermanent; therefore, it will go through constant change, and hence it does not make sense to be possessive of and attached to the body.

When we meditate on the impermanence of our physical existence, we should meditate on the body as a collection of grosser limbs which consist of more subtle components. These components are themselves conglomerations of many atomic particles. We should then dissect these atomic particles until we arrive at the partless particle.

It is wrong to hold onto the notion of a self. This self does not exist regarding our own body or others'. This is how it is. Our notion of the self is based on our own body. The body is taught to be a singular entity. Hence, when we talk about self, we think of the self as one, since the body is one. When we meditate on the mindfulness on the body, we can contemplate the Bodhicharyavatara, which says, "The head is not the body, the arms are not the body, the nose is not the body", and so forth. Through a process of negating our body we finally conclude that there is no body to be discovered. Then we simply allow our mind to rest in the state of not finding our own body.

In this way, we should look profoundly into our body and try to see its impermanent nature. In the same way, we should try to understand the suffering nature of our own body, the emptiness of our body, and the no-self nature of our body. If we reach an understanding concerning our body in all these ways, we will achieve the insight of the vipassana meditation.

It is vital to distill the essence of all the teachings that we have heard and put them into practice. When we involve ourselves with Dharma or meditation practice, it is important to remember that we should strike a balance between excessive tension and excessive relaxation. It is therefore recommended to alternate analytical meditation and concentration meditation. If we practice only concentration meditation there is a risk of falling asleep. When we feel drowsy, we should switch to analytical meditation. If we begin to feel a headache or tension while we are doing analytical meditation, we should switch to concentration meditation. It is very good to alternate between these two meditations.

The second of the four foundations of mindfulness is the mindfulness of feeling. The Buddha chose meditation on the mindfulness of feeling because human beings use their feelings to quarrel with each other. For example, most people like to feel healthy and happy for themselves but are happy to inflict sorrow and misery upon others. This happens between countries, religious traditions, races, and families.

Our fixation on feelings is the source of disputes, but when the Buddha looked for the existence of feeling, he could not find it. Instead, Buddha discovered impermanence and emptiness. But most living beings perceive feeling as permanent and real. Because of this, problems like quarrels, disputes, and wars arise.

If we get a sore, then merely dealing with the sore will not be particularly useful, but if we find the cause of the sore and do something, we will be able to prevent the sore from recurring. If we try to do something about disputes, wars, and quarrels, our effort will not be highly active, whereas if we remove to the source of the conflict or controversy, then we can prevent future wars and quarrels.

If feeling was truly existent, then it should truly exist either in objective phenomena or in the subjective mind. Consider three different people meeting a fourth person. One person might like the fourth; another might not; and the third might not care one way or the other. This shows that these feelings cannot be found independently in one single person. Similarly, a single dish tastes differently to different people. The same applies to clothes. Also, some people have higher standards of cleanliness than others.

A Tibetan story describes a man who fell in love with a woman. This man asked his friend, "Is my girlfriend truly pretty or not?" His friend replied, "No, your girlfriend is not pretty." The man argued, "When you look at my girlfriend from where you are standing, you are not able to see her beauty, but if you were to see her through my eyes, you would see her in the way I do." Objective reality does not possess attributes such as cleanliness, filthiness, happiness or sorrow; rather, these attributes are created by the subjective mind.

Buddha said that sentient beings of the six realms of existence perceive one reality in six different ways. Forget about the perception of the creatures in the six different realms, even within the single sphere of humans we have a vast difference in perception. For example, when the sun shines on my mother, then the sun has no concept of her as a mother, whereas when my father looks at my mother, he has the notion of a wife.

Feelings do not truly exist regarding objective phenomena. We need to understand that feelings are devoid of true existence, gain certainty in this understanding and implement it our practice. Do we doubt that feelings are empty? We should not let doubt remain, because otherwise we will not be able to enter the depths of meditation. We should try overcoming doubt. With a doubtless mind we can perform miracles. If we develop doubt when we want to jump across a small brook, we will probably land in the middle of it! The doubt will sap our strength and confidence, whereas if we have a very trusting mind when we leap, we will make it to the other side. This is because a trusting mind generates confidence. We should have confidence that we are able to meditate, and that we are able to enter the depth of meditation.

Many teachings on meditation have been expounded. Meditation should correspond to reality. We do not meditate on something that does not correspond to reality. It is not required to meditate on something that is false or unreal; such meditations are performed on a regular basis. For example, we meditate regularly on permanence, or on the self.

We have been meditating on four wrong views for a long time. Because of this, we have managed to create the evolution of samsaric existence. Here we are trying to meditate on the four correct views that act as an antidote to wrong views, leave behind samsaric existence and arrive at nirvana.

It is difficult for busy householders to attain a very profound experience of meditation, but upon hearing teachings and attempting to meditate, they will gain some transformation. During a solitary retreat, we leave behind telephones, TV, and all activities. The meditation practice will then create peace of mind and joy.

If a car is driven, it will move. But if the car is left as it is, it will not move. The five senses can be compared to drivers, the sixth sense consciousness, can be compared to the car. A car cannot be driven by many drivers at the same time, but we are driven by five drivers. Therefore, there are constant accidents. (Laughter.) When accidents occur and create "inner accidents," these inner accidents create more complications. Then the police arrive, along with mental pain and unhappiness

In the beginning, when we hear and study the teaching, we have to consider many elaborate instructions, but when it comes down to the practice of meditation, we should simplify these teachings so that the meditation practice can have an affect our being.

Later today I will teach you a yogic practice. The practice of the yoga should be followed by practice of breath awareness. We can count our breath five, ten or fifteen times. The practice of the breath awareness should be followed by the practice of the first of the four foundations of mindfulness. There are six types of breath awareness. The simplest is to follow the breath. As we exhale, the awareness runs parallel with the breath, and the same with inhaling. In this way, the breath is constantly embraced by our awareness. Breath awareness can be done five times in the beginning. When we succeed in doing this without becoming distracted, we can double it to ten.

Do you have any questions?

Question: I am wondering about the first mindfulness, the suffering nature of the body. Do you refer to illness and death? Is not suffering created in mind?

Answer: If there is physical suffering, we need to contemplate our body. If there is mental suffering, then we need to consider the mind.

Question: If you have pain in your body, should you

tolerate the pain?

Answer: When there is pain in a certain part of our body, we should try not to focus on that pain; we should focus on the whole body. If we focus on the pain, the pain may worsen.

Once, a Tibetan was struck by an eye disease. He went to consult a physician, but it did not help. Then he went to another physician who said, "Actually there is no eye disease at all, you do not need to worry. My diagnosis shows that you have a problem with your stomach. If you don't take care of your stomach you might get serious problems." After a while, his eye disease was completely cured because he was more worried about his stomach.

Another example is when we receive a hard massage to relieve a headache. While the masseur presses our head, the firm rubbing on the head is followed by tremendous relief. This comes from the pain created by the masseur.

Question: But if you try to focus on something else instead of your pain is this not mere suppression?

Answer: We can also observe the pain in our body, but this must be done without fixation, and without hope and fear. Then it is okay. But it is better to focus upon the whole body. But if there is no expectation, there is no problem in observing the pain. However, this is difficult to put into practice when we experience severe pain and illness. It is easy to talk about these things, but difficult to do.

Question: Can you describe the path of accumulation more specifically?

Answer: During the path of accumulation, we are involved in practices that allow us to accumulate a lot of merit.

Questioner: Is it not easy to become self-centered when you do this?

The path of accumulation, especially in the practice of the Mahayana, is not done for our own welfare. It is done to bring about good for all sentient beings. Therefore, there is no question of self-interest.

It is essential to recognize the actual path we are on. If we are on the path of accumulation, we should realize this, and accumulate merit and practice the four foundations of mindfulness. The second path is the path of application, also called the path of linking. It links us to the third path: the path of insight. On the path of linking, we attain the most purified mind. Here the mind is on the verge of becoming wise.

On the path of insight, we gain insight into ultimate reality. The next path is the fourth path: the path of meditation. On this path, we familiarize ourselves with the insight that was gained on the third path. The fifth path is the path of no more learning. When we enter the path of no more learning, we attain the state of Buddhahood. The five paths are the thirty-seven aspects of the bodhisattva path, so the four foundations of mindfulness belong to the thirty-seven aspects of practices of the bodhisattva.

Now shall we practice yoga outside?

Day Two

Listen to the following teachings by generating an altruistic state of mind. The main thing that we have been discussing today is the practice of the four foundations of mindfulness, which is the essential practice on the path of accumulation.

Buddha said that the body should be observed within the body, and we should thus gain insight into the reality of this body. Similarly, we should observe our feelings, our mind and phenomena in general, and try to attain new insight into them. Attaining this new insight is the attainment of vipassana meditation. Sentient beings usually fixate on their body or physical existence in terms of being permanent, clean, happy and having a self. Conversely, the yogi or practitioner of meditation will perceive his or her physical existence as impermanent, without self, with a suffering and empty nature. Therefore, it is essential to train the mind. Training the mind is called "lojong" in Tibetan. "Lo" means "mind," while "jong" means "to train."

While we are not enlightened, we perceive our physical existence as a single lump, permanent and with a self. This misconception generates conflicting emotions and discursive thoughts, which evolve into the accumulation of various forms of karma, which again is followed by misery. Thus, in this way we accumulate negative actions.

But as meditators, we try to perceive our physical existence in terms of impermanence, no-self, suffering, and emptiness. With this correct perception, we lessen the misery, eradicate it at the root, and obtain the omniscient state of Buddhahood.

The second mindfulness is that of feelings. Feelings should be understood in terms of our experience. Based on the experience of feelings, there evolve disputes, arguments, and quarrels. Nevertheless, we need to understand both the relative and the ultimate nature of feelings. The relative nature of feelings is impermanent; the ultimate nature of feelings is emptiness. When we experience a certain feeling after meditation, we should try to perceive our experience as an illusion.

During the meditation session, while we are meditating on the ultimate nature of feelings, which is meditation on the close mindfulness of feelings, we try to attain the three cycles of non-conceptuality. This means that there is no subject who feels, there is no object that is being felt, and there is no actual feeling. We should examine whether the feeling exists regarding objective reality, or if the feeling exists in the subjective mind, or if the feeling exists somewhere in between. Having analyzed the nature of the feeling through such investigation, we should alternate analytical meditation with concentration meditation.

Meditation on the four foundations of mindfulness is essential in connection with the path of accumulation. The compassionate Lord Buddha had very sharp faculties and was therefore capable of traversing the whole spectrum of the spiritual path within a single session, beginning with the four foundations of mindfulness. Hence, meditation on the four foundations of mindfulness is especially important for beginners on the path.

Then we arrive at the third foundation of mindfulness: the mindfulness of mind. All sentient beings possess a mind, and the mind should be understood in terms of awareness and clarity. Some people claim that the mind is the brain. Certain people think that the mind is in the heart. As far as Buddhism is concerned, the brain and heart act as a base for the mind. But neither the brain nor the heart is the actual mind. The Buddha explains that the mind forms the basis for samsaric cyclic existence. But this mind can also produce the state of enlightenment: nirvana. The nature of mind is awareness and luminosity.

Ordinarily, the mind creates the polarity of subjective and objective reality and conceptualizes something as permanent or impermanent. It also conceptualizes itself as separate from others. Clean is separated from dirty, ugly is separated from pretty, and pleasant sounds are separated from noise. The creator of all these polarities is the mind. Tracing everything back the mind, realizing that the mind is the creator of all these phenomenal experiences and appearances, and realizing the emptiness of this mind will allow us to realize the emptiness of all phenomenal experiences and appearances.

Most people believe that their mind is somewhere within the body, and based on this belief, they build the notion of a self. Now, we need to use our wisdom, and ask if the body is the mind. If the body is the mind, the mind becomes tangible. The body possesses four limbs, so perhaps the mind also possesses four limbs? The hand has five fingers; can the mind also have five parts? If we think along these lines, we will arrive at the certainty that the body is not the mind.

Then we should ask if the body is not the mind, is the mind then outside the body? If the mind were separated from the body, we would be capable of perceiving that mind. The Buddha said that mind cannot be found within the mind. If it did, then where do past thoughts go? If the mind exists, it should be inside or outside of our body, but if we tried to locate this place, we would not be able to do so.

Similarly, we can analyze where the mind comes from, where it abides and where it goes. Such analysis will bring us to the conclusion that the mind has no origin, no abiding and no cessation. Also, the mind has no shape or color. In this manner, if we analyze and investigate the nature of the mind, we arrive at an understanding of its emptiness.

The reason we need to meditate in these ways is because sentient beings have several wrong views. In order to counteract these wrong views, we use different methods of meditation. We gain certainty that the mind is empty and at the same time we transfer our analysis into meditation practice. This establishes the mind in terms of emptiness as well as clarity, or luminosity. This is the inseparability of emptiness and appearance. The mind that realizes this is wise. Such a mind is also the mother of the Buddhas of the three times. By using these terms, buddhas and enlightened beings can communicate the truth of fundamental reality.

When we have arrived at a profound certainty regarding the view, we do not need to perform further analytical meditation; we can do concentration meditation. If we study and hear this repeatedly, we will attain a deeper understanding. While I give teachings on the mindfulness of mind, your mind tries to grasp their meaning, and when you grasp the meaning, your mind thinks, "Okay, certain terms mean this or that." But if we turn within ourselves and look at the very mind that is grasping the meaning of these terms and phrases, we will not be able to capture it or locate its existence. This failure is the emptiness of the mind.

The mind is like a mirror. On the surface of a mirror we can see reflections. In the same way, all kinds of emotions can be on the surface of the mind, but we should not be concerned about whether these emotions are positive or negative; it is enough to observe their nature. When discursive thoughts arise, if we leave them just as they are, they will liberate themselves. If we can do this, this is meditation according to Dzogchen, and meditation according to the sutras.

In the same way, the mind should be perceived in terms of impermanence, no-self and emptiness. If we can perceive the mind as impermanent, without self and empty, then suffering cannot enter our mind. But if the four wrong views constantly occupy our mind, then our mind will know no peace and joy. Therefore, we should practice close mindfulness of our mind.

The fourth foundation of mindfulness is the mindfulness of dharma, which here means phenomena rather than the teachings. There are no dharmas other than the five aggregates. All dharmas can be found within the aggregation of the five skandhas. We can further reduce the five skandhas into composite phenomena and non-composite phenomena. When we meditate on impermanence, suffering, emptiness, and no-self, regarding our psychophysical aggregates, this is meditation on the dharmas. Sentient beings can see others, but not themselves. Therefore, it is easy to see the faults of others instead of our own, but in this practice, we are not trying to observe the psychophysical existence of other people; we are trying to observe our own skandhas.

Our five senses are open to external objective reality, and objective reality is very easily conceived, but these five sensory organs are not able to perceive themselves. Even this understanding that the sensory organs are focused outwards and perceive the faults and shortcomings of others, will bring tremendous benefit. It can give us a sense of respect for others. In the same way there will also arise respect for what others are saying, and because of this, we will be less proud and arrogant.

When we meditate on the mindfulness of dharmas, we should try to see that our five skandhas go through constant change. We should also view our five skandhas as having no self, and with a suffering and empty nature. All foundations of mindfulness are contained within the practice of the mindfulness of dharmas.

Question: I understand that you can talk about the impermanence of the body and feelings, but how can you speak about the impermanence of the mind when you cannot find the mind?

Answer: Some thoughts are positive, and others are negative. Positive and virtuous thoughts can change into terribly negative thoughts, like hatred, for example. This is the impermanent nature of the mind.

Question: So, are mind and thoughts the same?

Answer: There is no separate mind other than the very thought her an now. It is difficult to talk about thoughts as separate from the mind itself. Is the reflection in a mirror one with the mirror or separate from it? This is difficult to answer. Any other questions?

Question: But isn't the nature of thought dharmakaya?

Answer: If we realize the empty nature of the mind, that is, if we understand the empty nature of the thought or the emotion, this will be dharmakaya. A failure to recognize the empty nature of thoughts and emotions of the mind is samsara. While we are experiencing samsara, dharmakaya is already there.

Question: Then there is no samsara and no nirvana, no separation?

Answer: All that we have been talking about is made up by the mind. These concepts of dharmakaya, nirmanakaya, samsara does not exist. Mind you, we are now entering into a deeper level of the teaching.

Buddha said there is only one example of mind, and that is space, or sky. Usually sentient beings claim to have seen the sky, but this means they have seen nothingness. Seeing the sky is the same as seeing nothingness, or emptiness. As far as the suchness of sky is concerned, we cannot talk about it in terms of good sky, bad sky, good weather or bad weather. This is the reason that the Buddha kept silent for one week after enlightenment, without giving any teachings, because it is difficult to put into words.

Question: When you establish that mind is impermanent, can you also say that space is impermanent?

Answer: There are two different kinds of space, one is called composite space, and the other is called non-composite space. With non-composite space we cannot talk about permanence or impermanence. Composite space is impermanent because composite space performs certain functions. Anything that performs a function is impermanent.

For example, some non-Buddhist philosophies and doctrines claim that the creator of the world is God, and that God or the Supreme Self is permanent. This is impossible; they cannot be permanent and perform functions at the same time.

Question: Can you give an example of composite space?

Answer: Composite space can be found within our nose, within our mouth, within our body, as well as outside the body. Composite space facilitates certain activities.

Question: Is the space inside the entire universe composite?

Answer: Space is non-composite, but when we talk about composite space, it is created by human beings.

Question: Is it a concept?

Answer: Yes. For example, our conceptual mind creates the concept of some spaces being big and other spaces being small. The architect who built this house, would think about how to do this and plan before beginning construction. When it was completed, there was a space, this room. The amount of the space in this room corresponds with the size of this room.

Question: Can a composite space be natural? Like a cave?

Answer: Yes, that is also composite space, but made by nature.

Question: Physicists talk about space-time: space connected with time. Is there a similar concept in Buddhism?

Answer: Space is something created by our conceptual mind, and our conceptual mind also creates time. In this respect they are equal.

We cannot talk about space as being existent or non-existent. The actual nature of space is emptiness. This also holds true for all tangible objects like this table, which has come together through many causes and conditions.

To establish the emptiness of phenomenal existence and appearance, the Buddha gave the example of space to illustrate the emptiness of all phenomenal existence. But if sentient beings fixate on the emptiness of the space, this fixation will become their bondage. So, then the Buddha had to give a new example to liberate them from their new obsession, for instance, that phenomenal experiences and appearance are like illusions.

When scientists say that space and time are one, what kind of reasoning do they come up with?

Respondent: I have heard one example of space-time. Let us say you have a pair of twins, one is on earth, and the other is traveling in a spaceship at the speed of light. When the spaceship returns, the twin on earth will be older than the other twin.

The Buddha said this a long time ago. The Buddha said that a single day in one of the God realms lasts five hundred days in the human realm. It looks like scientists have reached the same conclusion that the Buddha reached 2500 years ago.

Question: You talked about the suffering nature of the body, feelings and mind. But sometimes you say that the true nature of mind is emptiness and luminosity, and now we are talking about the suffering nature of mind. Can you explain?

Answer: The nature of mind is suffering in nature because if we fail to understand the impermanent, no-self and empty nature of mind, we will experience suffering, whereas if we realize this, we will overcome this suffering. It is like an incompetent driver on the highway. This is dangerous and can create misery for everyone. But if he or she has good driving skills it can be lots of fun. Many people are not skillful drivers, so we must be careful.

Question: Can you give a short summery of the four wrong views?

Answer: We could say that fixating on permanence and singleness is the essence of the four wrong views. For example, when we refer to our physical existence, we say "my body." When we say "I," the thought of a single person comes to mind. Also, from birth until death we think there is a single "I" that will never change. Can you grasp my meaning? If you want to practice this after this session, will you be able to do so? This is important.

Question: So, do we have to go through all these questions?

Answer: Yes, this is analytical meditation. Various experiences might come while we meditate, but we should not ascribe much importance to these, whether these experiences are good or bad. This is important.

When we analyze the body down to the most subtle particle and realizes that these particles go through constant changes, we realize the conventional truth. This realization will help us to understand the ultimate truth.

Question: But how can you observe partless particles? You cannot see them with your eyes.

Answer: We cannot see them with our eyes, only with our mind during meditation. It is questionable if even the Buddha saw the partless particles that are the building blocks of the whole universe. But he saw them through his wisdom eye. This is a good question because when we cannot see something with our own eyes, we think that it does not exist. There is a wide range of phenomena that our physical eyes cannot perceive.

The Two Truths

Please prepare this session by generating a mind of enlightenment, bodhicitta, to benefit the limitless numbers of sentient beings. I rejoice in having the opportunity to come here and teach the holy teaching of Lord Buddha. Most of the participants in this audience know me, and this makes me especially joyful.

An important term in Tibetan Buddhism is "nang," which means "inner" or "interior." Happiness and misery should not be understood as coming from external objects. To attain ultimate and unchanging happiness, we need to realize our innermost being. We must strive to study the workings of the mind. When we realize our innermost being, we will realize the meaning of life and the meaning of the happiness that we experience in our life. In Buddhist teachings, the term "happiness" refers to authentic happiness.

In the beginning is it important to study the teachings of the Buddha. The ancient Indian master, called Digniga, said, "Initially we should exert ourselves in study, followed by a phase of reflection, which should be followed a phase of meditation practice." By engaging ourselves in the study of the Buddha's teachings, we will achieve peace of mind.

By gleaning wisdom from listening and studying, we can cut through doubt about the ultimate truth and acquire a determined mind. When we have gained certainty of the ultimate truth through listening and studying, as well as through reflection and contemplation, we should implement this certainty by uniting it with the phase of meditation. By relying on the wisdom that comes from meditation, we will be able to uproot disturbing emotions.

The Nyingma tradition of Tibetan Buddhism places a great deal of emphasis on analytical contemplation, which is the initial process of listening and studying. If we initially do not acquire the wisdom that comes from profound analysis, it is impossible to gain wisdom from meditation. If concentration meditation is not united with analytical contemplation, for example by only favoring analytical meditation, the Tibetan expression "idiot meditator" may be applicable. No benefit will come from such meditation. So, we should unite analytical contemplation with concentration meditation. Then, we should only do concentration meditation. I brought this up to underline the importance of the processes of listening, contemplating and meditating. I studied the teaching of the Buddha for ten years, and then meditation came quite easily.

As sentient beings, we are extroverted. We tend to perceive external objective phenomena through our senses. Therefore, we are not able to turn our mind inwards and look at ourselves. It is easy for us to see the dirt on somebody else's face, but it takes an effort to see dirt on our own face. The same goes for the sense of hearing. Our bodies make numerous sounds that we seldom hear, although we easily hear noises from outside.

Because of the function of sentient beings' five senses, we can develop a lot of discursive thoughts. The mind that is occupied with rambling thoughts is a deluded mind that tries to establish what is pure and what is impure, what is right and what is wrong, what is deluded and what is not deluded.

The deluded mind tries to decide what we see and hear by using our senses. But the mind of the Buddha perceives external phenomena in a completely different way: as lacking true existence and characteristics. Phenomena that have no characteristics do not exist. To quote the Heart Sutra: "The "I" does not have any true characteristics; the ear does not have any true characteristics; the tongue does not have any true characteristics." This can be applied to all sensory organs, to the sensory consciousnesses, and to the mind — they all lack true existence. If all these things lack true existence, then what is the truth? According to the teachings of the Buddha, there are two levels of truth.

The first truth is relative truth; the second truth is

absolute truth. The Tibetan word for relative truth implies "all" and "without essence." All samsaric phenomena are impermanent. Such phenomena can be very deceptive. It is easy to observe that all phenomena are impermanent; we can see an infant be born and gradually grow into a toddler, adolescent, and adult. Also, our feelings change. Sometimes we experience joy, sometimes misery. Impermanence applies equally to the external element of our environment.

It is difficult to find ultimate fulfillment. We can aspire to become wealthy and think that we will be happy by the time we have a certain amount of money in the bank. However, as soon as this happens, we want to have even more. It is therefore difficult for a samsaric being to attain ultimate fulfillment.

The Buddha said that lacking something is an illusion, and so is not lacking something. When we lack something that we want, we are miserable. This situation changes when we obtain something that we want, but we cannot guarantee our happiness then because new miseries will accompany the possession of new things.

All discursive thoughts can be traced to the three disturbing emotions: attachment, anger, and ignorance. The presence of rambling thoughts in a mind that is filled with these emotions makes it difficult for us to attain the omniscient state of the Buddha.

To realize relative truth, we must understand impermanence. Impermanence should be understood by considering birth. Birth is followed by destruction. If we, as meditators, realize the meaning of relative truth in this way, we will receive immense benefit even if we lack realization of ultimate truth. However, if we believe in the permanence of relative truth regarding our loved ones, regarding our spouse, with regard to our friends and family, or material objects, we will suffer. But again, if we realize the impermanence of relative truth with regards to all those things, we will be at peace.

If we had observed the physical existence of Buddha

Shakyamuni, we would have seen the nature of impermanence affecting his body, but the mind of Buddha Shakyamuni is enlightened and does not know the miseries of birth, old age, sickness, and death.

The view that holds onto permanence, true existence, and the singularity of external phenomena, is a perverted view. In contrast, if we realize the impermanent, selfless, empty, and suffering nature of external phenomena, particularly regarding our physical existence, our mind will not be perverted.

To understand the meaning of relative truth, it is essential to realize the meaning of impermanence. Instead of trusting objective phenomena, we should realize that external phenomena do not possess any absolute happiness. They are tainted by misery and suffering. If we realize the impermanent nature of the objective reality of objective phenomena, such a realization corresponds to the universal truth. If this understanding develops into the realization of the emptiness of the true existence of objective phenomena, this is the realization of emptiness, the absolute truth.

The ultimate truth lies beyond the domain of expression and description. Absolute truth cannot be expressed because our mind is powerless to do so. Our mind knows only two things: the extreme of existence and the extreme of non-existence. Our mind cannot go beyond these two extremes. For example, if we cannot see something, we will not believe that it exists. The same applies to our sense organs. For example, the ear is rather small, with only a small aperture, so there are an infinite number of sounds that we cannot hear. We believe in the sounds we can listen to; we do not believe in the sounds we cannot hear. The same applies to the nose, tongue, and the skin; their capacity to discern is very weak. Because of this, we are not able to understand all phenomena.

Earlier I said that the sense organs lack characteristics. Because of this, our sense organs are incapable of perceiving the whole spectrum of reality. Therefore, the Buddha said that the sense organs lack characteristics or true existence. One

Tibetan scholar said that if our eyes were placed in a different position, for example vertically, then our reality would be completely changed. When the Buddha said that the three realms are only in the mind, this means that the actual determining factor is our own mind. objective reality does not determine phenomena. They are determined by how our minds perceive them.

If we close our eyes and prevent our sense organs from being distracted, this is a kind of meditation. In the sutras, the Buddha talks about threefold meditation or samadhi meditation ("one-pointed concentration"). The Buddha talks about the samadhi that is associated with the three gates of the body, speech, and mind. For example, if we open the gates of our mind or sense organs, then many discursive thoughts will come through. But if we shut the gates, then the discursive thought will be blocked from our mind. The Buddha instructed how to practice closing the gates of our body, speech, and mind. He said that we should sit still, remain silent, and concentrate. If we could practice this simple meditation technique in a quiet place for seven days, then we will undoubtedly be able to suppress our conflicting emotions, at least while we are meditating. If we cannot do this for one week, then we probably will not be able to gain control over our disturbing emotions.

Our many past lives have made us familiar with our disturbing emotions. Therefore, it is crucial for the meditator to use mindfulness to look within the mind. This is meditation. In this way, we can practice meditation in formal sessions and implement whatever meditative experience we have gained into the informal period of our daily life. When formal meditation sessions are supplemented with post-meditation practice, then we are not only able to suppress and gain control over our disturbing emotions, but we will be capable of eradicating the root of the disturbing thoughts and feelings. It is therefore essential to combine the actual meditation sessions with post-meditation sessions.

This has been a very brief presentation of the relative

truth and the ultimate truth. Do you have questions?

Question: Is analytical meditation an absolute necessity for any real meditation experience?

Answer: The Buddha teaches about the emptiness of self. We should not accept the teaching of the Buddha at face value; we should thoroughly analyze the teachings. There is a reason the Buddha gave the teaching on the emptiness of the self, and we need to realize the validity of this reason. To do this we must analyze and use our investigative powers. For example, in the practice of being mindful of our body, we should observe our body and try to determine whether there exists a self within the body or not. The Indian Buddhist master Chandrakirti laid out the seven-fold reasoning of no-self of the chariot. If we meditate upon this seven-fold reasoning, then we are doing analytical meditation.

Since infinite time we have been accustomed to thinking that the ego exists. Whatever we do is based on the true existence of a self. We put a tremendous amount of trust into this notion. We trust what the "I" thinks is true, what the "I" states is true. Whatever the self does, we think it is right. If we build the ego in this manner, then this self will become so huge that it makes it difficult for us to see others.

Because of the law of interdependence, it is impossible to experience happiness for ourselves without experiencing happiness for other sentient beings. This implies that our experience is intimately connected with that of our fellow beings. Therefore, the Buddha claims that the existence of the self is responsible for suffering. The Buddha has also said that the altruistic mind brings about benefit for all living beings. To trust the teachings of the Buddha, we need to study, listen, reflect, and meditate on them, then we can become convinced of their validity. This is the foundation of the teaching of the Buddha. Everybody knows this, but it bears repeating.

I believe that many of you are quite knowledgeable on this topic and that many of you have been practicing for many years. You are therefore a most receptive audience. It is crucial for a teacher to share his understanding with such an audience.

Question: But you can study for a lifetime without being finished. When do we know that we should stop learning and go into retreat instead?

Answer: When we gain a profound certainty about the emptiness of self, we can drop our studies and apply this understanding to our meditation practice. But until we develop this profound certainty, we should continue our study. But if we still pursue our academic study through listening and reading after we have realized the meaning of the view, this is no point, because we have found our lost elephant. During the time of the Buddha, the elephant was a special and beloved animal. That is why the elephant is used as a symbol in the Buddhist texts.

Question: I am a bit confused about the term "study" in this context because the way it is being presented it seems to imply more than an intellectual understanding — that there is insight as well, that must be gained through meditation. Can you explain a little bit more about the meaning of study in this context?

Answer: If we can assimilate the teaching, when we hear instructions from a meditation master, this teaching will create peace in our mind, and this peace will permeate our body and our speech. Therefore, the sign of having studied and heard teachings is the experience of peace. And the sign of whether we have meditated is the absence of discursive thoughts.

By relying on the phase of studying and listening we are likely to experience shamatha. But such a process alone will not guarantee the realization of vipassana or insight meditation. Giving rise to the experience of shamatha meditation will bring us closer to the successive meditation experiences that will lead us to the experience of vipassana meditation.

For example, while we are studying and listening,

instead of letting our mind become distracted, focus on what we are studying and hearing; this constitutes the practice of one-pointed concentration. Also, because the objective focus of our meditation is a virtuous object, because we are studying Dharma, our mind will be protected from non-virtuous objects, at least while we are studying. This type of practice will constitute the practice of both the Dharma and meditation.

Buddhist practice should not be understood only as escaping to an isolated retreat and staying in a small hut. Any method that will lessen our discursive thoughts or conflicting emotions constitutes Buddhist meditation practice. If the phase of study and listening allows us to exclude rambling thoughts, then this also constitutes a practice. To use an example, compounds that cure illness are called "medicine." But if these compounds cannot eliminate illness, we cannot call them "medicine." If we can lessen or prevent our discursive thoughts from occurring, whether from listening to the teachings or contemplation or meditation, then this is the practice of meditation.

Before we enter the gates of Dharma, our minds entertain many polarities and extremes such as existence, non-existence, good and evil, and so on ad infinitum. When we enter the Dharma, the creation of such polarities stops, and we will not look upon study and listening as not being meditation. We often think that one aspect of Dharma is not meditation, whereas another is genuinely linked with meditation practice. Creating polarities within the Dharma will interfere with the practice, but if we understand the meaning of Dharma through the process of study and listening, it is possible to unite all the trivial acts that we perform in our daily life — such as waking up, walking around, sitting or sleeping — within the practice of Dharma. Everyday actions can be transformed into virtuous actions. This transformation can happen because we know how to do so.

Sometimes we think that we can only meditate by

separating ourselves from society, but it is possible to meditate within society. We do not need to distance ourselves from regular life. For example, eating is an ordinary activity. The act of eating can be united with meditation, and if we are eating with our totality, with our whole being, then the act becomes whole and total. Then we know the meditative art of eating. By eating in this way, the food becomes tastier and more nutritious. For example, if the Buddha were to eat bad food, even the grass that horses eat, he would be able to extract nutrition from that food as if he were eating very wholesome food. That is because his body, speech, and mind are taking part in the process of eating. Also, if we implement our meditation practice with walking, eating, sitting and so on, then our mind will calm down.

Question: Sometimes I feel vipassana is like going through lists, like the sevenfold reasoning of emptiness. In a way, it becomes so familiar that the vitality is lost. The process seems to become mechanical and boring. How should I avoid that?

Answer: To avoid experiencing boredom we need to alternate analytical meditation with concentration meditation. Most of the people of Tibet spend their lives high up in the mountains. They are eager to see the big cities, and one day maybe they find themselves in such a city, but after having been there they want to go back to the pure mountains. It is like this. We go in circles; this is samsara.

When we develop a sense of weariness for the discursive mind, our mind will not be so interested in producing thoughts. Therefore, a certain amount of tiredness is desirable. However, the conceptual mind does possess certain positive qualities, and therefore we should not condemn it. The conceptual mind allows us to make the journey from the discursive mind to the non-discursive mind. In this way, the discursive mind forms a basis. Also, we should not condemn individuals who are entertaining rambling thoughts by thinking that "I have fewer discursive thoughts than that person."

Chinese Buddhists, especially monks and nuns living in monasteries, are strictly vegetarian. When we meet such practitioners, some will brag about their vegetarianism and look down upon those who are not vegetarians. If our vegetarianism gives rise to such arrogant thoughts, then this practice has not done much good, other than not eating meat. Those vegetarians should develop compassion towards the non-vegetarians, because of their craving for meat.

In the same way, practicing humility towards all sentient beings is crucial. If I, as a Buddhist, think that I have a philosophy that is more profound than that of others, or hold that my religion is more genuine than theirs, this will increase ego and arrogance, which will lead to the condemnation of others. If this is the case, then my engagement in Buddhist practice does not serve any real purpose.

As we practice, a gradual shift will take place in our mind, helping us to generate a sense of love and compassion even towards an enemy. This shift occurs because of a transformation of attitude. We may think somebody is our enemy, but the nature of an external enemy is neither friend nor enemy. The actual nature of the so-called enemy eludes being both friend and enemy. If we study the Dharma through listening and hearing, reflection and meditation, and acquire the corresponding wisdom, this wisdom will have the power to change our mind to perceive the reality as it is, not in a limited way. Also, medicine is neither medicine nor poison. It depends on how a drug is taken.

Whether we perceive the phenomenal world as pure or impure depends solely on our perceiving mind. We cannot describe the external world as pure or impure. The external world escapes both states of purity and impurity because, in the final analysis, it is the perceiving mind that decides whether it is pure or impure.

This world can be a paradise or a hell. As the Buddha said, "I have shown you the path to liberation. Now, whether you gain the enlightenment of liberation or not is your own responsibility." This means that our attitude and perspective are the most crucial elements. As we said earlier, the phenomenal world of the three realms is nothing more than a creation of our mind.

If we understand these teachings, then wherever we are can be paradise. If we do not realize this, we will go through hell on earth. If we lack this understanding, then even if we were to meet Amitabha, the Buddha of Boundless Light, we will not be able to recognize him. But if we realize this meaning, then the person next to us transforms into the Buddha of Boundless Light.

In the sutras, the Buddha says that the nature of all living being is sugatagarbha, Buddha-nature. In the tantric teachings, the Buddha says that all phenomenal experience and appearance is infinite purity.

The Great Perfection

Today I would like to comment on a text written by the omniscient Jigme Lingpa, called *Perceiving the Naked State of the Genuine Reality of the Great Perfection*. This text is about revealing the genuine reality, or nature, of the mind. It is found in the Nyingmapa School of Tibetan Buddhism and is a well-known but advanced teaching known as the Great Perfection or Dzogchen in Tibetan.

If we ask whether the view of the Great Perfection lies within nirvanic peace or within samsara, the answer is that it does not lie within either of these extremes. If we want to search for the view of the Great Perfection, we must search within our own mind. The view of the Great Perfection is found within the mental continuum of every sentient being. It is endowed with the qualities of emptiness and luminosity. Yet the Great Perfection is not something that can be analyzed in terms of how it is constructed; it is, by its nature, non-constructed. If we were to ask whether we could discover the Great Perfection by transforming our present state of mind into another state of mind, the answer is no. Apart from our present mind, there is nowhere else we can look to find the resultant enlightened qualities of the Great Perfection.

Our mind, which is endowed with awareness and intelligence, is always occupied by all kinds of actions, daily activities such as working, standing, sleeping and sitting. The term meditation does not mean to be distracted from the nature of the mind, but to recognize this nature and try to retain this recognition. By doing this, the one meditating may experience a blissful mind, a clear mind, and a non-conceptual mind. We must be very skillful to retain the continuity of the recognition of the nature of the mind, and we should not exert excessive effort or forcefully try to settle our mind into such a state. Rather, in order to sustain the view of the Great Perfection, we should cultivate relaxation. If we do not apply a skillful method, we will lose the meditation.

Let an example illustrate this: Somebody who is imprisoned experiences discomfort, unease and restriction due to being confined to a small cell. Similarly, if we try to seize the true nature of the mind and forcibly sustain it, tension will arise in the mind of the one meditating.

When we try to meditate on the view of the Great Perfection, we come across many emotional and conceptual thoughts. For instance, when we come across a positive impression, we should try not to cultivate attachment to this thought. Instead of being overwhelmed by the presence of a positive feeling, which we easily do by only observing the surface of the thought, we should instead look directly at the thought's very core or essence. This applies in the same way to negative emotional complications such as anger and so on. By focusing on the nature of thoughts, the one meditating will understand that the essence of thoughts is fundamental awareness and wisdom.

The tradition of the Great Perfection maintains that by looking at emotional thoughts in this manner, we will achieve a vision of genuine reality (Skt. dharmadhatu). This suggests that the individual should look at the true essence of emotional complication, whatever it is, to perceive true reality.

But when it comes to the main practice, we often experience certain difficulties. It is not as easy as I have just explained. When we look at the very essence of emotional or disturbing thoughts, we should not evaluate them. We should look at the face of emotional thoughts in the same way as an elderly person watches children playing. Elderly people will not try to evaluate children's play by saying that it is good or bad; they will be indifferent to whatever occupies the children. We should look at our emotional thoughts in the same way.

This manner of meditation gives us a very intimate familiarity with the nature of mind. The individual's mind becomes liberated both from the concept of duality, which tends to grasp onto the superficial reality of the perceived objective phenomenon, and the perceiving phenomenon i.e. the mind. So, we are liberated from both grasping at the reality of the perceived world and the grasping of the perceiving mind. In turn, the emotions are set free. The individual becomes capable of reversing all kinds of grasping onto different forms of wholesome and unwholesome thought, and not to regard wholesome thoughts as something to be seized or unwholesome thoughts as something to be abandoned. At this point, the individual who is meditating experiences liberation into genuine reality. Emotional or conceptual ideas will cause no difficulty at all, whether they are positive or negative.

The meditating individual who manages to acquire such a meditative experience has traversed the seven impure bodhisattva levels. These are called impure because on those spiritual levels the individual is still contaminated with a subtle grasping at duality.

When it comes to realizing the view of the Great Perfection there are many pitfalls, errors, and mistakes into which we can fall. We said in the beginning that the nature of the view of the Great Perfection is emptiness. Because of this, some individuals grasp at the very concept of emptiness. They release their grasping onto the apparent reality but grasp instead at the very concept that was meant to release the grasping. This is a tremendous mistake. It is termed affirmative negative: we refute grasping at the existence of reality, but then affirms (grasps onto) this negation or emptiness.

The Buddha taught the teaching of emptiness to shatter grasping onto the reality of existence. But if an individual falls into the view of affirming negative, the Buddha specifically said that there is no other antidote to cure this spiritual disease of such people. If the medicine itself has turned into poison, there is no other antidote that can be applied. The Buddha said that "unwise people who are not skillful enough to perceive emptiness will suffer a tremendous loss."

One should recognize emptiness as something that is

free from extremes. We can apply this to the true nature of mind in which awareness and wisdom are fundamentally inherent. The exact nature of mind is free from the four extremes; it is not existent, it is not non-existent, it is not both existent and non-existent at the same time, and it is neither something other than existent or non-existent. In our previous discussion we only covered to first two extremes. Therefore, there is no origination and no cessation. There is not something that comes or something that goes.

The true nature of the mind is not masculine, feminine, or neutral. The nature of mind is empty of characteristics such as shape, color, and so on. Furthermore, the nature of mind belongs neither to the category of nihilism nor to the category of eternalism. It is inexpressible and inconceivable.

As an example, we cannot say that we have seen empty space. But we can still talk about space as a concept. In the same way, someone who has realized the view of the Great Perfection, as many individuals have done in the past, will try their best to find the most appropriate examples to express their spiritual experiences to their students. But despite all their efforts in trying to find suitable examples, they fail to give an exact explanation which communicates the true nature of mind. Therefore, we should be careful not to err when it comes to the view of the Great Perfection. We should take care to sustain recognition of the Great Perfection in all forms of activities.

To implement the view of the Great Perfection, there are two forms of meditations: shamatha and vipassana. But these should not be understood as the common shamatha and vipassana that we talk about in the context of the sutra level. Shine, calm abiding meditation, means a pacified mind. The true nature of our mind is, from the very beginning, completely undisturbed by the presence of gross and subtle forms of conceptual complications.

If we have a glass of muddy water and we let the water come to a rest, the water will resume its original transparency. But if the water is disturbed, the clarity will again be lost.

Similarly, our primordial state of mind retains inner transparency, which is termed luminosity. If we learn to leave the mind undisturbed, the mind will assume this original transparency. Again, if we allow the mind to be disturbed by the presence of disturbing thoughts, the mind will lose its original transparency.

The shamatha meditation of the tantric teachings of Buddhism is different from the shamatha meditation found in the sutra approach. In sutra shamatha meditation, the individual who meditates pacifies emotional complications by applying certain antidotes, but in the shamatha meditation of tantric Buddhism the mind is perceived as being free from the gross and subtle complications from the very beginning, and therefore there is nothing to pacify.

Vipassana meditation in the context of tantric Buddhism is described as looking at the non-dual state of mind, to experience that the mind is empty of the quality of the perceived and the perceiving mind. Gaining this experience is termed gaining insight into the non-duality of the mind.

Again, vipassana meditation according to tantric Buddhism is not the same as vipassana meditation according to the sutra level, where the one meditating first performs an analytical meditation and then tries to rest in the discovery that he or she has made. According to the vipassana meditation of tantric Buddhism, we gain insight into the non-duality of the mind which is free from both the perceived phenomena and the perceiving mind.

Within the Great Perfection meditation, there is what is called formal meditation and informal meditation, or post-meditation. In formal meditation, the individual tries to sustain recognition of the view by practicing mindfulness. In post-meditation, the individual brings his or her meditative experiences gained in formal meditation into his or her actions of body, speech, and mind.

During formal sitting meditation practice, we apply the mental faculty of mindfulness. But the mental faculty of mindfulness should not be understood as the common mindfulness of which we are all familiar. This is a unique kind of mindfulness. In Buddhism, the common interpretation of the term mindfulness is to keep in mind what shall be cultivated and what shall be abandoned. In the context of the Great Perfection the term mindfulness should be understood as there being nothing to cultivate and nothing to abandon.

When we try to sustain the view of the Great Perfection, we should not worry about being distracted. If we discover that we are distracted, we might develop frustration or sadness, but this is not appropriate. Neither should we apply excessive effort, as this will only disturb our mind. In brief, while we are trying to sustain the very recognition of the formal meditation, we should release our body, speech, and mind from any fabricated effort. If the individual who is meditating can meditate in this manner, then the technical term non-meditation is applicable.

In meditation we can therefore reach the state of non-meditation. But the terms meditation and non-meditation are dualistic, and the actual state of Great Perfection meditation is free from both meditation and non-meditation. In the view of the Great Perfection the individual neither grasps onto meditation nor non-meditation.

By meditating in this manner, the individual who meditates might experience three kinds of meditative experiences: bliss, luminosity, and non-conceptuality. The experience of bliss occurs when the mind becomes completely free from the three levels of suffering and simply merges with the fundamental state of mind, experiencing tremendous bliss. The experience of luminosity occurs when the mind becomes tremendously clear, without any contamination of dullness, agitation or an undercurrent of thoughts. The term luminosity should not be understood as a visual clarity of visual sensory experiences. The luminosity that arises during meditative absorption and the clarity we might experience when we are not meditating do not correspond at all. The third meditative quality that might be experienced is termed non-conceptuality. When we are beginners in meditation, many conceptual thoughts will occupy our minds. But as we progress in meditation, meditation will culminate in the experience of non-conceptuality. Then, our mind is no longer beleaguered by conceptual complications.

If we have beautiful experiences, there is always the danger of developing attachment or grasping, but we should not create a sense of attachment to the three meditative experiences detailed above. If an individual develops attachment to the first meditative experience of bliss, it is said that he or she will take rebirth in the desirous god realm. If an individual attach himself to clarity, he or she might end up in the form god realm. If he or she clings to non-conceptuality, then he or she will end up being born in the formless god realm. Clinging is therefore not regarded as being beneficial. We should therefore not try to meditate with the goal of achieving these three beautiful experiences, because the goal-oriented mind will spoil the meditation.

If meditation on the generation phase is not embraced by meditation on the completion or dissolving phase, the mere generation phase of the practice of tantric Buddhism will not cause attainment of Buddha-nature. On the contrary, it is said that such meditation causes the individual to be reborn as a very evil-minded being.

Since the genuine view of the Great Perfection is simplicity free from mental constructs, it is always possible to confuse this form of meditation with other similar experiences.

Present mind, or present awareness, is primordial awareness in its ultimate mode of existence. A non-referential view should embrace this primordial awareness. If we meditate correctly as outlined, we will eventually reach a culmination where there remains no agent, no action and no object on which to meditate. The duality of the subject and object simply disappears and becomes a non-dual experience.

Generally, individuals feel that they know what existence is and what non-existence is, but nothing beyond this. They claim that, if something exists, it cannot be non-existent. Similarly, if something is non-existent, it cannot exist. Our perception is based on the perception of existence and non-existence: nihilism and eternalism; if it is nihilism it cannot be eternalism, if it is eternalism it cannot be nihilism. An analogy might be one individual who knows two other individuals. They arrive at the house of those two, and then state that he or she meets either one person or the other. The scope of our present mind is very narrow; therefore, we are not able to embrace a state of mind that is free from all extreme complications. Our present deluded state of mind is therefore transient, and the true nature of our mind is primordially liberated.

When it comes to the primordial awareness, we cannot talk about union and non-union. The view of the Great Perfection is free from all kinds of sectarianism, bias, and partial attitudes. The view of the Great Perfection is also free from denigration and exaggeration. So, the view of the Great Perfection is free from mental activity. It is inaction. It is the pinnacle of all views, meditations, and conducts. So, therefore, the individual who meditates can realize the genuine view of the Great Perfection while sleeping comfortably in bed! (Rinpoche jokes and the audience laughs). The view of the Great Perfection is free from expression; nevertheless, I am expressing something. There is nothing to understand, but at least we understand this at some level.

This form of meditation can sometimes create difficulty if it renders our mind into total confusion. It is therefore important to sustain the continuity of awareness. Awareness is not something we need to cultivate. The quality of awareness is inherent in the very nature of our mind, as stated before. It is simple to recognize it and then sustain this recognition.

In the past, many individuals evolved into very spiritual beings by being spiritually crazy. They were called holders of the lineage of crazy wisdom. If we like, we can also participate in this spiritual community of mad people (all are laughing), but we must be genuinely spiritually mad, not just pretending, or be psychologically mad. I myself would like to enter this mandala of mad enlightened people, but to do so is quite difficult.

When we meditate on the Great Perfection, we should not worry if emotional or conceptual complications pop up. It is good when many emotions and thoughts arise. If we let these thoughts arise without trying to abandon or suppress them, they will exhaust themselves.

Hope and fear should not interrupt our meditation on the view of the Great Perfection. If they do, they bind and interrupt the meditation. We should not fear the presence of emotional complications and conceptual thoughts. Just let them vanish on their own.

I am not somebody who has genuinely realized the view of the Great Perfection, but I have tried my best to explain this view to you. Do you have any questions?

Question: You said in the beginning that the shine meditation of the Great Perfection is different from that of the sutra texts. Should we work on shine in terms of sutra first, and then go on to vajrayana?

Answer: Yes, we should proceed in a gradual manner through the yanas. As we say, we should practice shamatha as it is presented on the sutric level and then proceed to practice the shamatha and vipassana that is presented on the tantric level. Sutra teachings act like a steppingstone towards tantric practice.

Question: Can you give me a definition of emotion and thought? I see emotion as something I feel and thought as something that is in my mind.

Answer: Actually, Tibetan has the same word for both thought and emotion—"namtok." "Nam" refers to the object that induces the emotion or thought in the individual, "tok" refers to the emotional state of mind. Can you give me some examples of emotions?

Questioner: Anger.

Rinpoche: And thought?

Questioner: Fantasizing about the future and thinking about the past.

Rinpoche: This is also the answer to your question.

Question: Aren't these emotional thoughts connected with desire? Do you produce thoughts if you have a desire?

Answer: Yes, the presence of desire gives rise to further thought patterns and emotional complications, which again give rise to further karmic implications. "Namtok" means that we cannot have a thought without having a stimulant "nam". Without the stimulant, emotional complications will not arise. This is due to the law of interdependency — cause and effect.

Questioner: Will there be no anger either?

Answer: Right, because everything arises due to the coming together of causes and conditions. Before being enlightened, you can say conventionally that the emotional state of mind exists. When the individual enters the meditation of the Great Perfection and experiences a genuine meditative experience, then his or her mind is completely absent of emotional complications and conceptual thoughts. But when the individual leaves meditation and enters post meditation, then these emotions begin to come back.

Question: Can you say a little bit more about how to investigate the essence of thoughts?

Answer: We should not try to prevent ourselves from giving rise to emotional and conceptual thoughts. If they pop up, let them pop up, but then try to look directly at the essence of the thoughts without evaluating or judging them; just simply look at them. Encounters with thoughts should be embraced with a profound sense of confidence and certainty. This is important.

The content of emotional thoughts can differ, but when the one meditating penetrates the core of any thought or emotion, there is no difference between good and bad thoughts. On the inner level, both good and bad thoughts share the same essence of clarity and intelligence. Therefore, we should not try to cultivate good emotions and abandon bad emotions. This principle applies to formal sitting meditation.

Question: What is the purpose of these observations? What is the ultimate goal?

Answer: The ultimate goal is to be emotionally liberated, to observe the essence of the thought, so that we will not become victims of either positive or negative emotion. If we experience emotional thoughts such as attachment, aggression or aversion, we will end up creating certain karma. Creating karma creates certain misery and pain within us. To prevent this, we must prevent the karmic complications, and to prevent these we must prevent emotional difficulties. In order to prevent emotional complications, we must look at the nature of the emotion. The emotion will then simply liberate in its own place.

Also, the individual is not able to experience serenity if the mind is constantly affected by the presence of conceptual thoughts and emotions. I know a woman in Taiwan who told me that she loves her husband and wants him to look nice. But when he does look nice, she becomes afraid of losing him to another woman. Therefore, sometimes she chooses not to iron his clothes, so that he will not look like a gentleman. But when she sees him in bad shape, she experiences a dilemma. Like Hamlet's dilemma in Shakespeare's play: "to be or not to be"; to iron or not to iron! (Laughter.) It is not good to entertain so many contradictory thoughts. It is best to come to a decisive conclusion, either by ironing or not ironing. (Laughter.)

Question: You said that when the mind experiences bliss it becomes free of the three levels of suffering. Were you referring to the suffering of suffering, the suffering of change, and all-pervasive suffering?

Answer: Yes, that is what I meant. The suffering of suffering is what we experience when we become injured or ill. The suffering of change is the fact that even pleasant experiences will end in suffering, and all-pervasive suffering is caused by the fact that on a subtle level all phenomena are subject to subtle change and degeneration.

Question: Is being born in the desire god realm or the formless god realm to be regarded as spiritual progress?

Answer: It is not necessarily good to be born in the god realms. In order to have the best prospects for spiritual development, it is best to be born a human being. The reason there are many levels in the god realms is that the mind of the individual develops further and further. When the individual has reached the fourth level of the formless god realm, the individual has reached the peak of the samsaric mind. In total, the god realms consist of seventeen levels. But the god realm has certain disadvantages in terms of being a foundation for spiritual practice.

Question: If you were brought to the peak of the samsaric mind, what can you do with it? Can you make other people happy?

Answer: Someone who reaches this level of mind is free from the first two levels of suffering, but the mind of such an evolved being still experiences all-pervasive suffering. But if that mind becomes altruistic, generating bodhicitta, then that highly evolved mind can be utilized to benefit others as well as itself. The goal of the meditating Buddhist is not to reach the peak of samsaric mind, but rather to transcend it, to experience total liberation from the vicious circle of samsara.

Question: When you take the bodhisattva vows, you say that you will not attain enlightenment before other beings have attained enlightenment. That will never happen. (Person laughs.)

Answer: The reason for taking the bodhisattva vows is that when we become enlightened, and you will be, we remain neither in the extreme of nirvana nor the extreme of samsara. If we can genuinely and honestly do this, then the tremendous scope of this mind will hasten our enlightenment. So, you don't need to worry.

If an individual claims that he or she will create well-being on the face of the whole earth, then his or her mind has genuinely embraced an altruistic attitude. This individual will experience a tremendous ease and comfort within himself or herself. The inner serenity of such an individual will benefit everyone he or she encounters. Not only that, the scope of this mind has become so expansive that there remain no exclusions; it becomes an all-inclusive mind.

Cho Practice

Initiation

Initiation, or empowerment, belongs to the tantric tradition of Buddhism. The cho practice is a practice of the Prajnaparamita in its extended version, its middling version and its simplified version. All instructions that are contained within the whole body of teachings of the Prajnaparamita given by the Buddha are contained within the practice of cho.

The source of cho is the great Tibetan female master known as Machik Lapdron ("the only mother"). Machik Lapdron was prophesied in name by the Buddha in the sutra that distinguishes purity and impurity. The Buddha also prophesied her in the tantric teachings by mentioning her name, Lapkyi Dronma (Labdron), and saying that she would be a teacher and an emanation of the mother of transcendental wisdom. Drolma means "torch" — the torch from Lap. She was also prophesied by the great Indian master Padmasambhava as the emanation of Yeshe Sogyal. In most sutra and tantric teachings of the Buddha, her great spiritual accomplishment is mentioned.

The cho practice that comes down from the great mother Machik Lapdron has been transmitted through three lineages: the sutra lineage, the tantra lineage and the combined sutra and tantra lineage.

The sutra lineage of the cho practice can be traced to Buddha Shakyamuni — the historical Buddha, who passed it down to the bodhisattva Manjushri. Then gradually, this linage was transmitted to the great masters Nagarjuna and Arya Deva.

The source of the tantric practice of cho can be traced to the great mother Prajnaparamita. The great mother Prajnaparamita passed this down to the sambhogakaya Buddha Vajrasattva, who passed it on to the nirmanakaya female buddha, the Great Tara, who passed it onto Machik Lapdron.

The lineage that bears elements from both sutra and tantra can be traced to the bodhisattva Manjushri, who passed it on to Arya Tara. Arya Tara transmitted it to the great Indian female master known as Sukasiddhi. She passed it to the chief student of Nagarjuna, Arya Deva. Finally, it came to Padampa Sangye, who brought the lineage to Tibet where Sönam Lama received the transmission and passed it on to the great mother Machik Lapdron.

The reason behind expounding how the transmissions took place is to prove that this teaching has not been made up by some unenlightened individual. To practice the cho instructions according to the tantric tradition, we need to be empowered into the mandala of the cho practice. Since the cho instructions that will be given here pertain to the union of the sutra and tantra cho practices, empowerment is required.

The empowerment that will be given at this moment is bodily, verbal, and mental. The empowerment of the body of the deity is imparted on our body. The empowerment of Dharma is bestowed on the mind. The empowerment of mantra is imparted on the speech.

The audience should be fit vessels to receive this empowerment. A fit vessel is a purified mind that is ready to receive the blessings of the empowerment. You are a vessel. The nectar that is going to be poured into the vessel is the blessing of the empowerment. But if the vessel is broken or impure, whatever is poured into it will become contaminated. If we are to receive empowerment by allowing ourselves to be a fit vessel, it is essential to purify our mind.

The view of the cho instruction is emptiness. The action of cho is an unconventional action that is performed based on being free from hope, fear and hesitation. The voice of cho is uttering the mantra of the Prajnaparamita, OM GATE GATE PARA GATE PARASAM GATE BODHI SOHA.

One meditates on the cho instruction with the aim of breaking the grip onto the true existence of self or ego. All

136

aspects of Dharma can cut through the ego, but the cho technique has a unique way of doing this. We will now begin the initiation.

Please repeat the refuge prayer by folding your hands over your heart and visualizing them holding a lotus flower.

(Rinpoche leads the refuge prayer.)
With this verse we have taken refuge to the Buddha, Dharma and Sangha, and to the dharmakaya, sambhogakaya and nirmanakaya. Now, we will repeat the following verse, which generates the altruistic mind of bodhicitta. Contemplate at the same time how past masters in the same way have generated the altruistic mind of bodhicitta.
(Rinpoche leads the prayer.)

This completes the preparation of the initiation. The main empowerment will now be given. Machik Lapdron said the following words about this practice, "Your awareness should be relaxed, so that it is neither too relaxed nor too tense." When we can bring our mind to such a balanced state of relaxation, we can comprehend the view of emptiness.
When the empowerment of the Dharma is being imparted to our mind, we should practice the phowa transference that opens the space. The phowa practice that opens the space cannot be compared to other phowa instructions. To conduct the visualization of the phowa practice, you should stand up. Place your hands on the crown of your head. Visualize your entire body as a balloon filled with air. Then visualize a small ball of light, a bindu, white in color, under the sole of your right foot. Visualize a red bindu under the sole of your left foot. We will now offer the supplication to the masters of the lineage of the cho practice, and to the great mother Machik Lapdron.
(Rinpoche leads the supplication prayer.)
While I recite the following prayer, maintain your visualization, and the sense that your body is hollow. Pray to

Machik Lapdron that you will succeed in the cho practice.

(Rinpoche performs the melodious cho ritual of cutting through.)

Visualize the two white and red balls of light gradually moving upwards though your legs, arriving at your secret chakra where they mix and becomes the size of a small egg. Gradually this ascends through your navel chakra and heart chakra into the crown chakra. As it moves upwards it exits the crown chakra. As these bindus leave the crown of the head we should be careful about not creating attachment towards our body. Try to transfer your consciousness to space without any reference points. I will utter the sound "P'ET!" At this moment visualize your consciousness leaving your crown chakra into space without reference points and simply dwell in this non-referential state of mind.

P'ET!

Your consciousness has entered the realm of space. Sentient beings pervade all space. Wherever awareness pervades, so does dharmakaya.

Lower your hands. You might be a little tired now, but this will alleviate your disturbing emotions. Try to dwell without conceptual thoughts and emotions. You may sit down.

In the sutra teachings of the Buddha, such phowa practice is "the samadhi that perceives the crown of space," "the samadhi that encompasses the totality of space," and "the essence of space." If you can meditate in this manner, this meditation is known as the supreme meditation of the view.

Now visualize yourself in the form of the great Machik Lapdron. Now, for a moment, allow your mind to rest within the state of mind that knows no past or future thoughts.

P'ET!

This completes the bestowal of the Dharma empowerment upon our minds. Now comes the empowerment of the deity onto our body. This initiation is done through the medium of the torma ("ritual offering"). You should visualize the inseparability of the torma and the great Prajnaparamita and Machik Lapdron.

(Rinpoche prays.)

At this point you should visualize white light emanating from the forehead of the great mother Machik Lapdron and striking your forehead. This purifies all physical and karmic obstructions that you have created.

(Rinpoche leads prayers ending with the Prajnaparamita mantra OM GATE GATE PARA GATE PARASAM GATE BODHI SO HA and performs a mandala offering.)

At this point we should visualize a red syllable AH at the throat chakra of Machik Lapdron. It emits red light that strikes our throat chakra and purifies all negative obstructions we have created with our speech. Imagine that we have received the speech empowerment of Machik Lapdron.

From the blue seed syllable HUNG at the heart chakra of Machik Lapdron there radiates forth a blue light that strikes our own heart chakra and purifies all obstructive forces created by our mind. We should think that we have received the mind empowerment of Machik Lapdron.

At this point, visualize your body, speech, and mind as inseparable from the body, speech and mind of Machik Lapdron.

During the practice of cho we work to untie the knots in our energy channels. We do this by singing cho prayers with beautiful melodies, and we try to cultivate a mind that is free from attachment to reality. This completes the initiation. We conclude the ceremony with prayers for dedication of merit. I wish you all auspiciousness with the practice of cutting through the ego by using the practice of cho.

The empowerment of the cho practice, together with the instruction of the cho practice and the oral transmission of the cho practice is very well preserved in the Monastery where I come from. The Dzogchen Shirasing Buddhist College is famous all over Tibet. Thousands of monks study there. But when it comes to giving the empowerment of the cho practice, they invite a lama from my Monastery to give teaching on the cho. Thank you.

Talk held in English by Rinpoche

I am afraid my English is not that good. It would have been much better if Lama Changchub was here to translate. Many years before, in Karma Tashi Ling, we also did cho practice, and gave some initiations. I remember Aksel and Jørgen were there. In Tibetan Buddhism, lineage is significant. I have a good lineage of cho practice from my master.

If we experience a problem with our body or mind, we should know what to do to have a happy life, as well as enlightenment. For cho practice, bodhicitta is particularly important, as well as the view of emptiness. We should also take refuge in the Buddha, Dharma, and Sangha, as well as making offerings because merit is significant. We also need to practice forgiveness and the six paramitas.

We all experience unpleasant emotions and bad karma. These are caused by the ego-clinging that arises in our mind. If we change our mind, we will improve our lives. Because we are talking about how to face our life. If we experience problems in relationships, such as family, friends, and partners, or problems with housing, our job or money, we will experience a lot of suffering. If we have all these things, we may feel afraid that we will lose them. Usually, people think that money and power, as well as friendships and romantic relationships, are significant. If we are having problems in these areas, we often get angry or worried.

When we do practice, we must actively change for the better. Tibetans talk about the mind very often, but I think that action is also significant. We have both aspirational and engaging bodhicitta. To generate aspirational bodhicitta, we can think about all sentient beings, all our important relationships, our father and mother and so on, but we must also remember engaging bodhicitta, to do some actual action.

Generally, if somebody gives us trouble, we get angry, but instead we should improve our realization of compassion and wisdom. When we become more compassionate, we reduce our selfishness. When we learn the Buddhist view of emptiness, we will experience less bad emotions and karma, like jealousy, because ignorance subsides and weakens the attachment to the self.

Vows are important. If we have Samaya, I think we are purer in body, speech, and mind. If we do not have Samaya, there will be a little impurity in our body, speech, and mind. For example, I do not want to drink alcohol. Some monks think that they have a very lofty view and practice and that it is okay for them to drink ambrosia with alcohol. They also end up interacting inappropriately with women and other bad things. Unfortunately, in Buddhism, there are a lot of masters like this. This is not good. Therefore, pure Samaya is a necessary basis.

In Buddhism, we say that space allows for the four elements, wind, water, earth, and fire. So, we can say that all phenomena come from space. If we practice without Samaya, there will be no proper practice. When the Buddha reached enlightenment, he said "If there is Samaya in this world, there will be Buddhism, if there is no Samaya, there will be no Buddhism."

Westerners always talk about being free, holding freedom to be especially important. But can we be free if there is ignorance and attachment? If there is anger or other bad energies, will there be freedom? I do not think so. We should control our bad emotions, and this is Samaya.

In a way, there is good freedom and bad freedom. The freedom that stems from compassion, wisdom and good intentions is a good freedom. In Taiwan, people sometimes experience the effect of too much bad freedom. The news is free, but often they just talk about bad things. This leaves people without hope. Also, in our practice, we should not act completely freely, we should keep a check on what we say, think and do. We need to improve ourselves. This is important.

Cho practice is about cutting the ego, the evil Mara. I do not think there is any external evil. There is no big demon out there. The problem is selfishness. In cho, we say that there are four demons. The first is the tangible Mara, the demon of form. We generate attachment towards the forms we like and aversion and hatred towards the forms we dislike. This happens inside our minds, like water becoming dirty.

When we rely on emptiness, there is no subject or object. But when we do not, there is ignorance, and when we open our eyes, we see forms and thus generate attachment or aversion. Ignorance, attachment, and aversion are called the three poisons.

We have sensory experiences; we see, hear, and taste. For example, chocolate is not a demon, but too much of it will cause attachment. Many people have romantic partners. One partner is good — for example husband and wife living happily together, but if we want two or three, then we can become a demon ourselves, and cause a lot of problems. Problems can also arise from power and money. To counteract this, by eliminating the demon of selfishness as a cause, we cut through the three poisons and cut through bad karma.

Sometimes people are afraid of demons outside, thinking there are ghosts and places with no good energy, haunted places. For people who are afraid of the dark, it is okay to go to such places to do cho practice. But if there are tigers, then we should not go! If we go to do cho practice with a tiger, it might kill us. Padmasambhava would be okay with a tiger, but we will not. So, we stay away from doing such crazy things!

Cho practice is fascinating. The melodies are exceptionally beautiful, with drums, bell, and vajra. You should practice familiarizing yourself with it. Then it will sound nice. We are now going to do a Longchen Nyingthig cho practice. It is a nice one, not so long. We just did a cho practice from the Kagyu tradition which is a little bit different. In Tibet, we also use another long text, which is also from the Kagyu lineage. The Kagyu and Nyingma texts are sometimes interchanged. In the Kagyu lineage, many lamas practice Dzogchen, and in the Nyingma lineage, many lamas practice Mahamudra.

The Longchen Nyingthig text lists the necessary articles in the following way: To overpower the haughty demons, the skin of a fierce animal with all the claws still on its paws. A small tent. The Khatvanga trident for right conduct, which ascends through the Yanas; a human thigh bone for gathering the local gods and demons under our power; a Damaru hand drum, which overawes ideas and appearances; a handbell and small bell, which overpower the Dakinis, and a face veil made of strips of tiger and leopard skin and hair cuttings. In brief, we should prepare all articles necessary for the way of determined practice.

Questions and Answers

Question: My wife and I have been discussing where Buddha-nature is located. Is it found in the skandhas?

Answer: We should first understand what the Buddha-nature is. Then we can talk about where it is. It is more important to understand what it is. It is like saying, "there is a house over there, and there are some people inside." It is more important to know who the people are.

The Buddha-nature has three qualities. The first is emptiness. Talking about emptiness is difficult. Where is it? Where does it come from? Where is it going? We say it has no birth or death and is not coming or going. We cannot tell that the Buddha-nature is in the five aggregates. When we analyze the five aggregates, we find that they are empty. The second quality is luminous clarity, like wisdom. The third is compassion. Compassion is like the sun, shining in the sky, equally everywhere. So, the question of whether the Buddha-nature resides in the five skandhas is a difficult question to answer. Sometimes we say that the Buddha is our own mind. But what is mind? This just generates more questions. Sometimes, when we open our eyes, we can see a form, and this can be like liberation. The Buddha said that everything is possible in this world. We can think about colors, and we can see a lot of colors.

We say that form is emptiness, and emptiness is form.

Sometimes, I contemplate that everything is impermanent. Where is the form of yesterday gone? What about the eye faculty, eye consciousness, of yesterday, today and tomorrow? Are they the same, or are they different?

Question: According to the Sugatagarbha, they co-exist at the same time, yet appear separate, right? They seem to be different, past, present, and future, but ultimately, they are not separate. How do you explain the quality of Guru Rinpoche's mind, being beyond past, present, and future?

Answer: As one of the two truths, relative and ultimate, if we think regarding the ultimate truth, I do not believe that we can explain the nature of Guru Rinpoche's mind. If we talk regarding relative truth, past, present, and future will be different. If we talk about ultimate truth, there is no difference.

Let us say we are looking at the color white. I might like the white color, but you might not like it. There are different types of thought about form. It is a relative truth whether we like it or not. The ultimate truth is without like and dislike.

My students in Asia suffer greatly from problems related to work, family, education, and love. These things bring them suffering because they believe that if they get those things, they will be happy. They pray to the Buddha and the Bodhisattvas that these things should last forever, but forever is difficult to achieve. When we talk about love, everybody gets excited, saying things like "I love you forever," or, "Ahh... this is so sweet." But sometimes, as you know, emotions change, thinking changes, and then there is no forever.

Sometimes we talk about advanced teachings on emptiness, like the Dzogchen view, but problems are experienced in the relative. It is therefore important how we use our body, speech, and mind. If our thinking is right, then with wisdom, right speech and compassion, we will be happy. Sometimes we can look in the mirror, practice talking to the mirror, looking at our own face. If we look good when speaking, it creates a lot of good energy. Sometimes, I tell Aksel, when he is hungry, he does not look good but angry as if something terrible has happened. But he does not know that. I think he should change!

My practice is patience. I experience many obstacles, but mostly, my mind is very peaceful. This time we went on a trip around Europe, but in Germany, there were some problem with the train. We did not understand what was happening and asked many people. Some people said there had been a crash, and others said that there had been a terrorist, dressed up as a woman, but nobody could give us an exact answer. There was no proper information given. So, we had to take another route; eight hours became twelve hours, and two changes became five. At one point the train suddenly screeched to a halt, but again there was no information. We spent that whole day on trains. Despite this, we talked about how lucky we were to see a lot of different cities in Germany without having to pay, and about having a good time sightseeing. If we did not think like that, we could have become outraged.

Once, two Tibetan guys were going to an important party. They were wearing their best clothes, looking very smart, wanting to impress the girls with their singing and dancing, as well as wanting to have a good time drinking alcohol and having fun. But on the way, birds managed to shit on their stylish clothes. They considered going back to change clothes, but it was too far. Now going to the party did not seem so tempting because the girls might show dislike for their dirty clothes. One of the guys said, "I am not going to the party. Today is my unlucky day. This has never happened to me before. There is a lot of shit on my clothes, I feel angry, so I am going home," talking negatively like that. The other guy, being more open-minded and happier, said, "Thank God cows were not given wings; otherwise I would have had a big problem!" So, he went to the party alone and enjoyed himself, nobody gave him any negative comments. Sometimes, things happen, so we need to change our mind. This is just a story. In

Tibet, there are many stories like this. In the book I wrote in Mandarin, I told a lot of such stories, but I have already forgotten some of them.

Question: I think the idea of training in offering and cutting through is not very developed in many European religions and cultures. Do you think we could utilize these things more?

Answer: People in Asia enjoy making offerings very much and understand that merit is significant. In the West, they are more interested in meditation. If I ask Europeans to make some offerings or to give something away, it seems like this can be a little more challenging compared with Asians. Sometimes, when earthquakes are causing big problems, the Taiwanese and Japanese people are ready to donate a lot of money to help. In Tibet, many masters are building houses for old people. When we are old, we too can go there. The monasteries have constructed a lot of such homes now. Before, in Tibet, many young children were forced to go to the cities to labor and did not receive any education. Today, many organizations are setting up schools and making education freely available for children.

Part Two: Longer Teachings

Commentary on Lama Mipham's Gateway to Knowledge

Introduction

It is wonderful and fortunate that we have come together in this way to share the teachings of Lord Buddha. Therefore, I would like to express my gratitude to you all for being here. I am also very delighted to be in Norway, where everybody can enjoy democracy and peace. I would also like to express my thanks to everyone who organized this course at Karma Shedrup Ling.

The topic that we have chosen to discuss is a teaching composed by the Tibetan master Jamgön Mipham Rinpoche, also known as The Great Mipham. In Tibet, there are many Buddhist academic institutes and monasteries, and the primary curriculum studied at these institutions is for the most part written by the great master Mipham.

Lama Mipham was born in Eastern Tibet. At the age of seventy, he was widely known throughout Tibet as the emanation of the Buddha Manjushri. He was very learned in the sutric, as well as the tantric presentation of the teachings of the Buddha.

It is rare to be given an opportunity to speak on the topics composed by the great master Mipham. The Tibetan name for the text is Könchog. "Kön" means knowledge. If we would like to become an expert in the teachings of the Buddha, we should study this text.

The Buddha gave many teachings on how to counteract wrong views of fixation onto the self. This text presents ten topics that counteract such wrong views. The first topic is the five psychophysical aggregates (Skt. skandhas). The second topic is the eighteen elements (Skt. dhatus). The third topic is the sense sources (Skt. ayatanas). The fourth topic explains dependent origination. The fifth topic describes the correct and the incorrect. The sixth topic presents the faculties. The seventh topic explains time. The eighth topic is the Four Noble Truths. The ninth topic presents the different vehicles in Buddhism (Skt. yanas). The tenth and last topic concerns composite and non-composite. These teachings were presented by the Buddha from his own experience of interacting with his students, who had many ways of imagining a self. We should also meditate and become knowledgeable of the subjects of this text.

The Five Psychophysical Aggregates

Since we were born, we have had an intrinsic grasping onto the self. Our birth was immediately followed by the conception of the notion of a self which was then reinforced and continued. We then started to involve ourselves with all kinds of activities to provide happiness for this conceptual self and protect it from suffering. However, because of our notion of a self, all forms of disturbances occur.

If we examine this naive assumption of a self, we will not be able to discover a self as a separate entity outside our physical and mental existence. Sometimes we regard the self as being identical with our psychophysical existence. Sometimes we regard the self as being apart from our psychophysical existence. Sometimes we claim our body is well and our mind is peaceful. Such a claim shows that we already regard the self as something separate from the psychophysical existence. Sometimes we claim that somebody hit us. When we claim that we have been harmed by others, we identify the self with our psychophysical existence.

If we hallucinate and see a snake inside the house, how

shall we overcome this? To overcome this misconception, we must enter the room and sort out everything, shift things around and search for the illusory snake. Eventually, we will realize that we cannot find the snake. Similarly, we have the notion of a self in connection with our psychophysical existence, and we must search for this notion to see if it exists or not.

Our psychophysical existence consists of five aggregates. The first aggregate is the aggregate of form which includes our physical existence. What do we mean by "aggregate"? An aggregate is something that consists of several parts. The physical aggregate is a collection of many limbs and organs, particles and molecules. How is it produced? The basic causes that give birth to the physical aggregate are karma and emotional afflictions. The characteristic of the physical aggregate is that it can be destroyed or harmed. The rest of the aggregates relate to our psychology. The second aggregate is the aggregate of feeling, or sensation. The third is the aggregate of perception, the fourth is the aggregate of formation, and the fifth is the aggregate of consciousness. If we understand the functioning of the five aggregates, we can counteract the grasping onto the self.

The Aggregate of Form

The physical aggregates are subdivided into the internal and the external physical aggregates. What do we mean by this? Within the category of external physical aggregates, we find all kinds of phenomenal existence and forms, things that form a part of the external world. The internal physical aggregates refer to our own physical existence. Studying the internal physical aggregates enables us to lessen the grip of the notion of the self.

The Four Causal Forms

How do the internal physical aggregates of human beings evolve? They are based on the four causal forms which are the elements of earth, water, fire, and air. The nature of earth is solidity, and its function is to serve as a foundation. The nature of water is wetness, and its function is to hold things together in a cohesive manner. The nature of fire is heat, and its function is to prevent things from rotting. The nature of the wind element is movement, and its function is to mature. In the same way, the external physical aggregates arise by the four causal forms coming together. There is, therefore, a close connection between the internal and the external aggregates.

The Eleven Resultant Forms

The four causal forms give rise to the eleven resultant forms. The eleven resultant forms are classified into three groups: the five sense faculties, the five sense objects, and the eleventh form, the imperceptible form.

The first resultant form is the eye sense faculty. It is essential to make a distinction between the eye sense organ and the eye sense faculty. The eye sense organ acts as a foundation for the eye sense faculty. We can perceive the eye sense organ with our eyes, but we are not able to perceive the eye sense faculty. The eye sense faculty refers to a very subtle form of energy, so subtle and refined that we are usually unaware of it. This imperceptible energy activates the eye consciousness that contacts eye sensory objects through the eye sense organ. The rest of the sense faculties function in the same way.

The first sensory object is form, which is something the eye can see. Form includes all kinds of shapes and colors that our eyes can perceive. The second sensory object is sound, the sense object of the ear. There are many kinds of sounds, meaningful sounds and meaningless sounds, and so on. Odors are the sense objects of the nose. There are different kinds, like natural odors, fabricated odors, and so on. Taste, the next sensory object, is enjoyed by the tongue. Again, there are all kinds of tastes: sweet, salty, bitter, sour, and so on. The last type of sensory object is touch, the tangible objects sensed by the body.

This presentation of the eleventh resultant form is based on the philosophical viewpoint of the Vaibhasika. Having thus gone through the first and second sets of five we are left with the last resultant form, the imperceptible form. The imperceptible form has the characteristic of form but eludes our ordinary perceptions. For example, electric current belongs to the category of imperceptible form. The vows that individuals receive when they take ordination is also an imperceptible form. It is imperceptible to the individual taking the vow as well as to others.

The second philosophical school of Buddhism, Svatantrika, posits five classes of imperceptible forms that are objects of consciousness instead of the single imperceptible form of the Vaibhasika.

The first class of mental forms is the partless particle that acts as a base for all other particles. Gross material objects are analyzed down to the smallest particle, the partless particle. The partless particle cannot be perceived with our eyes, its existence can only be validated by mental analysis. The Buddha said that if the mind changes, then also the partless particle changes. Thus, the Buddha made it clear that the three realms of existence are a mere projection of mind.

The second class of mental forms is occasionally perceptible forms. These are magical creations, like illusions and dreams.

The third class of mental forms is form acquired through receiving, for example receiving vows on different levels.

The fourth resultant form is imputed form. For example, if we create a doll that resembles a person and name this doll after a person.

The fifth class of mental forms is forms that have power over certain things. This refers to an individual that has attained tremendous power in his or her meditation. For example, if such a person meditates that everything is blue, he or she perceives everything as blue. This can also mean having power over certain phenomena which the meditator can gain by very concentrated meditation on the four elements of earth, water, fire, and air. This is called the resultant form of having gained power over phenomenal existence.

To summarize, according to the Vaibhasika School of Indian philosophy we talk about eleven resultant forms, according to the Svatantrika School we talk about fifteen resultant forms. The physical aggregate is the collection of all these elements and is labeled "body" or "form."

The individual meditator should analyze the aggregate of form in this manner. Having analyzed form, which is comprised of so many elements, without finding the self, we should rest the mind in stabilizing meditation.

The Aggregate of Feeling

Next is the aggregate of feeling, or sensation. The characteristic of feeling is to experience something. There are three basic feelings: pleasant feelings, unpleasant feelings, and neutral feelings. We cannot find pleasant feelings within external or internal phenomenal existence. Pleasant feelings do not exist independently "out there" or somewhere "inside." The nature of feelings is impermanent.

If pleasant feelings were already established by external phenomena, then it would be impossible for different individuals to perceive other people differently. Some see a person as being pleasant, while others experience the same person as unpleasant. If we look at the person we regard as our beloved, then naturally this will induce a pleasant feeling within our mind. However, somebody else may look at our beloved with different eyes and experience another emotional reaction. Therefore, the pleasant feeling does not abide within the external object, because a single external object can induce both pleasant and unpleasant feelings.

Long ago in Tibet, there were two friends. One of them met a woman and fell in love with her. However, when he introduced her to his friend, his friend could not see any attractive qualities and said: "Why have you fallen in love with that woman?" His friends answered, "You should not look at the woman from your perspective; you should look at her from my perspective. Then you would see her attractive qualities."

Therefore, neither truly existing happiness nor suffering are present in connection with external objects, whether we try to look from another person's perspective or from our own. Happiness or unhappiness, pleasant or unpleasant feelings, do not exist as independent external objects. Similarly, we cannot find independently existing pleasant or unpleasant feelings in the inner perceiving mind.

If happiness is established in connection with the inner perceiving mind, then the individual should be able to experience happiness always. But clearly this is not the case, for sometimes the mind experiences unhappiness.

The Aggregate of Perception

Third is the aggregate of perception. This refers to characterizing phenomena as good or bad. The aggregate of feeling and the aggregate of perception are included in the aggregate of formations. Still, Buddha classified them separately. The reason for this is because so much conflict arises in society based on the aggregate of feeling and so many conflicts and arguments arise between different religious and philosophical schools based on the aggregate of perception.

Everybody wishes to have pleasant feelings and to escape unpleasant feelings. However, if we use unskillful means to fulfill our longing for pleasant feelings by harming other sentient beings, then this is regarded as destructive. Similarly, based on the aggregate of perception conflicts can arise between different religious communities. To prevent such conflicts, we should learn to respect the philosophical traditions of others, while regarding our lineage and tradition as something precious.

To lessen fixation onto any form of feeling, we should try to reduce the initial response to an object as pleasant or unpleasant. We should try to reduce the notion that our own religious or philosophical view is superior. We should at the same time try to lessen our feelings of aversion and lack of respect for other traditions and philosophical systems.

The Aggregate of Formation

The fourth aggregate is the aggregate of formation. The aggregate of formation signifies that something is being formed, a composition. The first type of aggregate of formation has to do with resembling. The second type of formation is neither a formation of mind nor a formation of an inanimate object. It is termed formation that is neither.

The resembling aggregate of formation should be understood as mental states. They are called mental states because they stem from the principal mind. It is complicated to classify the mental states. All kinds of thoughts, apart from the principal mind, are categorized within the category of fifty-one mental states. The second and third aggregates, feeling and perception also belong to the fifty-one mental states.

We differentiate between external and internal happiness. External happiness is acquired by collecting outer material objects and status. However, we are not able to obtain complete and perfect happiness by only collecting external material things. It is essential to develop happiness based on internal development. To be able to invoke inner peace, we need to know the difference between positive and negative mental states. What do we mean by positive mental states? They are any mental states that give rise to inner peace, happiness, and joy. What do we mean by negative mental states? They are any mental states that give rise to emotional turmoil and unpleasantness.

The conceptual states are beyond counting, but since the Buddha was very skillful, he summarized them as fifty-one mental states, which are again divided into six subgroups. The first is the five ever-present states that accompany all states of mind. The second is the decisive states because they prevent suspicion or hesitation. The third is the eleven virtuous mental states. These are primarily derived from non-attachment, non-aggression, and non-confusion. The fourth is the six root emotions. Why are they called this? Because these root emotions develop into all kinds of secondary emotional complications. The fifth is the group of twenty proximate emotions, named thus because they are close to the six root emotions. Sixth are the four variable emotions, called thus because they can change into a positive, negative, or neutral state, depending on the individual.

The five ever-present states are feeling, perception, intention, contact, and attention. As long as we are living human beings, these five mental events are always present, hence the name. They are called ever-present because when an individual gives rise to negative, positive or neutral mental events, these states are also present.

Next are the five decisive states. The first is interest, the second is determination, the third is mindfulness, the fourth is concentration, and the fifth is discernment. A mind in which these factors are inherent will enjoy decisiveness, free from hesitation and suspicion.

The third category is the eleven virtuous mental states. These are virtuous in nature, and we should practice these. The eleven virtuous states are faith, conscientiousness, alertness, equanimity, self-respect, priority, non-attachment, non-aversion, effort, non-violence, and non-confusion.

Next are the six disturbing emotions. These are desire, anger, pride, ignorance, wrong view, and doubt. They are also known as the six subtle emotions that have the potential to manifest on a gross level. If an individual possesses the six root emotions and allows these emotions to influence the mindstream, many other emotional complications will also arise.

Next are the twenty proximate emotions. These create disturbances in the mind of the individual, and we should strive to abandon them as much as possible. The first is anger, the second is resentment, and the third is spite. Then follows malice, jealousy, dishonesty, deceit, hypocrisy, avarice, haughtiness, lack of self-respect, lack of priority, torpor, restlessness, faithlessness, laziness, non-conscientiousness, forgetfulness, inattentiveness, and distractedness. It is essential to recognize these when they occur in our minds; this recognition allows us to abandon the emotion. It is necessary to know which feelings should be cultivated and which feelings should be abandoned. It is therefore critical to do "inner research" by observing our minds and recognizing these mental events.

The next four mental states are the four variable states. The first is worry, the second is sleepiness, the third is investigation, and the fourth is analysis. These final four variable mental states can turn into positive, negative, or neutral mental states. We should strive to change them into positive mental states.

The Aggregate of Consciousness

The aggregate of consciousness is a collection of eight consciousnesses. The term consciousness means being aware of something.

The Sense Consciousnesses

The eye consciousness, the ear consciousness, the body consciousness, the taste consciousness, and the smell consciousness are referred to as the five sense consciousnesses. The five sense consciousnesses are non-conceptual in nature. When the eye consciousness meets the sense object of form, characterized by shape and color, the eye consciousness can grasp the generality of that form. However, it is not able to distinguish the shape, the color and so on. Therefore, the eye sense consciousness is non-conceptual, as are the other sense consciousnesses.

When the mental consciousness, the sixth consciousness, is distracted, then despite this distraction, the five sense consciousnesses are able to perceive their corresponding sense objects. However, these perceptions will not be recognized.

Of course, there are specific causes and conditions that give rise to the five sense consciousnesses, but we are not going to discuss these here. We will do this later when we go through the eighteen elements.

The Mental Consciousness

The sixth consciousness is the mental consciousness that functions conceptually as well as non-conceptually. When we shut our eyes or block our ears, we are still able to perceive certain forms and sounds. These forms and sounds occur on the level of mental consciousness.

The conceptual mental consciousness can grasp the five sensory objects: form, sound, smell, taste, and touch. The mental consciousness is the primary consciousness. Because of this, the Buddha said that the mind precedes all phenomenal experiences. Therefore, the mind is the most important and we should strive to train this mind.

When we do meditation, such as the development and completion phases of tantric meditation, we are primarily employing the mental consciousness. All forms of spiritual practice connected with meditation are undertaken mainly by using mental consciousness. The mental consciousness can see shapes, hear sounds, smell odors, taste food, and so on. Therefore, our mental consciousness is employed during meditation.

We must make a distinction between the functioning of the mental consciousness and the preceding five sense consciousnesses. The functioning of the five sense consciousnesses is partial and confined. The mental consciousness is pervasive. It can grasp and perceive all sensory objects and is, therefore, the most important consciousness.

The Afflicted Consciousness

The seventh consciousness is referred to as the afflicted consciousness. The object of reference of the afflicted consciousness is the fundamental consciousness. Why is it called "afflicted consciousness?" Because this consciousness grasps onto the belief in a self. It is afflicted because it obscures the individual from seeing selflessness, leading the individual to perceive a self where there is none.

The afflicted consciousness is supported by many afflicted emotions, such as ignorance, belief in, and pride of self. Usually, the afflicted consciousness is inherent in the minds of individuals and is supported by these three emotions. However, there are occasions when the individual is free from these three emotions; they are not present when the individual enters formal meditation and realizes true reality. Someone who has previously recognized genuine truth in formal meditation will at death have a mind that is free from afflicted consciousness. Similarly, when someone experiences cessation, the mind of the individual is freed from the conflicting consciousness supported by the three emotions. Also, when someone attains the path of no more learning, the stage of Buddhahood, the mind of such an enlightened being is liberated from afflicted consciousness. Apart from this, afflicted consciousness always permeates our minds, even when we are unconscious or in deep sleep.

The Fundamental Consciousness.

The Tibetan term for fundamental consciousness is "the consciousness that is the basis for all" because this consciousness acts as the very foundation for all karmic complexes and patterns.

Suppose a person murders somebody. The act of murder has ceased when the person has died. But the karmic energy of having been involved with such a negative action is stored in the fundamental consciousness. In future, when the presence of the seed of the harmful act is aroused or stimulated by craving, the seed will sprout. The individual will then have to meet the negative consequences of having performed the adverse action in the past.

Not only are adverse actions stored in the fundamental consciousness; the energies of defiled positive actions are also stored here. Positive actions are termed defiled because they do not transcend dualistic thought. Because of this, the happiness that we experience is primarily created by ourselves, not by somebody else. So, everyone is responsible for their own happiness and suffering. Therefore, it makes sense to accumulate merit and engage in virtuous acts and to abandon non-virtuous actions.

The Continuation of Consciousness

Sentient beings wander in the cyclic existence of samsara because of the continuity of the five psychophysical aggregates. When we talk about the continuity of the five psychophysical aggregates from one life to the next, we are not talking about transferring the preceding psychophysical aggregates to the reincarnated psychophysical aggregates, but instead we posit a continuity of the psychophysical aggregates from one life to the next.

The preceding five aggregates are causes for the resultant five aggregates. It is a relationship of cause and effect; the aggregates are not propagated as such. It is not like entering an airplane in Norway and flying to America.

The texts give many examples to explain that the five aggregates are not transferred as a separate solid entity from one moment to the next. For example, let us say we place a line of candles in front of us, and light the first candle. If we use the first candle to light the next and so on, all candles will be lit, but it is not the case that the flame of the first candle jumps into the flame of the second candle. Still, the other candles are lit because the first was lit. As another example, let our image be clearly reflected in a mirror. It is not the case that the image has jumped into the mirror; the reflection is produced because of the presence of our physical existence, as well as the mirror. The teacher's knowledge can be acquired by the student, but it is not as if the teacher's knowledge jumps into the student. By learning from the teacher, the student can acquire the same knowledge as the teacher. When we create a figure from a mold, the original mold has a certain shape, but the mold is not transferring itself, rather the molded object receives the shape of the mold. We can produce fire by using a magnifying glass, but it is not the case that the fire of the magnifying glass jumps into the object that catches fire. In the same way, the five aggregates of the preceding moment act as causes for the aggregates of the present moment. But it is not the case that the aggregates of the preceding moment jump into the subsequent moment to ensure continuity. I have included so many examples to help us reduce our clinging to the idea of a separate self in the five aggregates.

It is easy to understand how the last four aggregates

propagate as causes and results in the next life; it is more difficult to understand how the first aggregate does this. When a person dies, the gross body ceases to function, but the subtle physical body remains. It is this subtle physical body that continues from this life to the next. When the individual goes through the bardo ("transition state") of death and enters the bardo of becoming, the individual possesses only four of the psychophysical aggregates. The mind of the individual is not completely without a body, the physical body is maintained on a subtle level by the mental body of the bardo. A sentient being wandering in the bardo of becoming will in the early stage experience the mental body from his or her previous life. If the past life was human, it will experience a mental human body. But if the individual is going to be reborn as an animal, then in the later stage of the bardo of becoming, the individual will experience the mental body of an animal. After going through the bardo of becoming, future rebirth awaits.

When the gross body ceases, the subtle body can carry certain information from the past life to the next. Some of the reincarnated lamas have marks on the body that resemble marks on the body of a previous life. This is taken as proof of the subtle physical continuity from one life to the next.

If we become knowledgeable about the five psychophysical aggregates, we will be able to counteract the assumption of the self as a unitary entity that maintains its continuity by jumping from the past life to the next.

Stopping Samsara

Why do the five psychophysical aggregates not cease to exist? Karma is the reason behind the unstoppable movement of the psychophysical aggregates from the preceding instant into the subsequent instant. If karma is not accumulated, then the continual flow of the five psychophysical aggregates will stop.

If we are going to stop accumulating karma, we must stop the emotional complications that give rise to karma. In order to eradicate the very root of the emotional complications, we need to get rid of our belief in a unitary self. This is done through the Buddhist view of dependent origination; everyone is the creator of his or her world, and each is the destroyer of this world as well.

If we continue to involve ourselves with samsaric existence, this involvement will never cease. However, if we do not identify ourselves with the existence of samsara, or renounce ourselves from involvement with samsaric existence, then we can stop at this very moment.

It is a little bit like a hamster that treads a wheel in a cage. The hamster becomes excited and keeps running. Samsara is a bit like that unless we stop. Not long ago, I chanced to see such a hamster, and this reminded me of the vicious circle of samsara.

Questions and Answers

Question: You said the eye sense faculty is dependent on the eye sense organ. Will a blind person not have the eye sense faculty?

Answer: When the sense organ is damaged, the subtle sense faculty is also damaged, and the sense consciousness will not be able to perceive the corresponding sensory objects.

Question: Is the eye sense faculty a completely visual thing? When we are dreaming, we can see pictures. Are these images separate from the eye sense faculty? We can also see forms when we visualize in meditation.

Answer: Dream appearances in sleep are not perceived through the eye sense organ and the eye sense faculty. They are perceived by non-conceptual mental consciousness. When the non-conceptual mental consciousness becomes deluded, it gives rise to the perception of a dream.

Question: Did you say that form comes from afflictive emotions and karma? I do not understand this.

Answer: Take our own physical existence as an example. The mind of a sentient being evolves from positive and negative actions. By accumulating positive or negative karma, the consciousness of the being is propelled toward the womb of the mother. However, this is not enough; the masculine and feminine energies that we receive from our father and mother must come together as well. Then birth is possible. Do you understand now?

Question: I understood that. Is this inner form? What about outer form. Is that the same?

Answer: When it comes to the external physical existence, we can say that it is the same in general, but there are exceptions of physical manifestations that sometimes do not follow the law of the karma.

Question: You talked about the four elements. Is the space element not included?

Answer: When we try to describe the first aggregate, the form aggregate, the fifth element, space, is not included. The reason for this is that space is regarded as a non-composite phenomenon. We cannot inflict harm on the element of space, unlike the aggregate of form.

Question: Are all basic emotions negative emotions? Are there no positive emotions?

Answer: Of course positive emotions exist! The eleven virtuous mental states are positive. The last classification of the fifty-one formations is the four variable states, and these emotions can also be positive. The second classification, the five decisive states are also virtuous states because they create a decisive, unconfused mind.

Question: How can worry, the first of the four variable

states be made positive?

Answer: If we have accumulated certain karma in the recent or distant past, and we remember it and develop a sense of worry of having accumulated certain bad karma, this becomes positive worry instead of negative worry. This worry, or regret, belongs to the five antidotal powers that can purify negative karma.

The Eighteen Elements

The second topic is the eighteen elements. Earlier, when we talked about form, we mentioned the five sense faculties and the corresponding sense objects. This makes up the first ten elements. The next seven elements are associated with the fifth aggregate, the aggregate of consciousness. This makes a list of seventeen. The last element is phenomena, which again consists of four sub-elements, the aggregates of feeling, perception, formation and the non-composite element. If we become knowledgeable in the field of the eighteen elements, we will be able to counteract the belief in a self that is the enjoyer of the experience.

The eighteen elements become more comprehensible if we classify them into three groups: the six sense faculties, the six sense objects, and the six corresponding consciousnesses.

The Six Sense Faculties

The first of the six sense faculties is the eye sense faculty. Remember, we are not referring to our ordinary sense organs, but the subtle sense faculties. Ordinarily, we are not able to perceive the subtle sense faculties. It is a bit like the high and low frequencies of sound that elude our sense of hearing. However, the subtle shape of the eye sense faculty can be seen by someone who has attained the divine eye by achieving profound realization. It can then be seen to have the form of a blue flower. This realization also makes it possible to see things that are far away, as well as the subtle forms of the faculties. This is the first type of clairvoyance.

The subtle form of the sense faculty of the ear has the curly shape of the branch of a birch tree. The subtle form of the sense faculty of the nose has the shape of two parallel copper needles. The subtle form of the sense faculty of the tongue is a crescent moon, resembling the curvature of the tongue. The subtle form of the sense faculty of the body is soft like a bird's feather. It permeates the whole body, and in the same way that a fire is hot from whatever direction we touch it, we can feel with all parts of our body.

Next is the mind faculty. The mind faculty is difficult to understand, and what exactly is the mind faculty in this context? When the six consciousnesses cease to exist, the mind faculty immediately arises as cognition of the object at hand. For example, assume the eye consciousness has become conscious of a certain form. At that very moment, the continuity of this consciousness is interrupted and replaced by the mind faculty that cognizes the form that was earlier perceived by the eye sense faculty and the eye consciousness.

The Six Sense Objects

The first sense object is form. Form is the object of the eye sense faculty. When we talked about the classification of the aggregate of form, most of these things were talked about. Therefore, I will just list the names for the sake of presentation. The sensory object of form is followed by the sensory object of sound. The third sensory object is odor, the fourth is taste, the fifth is touch, and the last is mental objects. The mental objects are a collection of the second, third and fourth psychophysical aggregates i.e. the aggregate of feeling, the aggregate of perception, and the aggregate of formation, in addition to imperceptible forms and all unconditioned phenomena. Space is an example of the last category. Also, the genuine nature of our mind is an unconditioned phenomenon and is also an example. Note that in the explanation of the five psychophysical aggregates the element of unconditioned phenomena is not included, but in the context of the eighteen elements it is.

The Six Consciousnesses

The first consciousness is the eye consciousness, the second is the ear consciousness, the third is the nose consciousness, the fourth is the taste consciousness, the fifth is the body consciousness, and the sixth is the mental consciousness.

So, all possible existence and experience are included in the presentation of the eighteen elements. If we become knowledgeable in the field of the eighteen elements, we can claim to know all phenomenal existence.

Causes that give rise to the Elements

Do these eighteen elements have causes or is there an agent that causes them to develop? The eighteen elements have causes, but there is no separate almighty agent that creates all the eighteen elements and the various phenomenal experiences.

In Tibetan, the word "phenomena" is referred to as "kham". The meaning of kham should be understood as potentiality. What kind of potentiality is inherent within the six sense organs? The six sense organs and their respective sense objects have the potential to give rise to the six corresponding consciousnesses. What kind of potentiality is inherent in the consciousnesses? For example, the eye consciousness has the potential to grasp perceived form. The others have a similar potential to grasp their corresponding sense objects.

Causes Giving Rise to Consciousness

The six classes of consciousnesses can arise upon contact between the six sense organs and the sense objects. Consciousness can also arise from the resembling cause, which is the preceding moment of consciousness that upon cessation gives rise to the next moment of consciousness. There is also a maturing karmic cause and an immediate cause that give rise to the six classes of consciousnesses. The main point is that the six classes of consciousnesses depend on the coming together of many types of causes and conditions.

Causes Giving Rise to Sensory Objects

The six sensory objects arise due to various causes and conditions. One set of causes that give rise to the existence of the six sense objects are the five great elements. Another cause that gives rise to the six sense objects is the maturation of the collective karmic cause. There is also a resembling cause.

Causes Giving Rise to Sense Faculties

There are four different causes of expansion that give rise to the six sense faculties. Why are they referred to as the four causes of expansion? Because by relying on these four causes, the individual can nurture the five sense faculties. The first cause of expansion is the consumption of appropriate food, the second is sleep, the third is cleanliness, and the fourth is meditation. From this, we can understand that the Buddha underlined the importance of taking care of ourselves by eating, sleeping, and cleansing, as well as practicing meditative absorption. The four causes that develop the sense faculties should be practiced in our daily life. We should try to consume nutritious food that benefits our body, and we should try to sleep at appropriate times. This will contribute to the development of the six sense faculties.

The Benefit of Meditating upon the Elements

The Buddha said that whoever is endowed with the six elements can reach enlightenment. In this context, the six prominent elements are earth, water, fire, air, space, and consciousness. What are the space elements? They are all the spaces and gaps that can be found within an individual.

The classification of the eighteen elements is presented primarily in connection with the beings of the desire realm. When we are within the desire realm, all the elements are functioning fully. Creatures in the desire god realm do not possess the sense organs of nose and tongue. Therefore, they are not able to experience the nose and tongue consciousness and are relieved from attachment to the sensory objects of odor and taste. The gods of the formless realm are deprived of all the rest of the eighteen elements apart from the last three, the sense faculty of the mind, the sense object of the mind, and the mental consciousness.

If we are knowledgeable about the classification of the eighteen elements, we will be able to do away with the assumption of the self as the cause of action. An action is the result of causes and conditions coming together.

Meditating upon the classification of the eighteen elements is also said to act as an antidote to arrogance and pride.

The Buddha said that to grasp the meaning of the non-conventional we must depend on the conventional; to understand the ultimate truth we need to become well versed in the functioning of conventional truth.

Questions and Answers

Question: What is the relationship between the sense consciousness and the sense faculty?

Answer: The relationship between the six faculties and the six consciousnesses is the relationship between cause and effect. The six faculties act as causes and the six consciousnesses act as effects.

Question: How do the faculties work concerning dreams and things that appear before the mind when the eyes are shut? Are these not part of the mind consciousness?

Answer: When the individual is dreaming, the five sense consciousnesses are not functioning. The dream is based on the mental consciousness. It is difficult to talk about consciousness because consciousness is not a solid object.

Question: But you talked about the cessation of the sense consciousnesses giving rise to the mind faculty?

Answer: The mind sense faculty is not included within the five sense faculties but still included in the list of six faculties. All the six consciousnesses are part of the mind faculty, and mind will act as a cause for the six sense consciousnesses. We talk about the six sense faculties acting as a cause and the six consciousnesses acting as a result, but sometimes the result will act as a cause. It is something like this: if one individual has a father and a son, then relative to his father he is referred to as the son, but in relation to his son he is referred to as the father. The collection of the six consciousnesses is a result, but we cannot say that they always will be a result; they can develop the mind element. When a seed is planted, we can say the death of the seed is the birth of the sprout; the death of the six consciousnesses gives birth to the mind faculty. This teaching reveals the law of interdependency that posits the validity of karma, cause, and effect. However, if we overanalyze it, such teachings can lead to a nihilistic attitude that considers everything to be non-existent. There is a Tibetan expression, "When we talk about the horse, we should not talk about the mule." When we talk about the relative truth, we should not start talking about the absolute truth.

Question: Is it possible to grasp this on the level of cause and effect? What happens after the six sense consciousnesses give birth to the mind faculty?

Answer: The cessation of the six consciousnesses gives rise to the mind faculty that cognizes. The mind faculty is the "knower." The subject matter is extremely complicated because so many consciousnesses are always taking place at the same time.

Question: Is there a subtle form of the mind faculty?

Answer: The mind element does not have any characteristics in terms of shape and color. There is no form, not even on the subtle level. We can summarize by saying that external phenomenal existence originates from the mind of the individual. Where does mind come from? It comes from the accumulation of karma, which again comes from accumulation of conflicting emotions.

Question: Can you say that the solar system and the universe have their own karma?

Answer: We can say that most things come from the accumulation of karma, but not everything. Take the small world (our own body) as an example. It exists because many causes and conditions have come together; the food that we eat, the masculine and feminine energy from our parents contribute to the existence of the body, as well as the consciousness from previous lives along with past karma. So, we can say that this small world is a by-product that we receive in this life. The same logic applies to phenomenal existence as well.

The Twelve Sense Sources, the Ayatanas

The third topic is the twelve sense sources. To be able to perceive the truth of suchness, the ultimate truth, it is important to comprehend and understand the functioning of conventional phenomena. Studying the subject of the twelve sense sources enables the individual meditator to counteract the notion of self as the enjoyer of experience.

The presentation of the twelve sense sources is not done to make things more difficult; it is an alternative representation of the eighteen elements. The first ten sense sources correspond to the five sense faculties and the five sense objects. The last two sense sources are the mind source and the mental object source. The mind source represents the seven consciousness elements. The mental object source represents the element of mental objects that contains the mental formations.

The Buddha used the three different presentations of the five aggregates, the eighteen elements, and the twelve sense sources, because different individuals are suited to varying degrees of detail. I am not going to elaborate on the presentation of the sense sources since these can be found within the eighteen elements.

Dependent Origination

The twelve links of dependent origination establish the view of the teaching of the Buddha. Saying that the view of Buddhism is dependent origination is the same as saying that the view of Buddhism is emptiness. The law of the twelve interdependent links makes it possible to claim that the view of Buddhism is emptiness.

Why is it called dependent origination? Because nothing can stand on its own without depending on other causes and conditions. All phenomenal experience and existence is a byproduct of things that depend on each other.

In conventional reality, all phenomena are subject to change and impermanence. This means that the true nature of any phenomenal existence is emptiness. If we understand the teaching on emptiness, it will be much easier for us to understand the unenlightened state of samsara and the enlightened state of nirvana. Some people think that if they understand the teaching of emptiness, then samsara will cease to function because its ultimate nature is emptiness. However, such a conclusion does not correspond with a correct understanding of the teaching of emptiness.

Somebody who has not realized the meaning of emptiness is unenlightened. Someone who has realized the meaning of emptiness directly is enlightened. This is the motivation for studying the fourth topic of dependent origination.

All external and internal phenomenal existence has the nature of dependent origination. Take for example a seed that gives rise to a sprout. The sprout will develop further into a plant through different stages and eventually wither. There is a connection between the cause and the effect. Also, the five great elements of earth, water, fire, air, and space, including the element of time act as causes that give rise to certain phenomenal existence on the external level. All these six great elements are contained in any given external object. An ordinary cup contains these six great elements. The cup contains the element of earth because the function of the element of earth is to stabilize. The element of water is also contained in the cup, but we are not able to perceive it. The water has a cohesive function that allows the cup to retain its form. The element of fire is also present in the cup. Similarly, the element of wind is contained in the cup because the cup can be moved from one place to another. The external space element and the internal space element are inherent in the cup; when they function together it is possible to place certain objects on certain things. The element of time is also included. Previously the cup did not exist, but at a certain point it came into existence. From a subtle perspective, the continuity of the cup ceases at every moment, and facilitates the unfolding of the subsequent moment. In this way, the six great elements make the external phenomena come into existence.

Also, internal phenomenal existence arises due to many causes and conditions. The primary cause of all internal phenomenal experiences is ignorance. Therefore, the ignorance that posits the existence of the self of the person is the first link of the twelve interdependent links. For example, if we have a sore on our hand, and the cause of the sore is removed, then the sore will disappear. However, if the sore is only treated symptomatically, the sore will not be perfectly healed. In the same way, if we are going to recover from the pain and misery of the unenlightened existence of samsara, we must heal the basic wound at its root; the ignorance that clings to the idea of a personal self.

The same ignorance that grasps onto the self of the person also seizes onto the sensing of others. Because of this, the individual develops attachment to self and aversion toward others. The mental continuum of such an individual consists of three basic emotions: the emotion of ignorance, the emotion of attachment, and the emotion of aggression.

The Twelve Interdependent Links

The Buddha said that all phenomenal experience and existence comes about from specific causes. By the expression "all phenomenal experiences" we mean the unenlightened state of samsara and the enlightened phenomenal experiences of nirvana. So, the Buddha did not only talk about the evolution of samsaric existence, but he also spoke about the development of nirvanic existence by relying on the Fourth Noble Truth. The Fourth Noble Truth of the path shows how to realize the Third Noble Truth, the truth of the cessation of conceptuality. This is the same as attaining nirvana.

The Buddha's teaching on the twelve interdependent links is a teaching on the first set of the two truths, the truth of suffering and the reality of the origin of suffering. It is essential for us to recognize the cause of unenlightened, samsaric existence. The cause of samsaric existence is the fundamental ignorance that is the first of the twelve interdependent links.

The twelve interdependent links are most easily understood as completed in three lifetimes. The link of ignorance, karmic formation and the establishment of consciousness are associated with the preceding life. From the fourth link, name and form, which signify the five skandhas, the link of the sense organs, the link of contact, feeling, craving, grasping and existence are traversed in the present life. The last two links, birth, and old age and death are completed in a future life. It is also possible to present the twelve links as completed in one or two lifetimes.

Ignorance

Ignorance should not only be understood as a lack of knowledge. Not recognizing some individual or object is not regarded as ignorance in this context. Ignorance is the opposite of primordial awareness. With primordial awareness we can see the genuine reality, but ignorance prevents us from doing this.

Primordial wisdom is twofold: the wisdom that realizes the selflessness of the person, and the wisdom that realizes the selflessness of phenomena. Correspondingly, there exists a twofold ignorance. Which ignorance should we identify with the first of the interdependent links? This is the ignorance that is incapable of realizing the selflessness of the person. In order to abandon samsaric existence, it is enough to understand the selflessness of the person.

For example, we can mistake a rope for a snake, but when we can realize that the rope is not a snake, this very realization releases the misconception of the snake. It is not necessary to destroy the rope in order to destroy the misconception of the rope as a snake. In the same way, it is not necessary to realize the inherent non-existence of the five physical aggregates. It is enough to understand the emptiness of the self.

For example, *arhats* belonging to the *shravakayana*, do not realize the emptiness of phenomena. They understand the selflessness of the person without realizing the selflessness of phenomena. This enables them to transcend the conditioned existence of samsara. Therefore, the root of the cyclic existence of samsara can be traced back to the fundamental ignorance of the emptiness of the self of the person. It is therefore essential to recognize that the root of all the mistakenness, of all the emotional complications, is the fundamental ignorance that grasps onto the existence of the self of the person. Someone who would like to attain liberation from the cyclic existence of samsara and attain the state of complete liberation, Buddhahood, should view this fundamental ignorance along with its entourage of emotional complications as something that is not worth pursuing.

Karmic Formations

The Buddha said in the sutras that "because of this, that has occurred." What he meant was that because of ignorance, karmic formations have occurred. Karmic formation should be understood as action. Karmic formations include virtuous karma, non-virtuous karma, and neutral karma. What do we mean by neutral karma? It is karma that cannot be changed. Actions of neutral karma act as a cause for rebirth in the higher realms, which are the Formless and Form God Realms. Other causes and conditions cannot destroy the karma of such actions, and therefore the individual must experience these realms.

The second link, karmic formations, comes about because of the first link, ignorance. Ignorance gives rise to attachment, aversion, and neutrality, and these emotional complications give rise to the karmic formations of the second link. Initially, because of ignorance, we grasp onto the reality of the self of the person. Grasping onto the existence of the self of the person establishes the self of others. We develop attachment to our self, our families, and our friends; anyone we see as belonging to "our side." Those who do not belong to "our side" we categorize as "others." In the worst case, the category of "others" becomes enemies. On these bases, aversion and dislike arise. It is because of the splitting of the reality into the duality of the "I" and "others" that desirous attachment, aversion, and other emotional complications take root. In this way, we end up accumulating correspondingly virtuous, non-virtuous, and neutral karma. Within the category of others, there will also be individuals we look upon as neutral. For these sentient beings, we might develop a sense of indifference, without any concern.

This is how the karmic formations evolve from the fundamental ignorance of the first link. We might think that it is necessary to have another link inserted between the first and the second link, a link of disturbing emotions. In some sense this is true, but the reason the Buddha did not do this was that if we just overcome ignorance, we will also be able to overcome the emotional complications that are caused by the ignorance.

Consciousness

During the evolution of the second link, the individual accumulates non-virtuous, virtuous and neutral karma. Positive karma causes the mind of the individual to experience the three higher realms. These realms are also included within the conditioned existence of samsara.

Negative karma causes the mind of the individual to experience the three lower realms.

There is a projecting consciousness, and there is a projected consciousness. Ignorance causes karma, and the karmic energy that is stored in the consciousness is termed projecting consciousness. If this energy is not exhausted, it will stay dormant in the mindstream of the individual. Then, when the right causes and conditions come together, perhaps lifetimes later, the individual will have to experience the corresponding result. This is the projected consciousness. The projecting consciousness acts as the cause that gives rise to the projected consciousness as a result. Because of this, there is a continuum of consciousness from one lifetime to the next. Karma acts as fuel for propelling the consciousness from one lifetime to the next.

Name and Form

At the moment of conception, the stream of the consciousness of the individual from the past life enters the mother's womb, together with the substances from the father and mother, and consciousness evolves into the fourth link: name and form. This starts the new life. Then, gradually the different stages of name and form develop.

"Name and form" is a technical term. "Form" refers to the first aggregate. "Name" refers to the rest of the aggregates: feeling, perception, formation, and consciousness. "Name" signifies the psychological and unobstructed character of these aggregates. "Form" bears the physical entity. Remember, here we are talking about form as a newly conceived child in the womb of the mother. This form is not distinct, and we cannot detect any human features.

The Six Sense Organs

Next is the fifth link of the six sense organs that start to develop as the fetus is growing. The evolution of the six sense organs evolves simultaneously with the six sense faculties.

Contact

Next is the sixth link of contact. Contact means meeting or touching. What kind of meeting takes place during the sixth link? It is the meeting of the six sense organs as a causal factor, the six sense objects, and the six sense consciousnesses.

Feeling

The seventh link of feeling evolves from contact. A feeling is defined as an individual experience. Depending on whether there has been contact with a pleasant or unpleasant object, the corresponding feeling will be pleasant or unpleasant. Neutral feelings are also produced in the same way.

Craving

The eighth link of craving evolves from feeling. We develop craving for pleasant feelings, which again creates aversion toward unpleasant feelings. Aversion towards unpleasantness is seen as craving to not experience unpleasant feelings. Beings of the form and formless god realms develop craving toward neutral feelings.

Grasping

The ninth link of grasping comes from having developed

craving for pleasant and neutral feelings and aversion toward unpleasant feelings. The individual will grasp at certain activities in order to experience pleasant feelings and avoid unpleasant feelings. This also applies to neutral feelings. There are four kinds of grasping: grasping at desirable objects, grasping at wrong views, grasping at forms of discipline or rituals, as well as grasping at a belief in the self. Grasping can develop toward all kinds of sensory objects, including form, sound, smell, and touch. The second form of grasping is grasping at wrong views. Any fanatical or unbalanced view that has fallen into the extremes of eternalism or nihilism is a wrong view. Grasping at rituals and disciplines is to claim that our own form of rituals and disciplines is superior to other traditions. Grasping at a belief in the self means that the individual believes that there exists something called a self and cultivates craving for this self.

Existence

The tenth link of existence comes about because of grasping and craving. The Tibetan word for existence signifies possibility. At this point rebirth is possible. The tenth link should be understood as the accumulation of strong karma that acts as the primary cause for future rebirth.

Birth, Old Age, and Death

Existence makes rebirth possible. Birth is the eleventh link. Birth causes old age and death, the twelfth link. The reason that the twelfth link contains both old age and death is that we can die without growing old, death can occur at any time.

Further Analysis of the Chain of Dependent Origination

Analyzing the twelve links further we discover that certain links belong to the category of emotional afflictions and certain links are associated with karmic formations that are generated on the basis of emotional complications. We shall look at how certain links are associated with the noble truth of suffering.

The Influencing Powers

The first, eighth and ninth links, ignorance, craving, and grasping, are associated with afflicted emotions. The second and tenth links, karmic formations and existence, are associated with the karma produced from afflicted emotions. All together, these links belong to the category of the second noble truth of the source of suffering.

The remaining seven links are associated with the first noble truth of suffering. These are the third to the seventh links, as well as the eleventh and twelfth link: consciousness, name and form, the six perceptions, contact, feeling, birth, and old age and death.

These three groups of the links — the links associated with the afflicted emotions, the links associated with karma, and the links associated with suffering — are referred to as the three influencing powers. We do not have freedom from influence by these powers. They are called the influencing power of emotional complications, the influencing power of karmic actions, and the influencing power of suffering. Gripped by the influence of emotional complication, suffering and karma, we become victims of these powers.

The Characteristics of the Law of Dependent Origination

All external and internal phenomenal evolution is based on the law of dependent origination. The evolution of external and internal phenomenal existence proceeds from one moment to the next with five unique characteristics. The first characteristic of the law of dependent origination is the absence of eternalism. The second characteristic is that it does not fall into nihilism because the very cessation of the preceding moment facilitates the arising of the subsequent moment. The third characteristic is non-transferability; the transition from the preceding moment to the next is not by way of transference. There is no solid entity that is transferred as a cause into the new territory of the result. The fourth characteristic is that by relying on a small cause we can obtain a tremendously great result. This should primarily be understood regarding the evolution of external phenomena. The fifth characteristic is termed resemblance of the cause and result. This means that we reap results according to the causes we have accumulated.

Attaining Enlightenment by Reverse Contemplation on the Twelve Links

The ascending order of the twelve links describes the evolution of the unenlightened state of samsara, as explained by the noble truth of suffering and the noble truth of the source of suffering. Contemplation on the twelve links in reverse order facilitates the evolution of the enlightened state. Meditation on the reverse order is termed the twelve links of genuine truth. In brief, the twelve links of genuine truth can be summed up by the third and fourth noble truth; the noble truth of cessation, nirvana, and the noble truth of the path that leads to the cessation of suffering.

The second set of the Four Noble Truths reveals how to develop an enlightened state. The fourth noble truth shows the path that leads to the cessation of suffering by breaking the links associated with emotional complications and development of karma as we discussed above. This is the nature of the noble truth of the path.

To simplify, there are certain links that are associated with emotional complications. By relying on the noble truth of the path, we can exhaust the five links associated with karmic and emotional complications. This gives rise to the noble truth of cessation. What has ceased upon attaining the noble truth of cessation? The remaining seven links of dependent origination stop at this point.

The Benefits of Meditation on the Twelve Links

This has been a brief presentation of the twelve links of dependent origination. If we were to expound on it, the subject matter would become overly complicated. Because of this, the Buddha suggested to meditate on the twelve links of interdependent origination as an antidote for ignorance.

If we study, contemplate and meditate on the nature of the evolution of samsara, we will be able to discover many things that we have not seen before. If we become knowledgeable in the field of the twelve links of dependent origination, it will counteract the naive assumption of a self as the sole creator of everything.

Questions and Answers

Question: How is it possible to grasp neutral feelings?

Answer: It is also possible to grasp at neutral objects. One example of such an object is the meditation that acts as a cause for rebirth in the higher god realms. The nature of such meditation is neutral. It is possible to develop grasping toward such meditation.

Question: Is the projective consciousness the same as fundamental consciousness, the alaya?

Answer: There is no contradiction in calling it fundamental consciousness. But to be precise, the presentation of the twelve interdependent links does not talk about fundamental consciousness. Consciousness should be understood as the fertile ground in which the seed of the karmic energies is imprinted. The second link is the link of karmic formations. The consciousness transports the energy of the karma. This presentation of the twelve links of interdependence is based on the highest Madhyamika view. Lower views, such as the Cittamatra School, talk primarily about fundamental consciousness.

Question: Where is the invisible world?

Answer: The tenth link, the link of existence or possibility that is acquired by the accumulation of powerful karma, is the cause of reincarnation, the eleventh link. The mind of the individual goes through the phases of the Bardo in the time between the tenth and the eleventh link.

Question: Are all links present at the same time?

Answer: The twelve links represent the relationship between cause and effect. When we plant a seed, and it sprouts into a plant, the plant will give rise to leaves, fruits, and flowers. It evolves through several stages. Similarly, ignorance, karmic formations, and consciousness act as causes that give rise to later stages. These later stages again act as causes for still later stages of development. Moreover, these will again serve as causes for other results. It is essential to understand that even if we say that ignorance is the root of samsara, it is not associated only with the beginning of samsara.

Question: My understanding may be wrong, but I think

we are always in this one lifetime. The twelve links are always there. However, if we talk about the three lifetimes, we are always present in steps four to ten. It is more like a didactic method, a method for understanding. It is not like we do not experience birth, old age and death only in future lifetimes. Of course, we experience these in this lifetime as well.

Answer: Yes, this is precisely what I mean. This is a good way of understanding it — the twelve links of interdependence act as cause and result. Their relationship is cause and effect. We cannot see both cause and effect in one single instant. The cause is associated with one instant, followed by the result in the next instant. For example, by depending on ignorance and the karmic formations of the individual's past life, present existence evolves, because of ignorance of the present life, future life evolves.

Question: Do karmic actions take two lifetimes to ripen?
Answer: Primarily the link of ignorance, the link of karmic formations, and the link of consciousness are completed in the preceding life. Links four to ten, from name and form up to existence, are said to be completed in this lifetime. The links of birth, old age, and death are completed in the next life. Now, there are two aspects of consciousness: projecting and projected consciousness. Projecting consciousness occurs in the past life, the projected consciousness occurs in the present life. This is how the twelve links are completed in the cycle of three lifetimes.

If we perform certain actions, for example the act of killing, the actual act requires a certain amount of time. This is the duration of the act of killing. The twelve interdependent links can also be understood to be completed within the duration of the act of killing, but this is not a valid presentation of the twelve links, and in this case each link is defined differently. For example, let us say an individual is involved in killing an animal. The link of ignorance, in this case, is defined as ignorance of what is to be cultivated and what is to be abandoned, what is positive and what is negative.

Question: Where can we stop the cycle of birth and rebirth? Where is the weakest link to cut the chain?

Answer: It depends on whether we want to stop the wheel of interdependent origination or if we want to turn the wheel of interdependent origination. If we want to stop, we must stop the link of ignorance, the first link. However, this generates much fear in the mind of the individual because by stopping the link of ignorance the "I" will be lost. The sense of self will be lost. This generates fear.

Question: Are the samsaric formations referred to in twelve links the same as the formations referred to in the skandhas?

Answer: Even though the same term is used in the context of the five skandhas as in the presentation of the twelve links, their meaning is totally different. In the context of the five skandhas, karmic formations refer to all kinds of mental events and factors that form or accumulate karma. In the context of the twelve links, karmic formations are the actual karma.

Question: You said that the self is not the cause of action. Does this mean that we are not responsible for our actions?

Answer: When we manage to counteract the assumption that it is the self that causes the action, we will not become irresponsible. The reason for this is that when we can see other individuals that are victims of grasping onto the self, our view of emptiness will be embraced by loving-kindness and compassion. Not only will we feel responsible for ourselves, but we will also want to take on the responsibility for other living beings because we can see their suffering.

This teaching is given to reveal the non-existence of the cause. During the time of the Buddha, non-Buddhist philosophical systems posited what was known as a Supreme Self, an Almighty Power, and to refute this philosophical viewpoint the Buddha bestowed the teaching of selflessness, the emptiness of self. There are two kinds of belief in a self. The first is the spontaneous belief in a self and the second is the imputed belief in a self. Every being possess the spontaneous belief in a self, but ancient Indian non-Buddhist philosophical systems posited an imputed belief in the existence of a supreme self. They believed in a cosmic self, pervading the cosmos, and that our self is a part of that cosmic self. This is a fabrication of philosophical ideas.

Question: Who is the creator of karma if there is no self?

Answer: If we realize the emptiness of self, then there is neither a creator of karma nor some self that experiences the karma. However, if we fail to recognize the emptiness of self, then that self will be both the creator and experiencer of karma. For example, I exist conventionally. If "I" ask somebody to bring a certain cup, the person might know of this cup and bring it. However, the label "cup" is not the cup; it is simply a label for the actual cup. There is a difference between the label and the cup itself. For when we analyze the label, we cannot find the existence of the cup.

If we are clinging onto the notion of a self, we will create karma and must experience the consequences of this. However, as soon we directly realize the emptiness of the self, there will neither be a performer nor an experiencer of the consequences of the karma.

Question: So, if you realize the emptiness of self, then you will not create non-virtuous actions, because you know that there is no self. However, if you do virtuous things, you also create karma. Shouldn't we create positive karma?

Answer: Is it necessary to believe in the self in order to create positive karma? We must make a distinction between fundamental consciousness and fundamental awareness. Fundamental consciousness is associated with the unenlightened state of mind. With realization, fundamental consciousness is transformed into fundamental awareness.

When an enlightened person performs positive actions, these do not come from the fundamental consciousness, but instead from the fundamental awareness. So, the virtuous karma is not produced by the self.

Respondent: And because there is no self that performs these actions, there is no karma. Is that the logic?

Yes, that is the logic. Super logic!

Question: But should we not be attached to the ones we love?

Answer: We need to distinguish between attachment and love or affection. Sometimes we mix these and think that attachment is something good, something needed, but attachment is not needed to benefit ourselves or others. Genuine love is needed. Attachment is something bad.

Question: Many people do things they think are good because they cannot see the consequences of their own actions. However, if we look at the consequences, their actions are not good. Their intention has not been negative, but because of ignorance, negative consequences follow. Can you comment?

Answer: Therefore, the Buddha said that we should not fall into the extreme of altruism. We should unify love and compassion with wisdom. Your example indicates that the person has good motivation but does not have the wisdom to see what benefits themselves and others.

The Correct and the Incorrect

The fifth topic in the Gateway to Knowledge is "the correct and the incorrect." What do we mean by the correct and the incorrect? First, we will talk about the term correct. In Tibetan, this term signifies possibility or opportunity. The

Tibetan term for incorrect signifies impossibility. If we perform virtuous karma, this leads to happiness. This is correct. If we accumulate unwholesome, negative karma, this makes it impossible for us to experience happiness. This is incorrect.

All fields of worldly knowledge are about knowing what is correct and what is incorrect so that we can engage in the correct and stop doing the incorrect. In Tibet there exist many different fields of knowledge, but in this context, we talk primarily of inner science. By "inner science" we mean the teaching of the Buddha.

If we possess a correct view, then we can attain liberation. On the contrary, if we maintain an incorrect view that does not correspond with reality, it will be impossible to attain enlightenment. There are basically two incorrect views, the false view of nihilism and the wrong view of eternalism. If we cling to the wrong view of eternalism, it is not possible to attain liberation.

A correct view is the balanced view of the Middle Way that falls into neither the extreme of nihilism nor eternalism. This view enables the individual to attain liberation and enlightenment.

Some ancient Indian, non-Buddhist philosophical traditions possessed a mistaken view of nihilism and eternalism. For example, the Tirtikas held an eternalistic view. They believed that an agent, a permanent cosmic Supreme Self, was the creator of the universe. They thought that this eternal cosmic self was the creator of both the world and the human beings within. They believed that if we pleased this cosmic eternal self by offering and worship, we would be drawn to the realm of this cosmic self. This view is refuted by Buddhism.

Jaintempa was another ancient non-Buddhist view that was nihilistic. This non-Buddhist school fell into the view of nihilism because they claimed the non-existence of past and future lives. They also claimed that the sun rose in the east in a natural way devoid of causes and condition. They claimed that the downward movement of the water of a river occurred naturally without causes and conditions. They claimed that roundness is not created by anybody or any causes and conditions but is so naturally or randomly. They made the same claims regarding the sharpness of the thorn and the beautiful feathers of the peacock. In this way, they came up with many examples to validate their viewpoint.

It is crucial to reflect, contemplate and enquire into the eternalistic and nihilistic views. By penetrating these, we will avoid developing any sense of trust in these extreme views.

Traditional Buddhist Schools of Ancient India

In ancient India there were four philosophical schools of Buddhism. It is essential for us to grasp the philosophical viewpoints of these four different Indian Buddhist traditions. These schools are called Vaibhasika, Svatantrika, Cittamatra and the Madhyamaka. All these systems tried to establish the genuine reality in terms of the two truths, the relative and the ultimate truth.

The Vaibhasikas claimed that all gross phenomenal existences within the perceived world as well as what exists within the perceiving mind is the relative truth. This relative truth was defined in terms of the smallest particle that cannot be divided and regarded as the ultimate truth of the perceived world. Similarly, concerning the perceiving mind, the Vaibhasikas dissected the consciousness until they found what is known as the partless instant of consciousness. The discovery of the twofold particles of the perceived world and the perceiving mind was the ultimate truth of the Vaibhasikas.

The followers of this school of thought were able to establish the emptiness of the gross elements of the perceived world and the perceiving mind. But they were not able to establish the emptiness of the partless particle and the partless instant because they regarded these as the ultimate truth.

They did not believe in the usage of the term self-awareness; that consciousness is capable of being aware of itself. They believed that there are no hindering factors between the individual consciousness and the phenomenal objects perceived by the consciousness; that the consciousness grasps the object without any hindrances.

The Vaibhasikas did not believe in the collection of the eight consciousnesses, but classified consciousness as having six parts. This school also claimed that non-composite phenomena, phenomena that are neither physical nor mental, were substantial. As a remark, there are many phenomena that are neither physical nor mental, for example, the power of the life force.

They believed that their own view had its own unique characteristic, with a unique position, and so held onto claims and viewpoints.

The Svatantrikas claimed that all things that can perform a function belonged to the ultimate truth, and that all things that cannot perform a function belonged to the relative truth.

The third school was the Mind Only school, or Cittamatra. They claimed that consciousness was the ultimate truth and that the phenomenal external experiences that are reflected or projected by the mind are the relative truth.

The Middle Way School established the true reality through the two truths of the relative and the absolute truth. The ultimate truth is emptiness, the relative truth is all appearances.

The Vaibhasikas and Svatantrikas managed to establish the emptiness of the gross phenomena, but they did not determine the emptiness of the partless particle. Therefore, there was still an object to grasp onto.

The Mind Only school of Cittamatra managed to establish the emptiness of external, perceived phenomena but did not realize the emptiness of the perceiving mind, because they believed that the mind was the ultimate truth.

The Middle Way School managed to establish the emptiness of the perceived phenomenal world as well as the emptiness of the perceiving mind. Therefore, no internal or external object remained to which they could cling.

All the non-Buddhist schools of ancient India can be categorized as believing in either the eternalistic or the nihilistic view. All Buddhist schools of philosophy can be categorized into these four major classifications.

In this manner Lama Mipham explains about the schools of ancient Indian Buddhist thought and philosophical systems in The Gateway to Knowledge. What is important, however, is to know what is correct and what is incorrect. In other words, what we should do and what we should not.

Questions and Answers

Question: Is the view of the Tirtikas the same as Christianity?

Answer: I was not referring to the view of Christianity; I was simply referring to the view of an ancient Indian non-Buddhist philosophy. During the time of the Buddha, there were many philosophical confrontations in terms of debate and argument between Buddhist and non-Buddhist philosophers in order to establish the genuine reality. In the fifth topic of The Gateway to Knowledge, Lama Mipham talks about the correct and the incorrect, and explains the non-Buddhist view and various philosophical views found within Buddhism.

Question: The text talks about the seven dependencies, and the fifth is dependency of control, which says that it is not possible to take possession of the precious view and the seven precious possessions in the physical body of a woman. What does this mean?

Answer: I did not talk about this subject although it belongs to the subject of the correct and the incorrect. The text says that we are not able to attain the spiritual realization of arhathood with a female body. This statement is from the perspective of the Hinayana. This is different from the perspective of Mahayana and Vajrayana, which claim that arhathood is not the ultimate realization. Also, the text says that we are not able to attain the state of a universal monarch with a female body. Again, this statement is from a Hinayana perspective that emphasizes the body, instead of the mind, as in the case of Mahayana and Vajrayana. I did not talk about this because I thought it would confuse you. You will also discover in some texts belonging to Hinayana how to avert the development of desirous attachment to the opposite sex, usually a woman, because the Buddha's students were primarily men. The teachings suggest viewing the woman's body as something conditioned, as something impure to prevent the practitioner developing obsessive desirous attachment. But the Buddha also said that if the practitioner was a woman, she would have to do the opposite, viewing the men's physical existence as something impure in order to suppress her desirous attachment.

Question: Is desirous attachment something we should suppress?

Answer: Meditation on the impurity or the shortcomings of the opposite sex enables the individual meditator to temporarily subdue the disturbing emotions of desirous attachment. We use the word suppress because the pacification is just temporary, it can recur at any moment. To be able to cut the very root of the desirous attachment from developing onto an object, we need to realize the emptiness of the self.

The followers of the tradition of the Hinayana tried to suppress the emotional complexes, but according to the Mahayana tradition, we do not suppress these emotions, we simply let them go where they want to go. We act indifferently toward the emotional complications. This is a different approach. Can one of you list all the five skandhas for me?

Respondent: Form, feeling, perception, formation, and consciousness.

Where is the self?

Respondent: Nowhere

Then where is it?

Respondent: It is a mental formation.

Then who constructed the mental formations? Are the rest of the five skandhas also constructed by the mind in the same way as the concept of the self? Who made the mind?

If the "I" is the creator of the mind, then that supreme self must be eternal. The energy of the mind is released by the accumulation of karma that is based on emotional complications. Karma acts as fuel for the mind. If we reflect upon and contemplate how samsara evolves because of karma and emotional complications, we will be able to attain a deep certainty about the evolution of samsara. We will then want to renounce samsara, and instead develop an aspiration toward attaining the opposite, the state of nirvana, enlightenment.

Question: Earlier you referred to nirvana and enlightenment. But are nirvana and enlightenment the same thing?

Answer: Actually, the term nirvana is a very general term. It is used to describe enlightenment according to the different *yanas*. When we refer to enlightenment, or Buddhahood, this is a specific term that refers to the full enlightenment that neither abides in the peace of nirvana nor in the pain of samsara. This is the definition. So, there is a difference.

The Faculties, Indriyas

So far, we have gone through five topics: the five physical aggregates, the eighteen elements, the twelve sense sources, the twelve links of dependent origination, and the correct and the incorrect. We will now discuss the sixth topic of the twenty-two faculties (Skt. indriya). The term indriya, which in English means faculty or power, should be understood as having power or influence over something. For example, an individual has power over his or her belongings.

Generally, we grasp onto the self. We think that there is some kind of self that possesses the physical and mental aggregates. If we become well versed in the classification of the twenty-two faculties, we will be able to counteract this naive belief in a self that possesses control.

The first is the eye faculty that has the power to grasp visual objects. The second is the ear faculty that has the power to grasp sounds. The third is the nose faculty that has the power to grasp smell. The fourth is the tongue faculty that has power to grasp taste. The fifth is the body faculty that has power to grasp texture. The five sense faculties have the power to grasp their five corresponding objects of the present, but they are unable to grasp sense objects of the past or future.

The eye faculty and the ear faculty can sense their respective sense objects without touching them, and it does not matter whether the sense objects transcend the size of these sense faculties. Even if the sense object is small or large, the sense faculties can sense them. The other three sense faculties must meet their corresponding sense object directly, and the sense objects must match the size of the sense organ. If they are too big or too small, the sense faculties are not able to sense them. The sense faculties are not capable of grasping onto the sense objects by themselves; this is done by the following faculty, the faculty of the mind.

The faculty of the mind has the nature of consciousness.

The mind consists of the conceptual mind faculty and the non-conceptual mind faculty. It acts as a basis for its corresponding sense objects, the phenomena. The relationship between these two is that which support and that which is supported. The mind faculty is formless and immaterial, and therefore capable of producing a limitless range of phenomena in terms of size, color, and shape.

The seventh faculty is the life force faculty. The life force faculty performs two primary functions; it enables the individual to remain within society and share human characteristics with others, and it allows us to sustain our life as long as we are alive.

The eighth and ninth faculties are the male and female faculties. The male and female faculties create the distinction between man and woman. The male and the female gender faculties have the power of creating conception, and the potential to experience a sexual orgasm.

Death can occur in three ways: because the life force has run out, because the stock of merit has been completely exhausted, or because the karmic actions have been completely exhausted. Death that occurs because the life force or the stock of merit has run out can be postponed. But death that happens because of karma cannot be prevented. To lengthen our lives, we can do long-life practice, based on long-life deities. Receiving empowerment of long-life deities can lengthen a life force that is about to cease. To postpone death that occurs because of running out of merit we can practice giving to those in need and make offerings to highly evolved spiritual beings. This type of practice also includes other elements such as abstaining from harming other sentient beings. This enables us to accumulate merit, which again lengthens our lifespan. There is also the practice of the giving of fearlessness. But the cause of death that occurs because of karma is impossible to stop; it is like a forceful river of water. At this moment, even if the Buddha of long life appeared in front of us, he would be helpless to increase our lifespan.

The tenth faculty is suffering, the eleventh faculty is

pleasure, the twelfth faculty is mental pleasure, the thirteenth faculty is mental pain, and the fourteenth faculty is neutral sensation. These faculties are associated with feeling. The faculty of suffering and the faculty of pleasure are strictly associated with feelings of the body. These five faculties belong to the category of mental events. They have the power to make the individual experience the consequences of karmic maturation.

Next are five faculties associated with enlightenment. They are faith, effort, recollection, concentration, and wisdom. These faculties empower the individual to acquire all necessary qualities needed on the path to enlightenment.

The twentieth faculty is the will to know the unknown. This faculty comes about when the individual attains the path of seeing. This brings insight into the unknown. The mind of a practitioner who has reached the path of seeing is also endowed with the presence of other positive faculties of playful mind, pleasure, joyful mind, indifference, and mindfulness. Thus, altogether nine faculties are present within the mind of the individual who has arrived at the path of seeing. These nine faculties empower the individual to see things that he or she has not seen before, gaining insight into the unknown reality.

The twenty-first faculty is termed "that which is unknown." The difference between this faculty and the former lies between the path of seeing and the path of meditation. At the path of seeing, the individual develops insight into the unknown reality. This insight is further stabilized when we move to the path of meditation. Earlier glimpses into genuine reality are now further familiarized through meditation and this leads to the final faculty of omniscience. The presence of the nine faculties on the path of no more learning empowers the individual to attain omniscience.

Seven of the faculties are physical. These are the five sense faculties and the male and female faculty. The others are non-physical. One faculty, the mind faculty, is immaterial and has the nature of consciousness. Ten faculties are mental factors; these are the five faculties of purification, faith, effort, mindfulness, concentration, and wisdom, and the five faculties of misery, pleasure, joyful mind, unhappy mind, and indifferent mind. The faculty of life force is categorized as a formation that is neither because it belongs neither to matter nor mind.

There also exist other classifications: faculties that are defiled and that are undefiled, those that are virtuous and those that are non-virtuous, and those with a neutral nature.

Questions and Answers

Question: Is it possible to reach the state of omniscience without being enlightened?

Answer: No. We become enlightened when we reach the path of no more learning. Attaining omniscience is the same as being enlightened.

Question: The faculties numbered ten to fourteen were mental events without being mind. Can you explain?

Answer: We must make a distinction between mental events and mind. The difference between mind and mental events is the difference between the ruler and his attendants. The mind is the ruler, the mental events are the attendants.

Question: How is the ruler in control?

Answer: The primary mind represents the king in our example. The mental events represent the ministers and entourage. If something goes wrong with the king, this will also affect the subjects. If the primary mind is positive it is possible to transform the rest of the mental events, but if the primary mind has become negative, then all the mental events will also be negative. Therefore, the primary mind is illustrated as the king. The primary mind is the six sense consciousnesses. The mental events are the fifty-one mental events.

Time

The seventh topic is the analysis of time. When we analyze time, we not only discover past, present, and future, but also that time is not intrinsically existent. It cannot exist by itself but is created from external references.

What do we mean by the past? When phenomenal experience has ceased to exist, we term this the past. When phenomenal experience is enduring, we term this the present. When phenomena have not yet unfolded, we term this the future. In this way, we can understand the past, present, and future. We can also show this with another illustration. When cause and effect have subsided, this is referred to as the past. When the cause has enacted, but the effect has not yet arisen, this is termed the present. The future is defined as the cause being present without being enacted, and the result not yet arisen.

The first Buddhist philosophical school, the Vaibhasika, claimed that the past, present, and future exist substantially. Other schools, the Svatantrika, the Mind-Only School, and the Middle Way School, stated that time is merely a conceptual construction.

The shortest period is referred to as the indivisible time unit. In this minute moment there is no distinction between the past, present and future. One hundred and twenty such indivisible instants are called one moment. One moment is defined as two pulse beats of a healthy person. Sixty moments are one minute. Thirty minutes are one period and thirty periods make twenty-four hours. This view belongs to the general sutra presentation of the Buddha and is agreed upon by all Buddhist schools. We can also define time from the movement of the sun, the seasons, and the moon.

Enlightened beings realize the evenness between the ultimately smallest instant of time and exceptionally long timespans. Because of this, they can develop altruistic motivation in the beginning, undergo training in the middle, and experience enlightenment at the end. They can demonstrate enlightened activity within one such smallest instant because the shortest and the longest moments of time have become equal.

Because the ultimately smallest unit of time cannot be divided, it is called partless. Similarly, regarding the mind, we have the indivisible partless consciousness. Time can then be defined with reference to these. Since these are indivisible, it follows that time is empty.

Analysis of subtle forms requires a delicate time system, but grosser forms of external phenomena require larger units of time. Buddhism explains that the phases of the formation, endurance, destruction, and the following emptiness of the universe take eighty eons to complete. Eighty eons make one great eon. This is the largest time unit in Buddhism. Right now, we are in the enduring phase of the universe. It has not yet entered the phase of destruction. But other universes may go through different phases than ours, perhaps being in the phase of emptiness or creation.

Questions and Answers

Question: Do you know that the internal clock of a computer operates thousands of times quicker than the ultimately smallest instant?

Answer: I do not have much knowledge of the time aspect of computers, and I do not know the speed of computers. Since I do not know the speed of computers, I cannot compare this to the smallest unit of time that the Buddha talked about.

Questioner: But I know the speed of computers.

That is very good. We can talk about it. When I snap my

fingers, there pass sixty smallest units of time. How is this compared to the speed of a computer?

Questioner: Maybe one thousand.

Then the computer seems to be faster. But we can trace back as much as we can, but we will always reach a point where there is no past, present, and future.

Questioner: I think quantum physics describes the same kind of experience—when the past, present, and future break up.

Are you referring to the atom?

Questioner: There are smaller particles than that, and when they split, it is not possible to say what happens in what order so to speak.

This is what the Buddha said two thousand five hundred years ago. At the ultimately smallest unit of time, the cause-and-effect relationship falls apart because we cannot separate the past, present, and future. When scientists observe such phenomena, time seems to be lost. In other words, when the notion of the past, present, and future is lost, this is what is referred to by the Buddha as the smallest indivisible unit of time. Because the boundaries of time disappear, this leads to the discovery of emptiness.

Question: There are two different ways to explain the past and the future. Can you elaborate?

Answer: Time is non-substantial, but in order to posit the existence of time, we must create substantial examples, for example like the seed and the sprout. When the seed and the sprout both have ceased, this cessation is regarded as a past moment. When the cause, a seed, has given rise to the result, a sprout, this is regarded as the present moment. When the cause is present but the necessary conditions to obtain the result are lacking, this is termed the future. When we analyze time we usually talk about cause and effect, but time can also be analyzed from other perspectives. If we are going to examine time from a broader perspective, then cessation is regarded as the past moment, the birth is regarded as the present moment, and the unborn is viewed as the future moment.

The Four Noble Truths

We shall now discuss the eighth topic in The Gateway to Knowledge that concerns the Four Noble Truths. By becoming knowledgeable in the analysis of the presentation of the Four Noble Truths, we will be able to overcome our naive assumption that the self is something defiled that is being purified on the spiritual path.

The Buddha gave three important sermons; we say that he turned the wheel of Dharma three times. The teaching of the Four Noble Truths belongs to the first teaching the Buddha gave to the five noble disciples. The first noble truth is suffering. The second noble truth is the source of suffering. The third noble truth is the cessation of suffering. The fourth noble truth is the path that leads to the cessation.

It is essential for us to recognize suffering to abandon the source of suffering, the second noble truth. To do this, we need to actualize the third noble truth, the noble truth of cessation. Cessation is done by relying on the fourth noble truth as the path.

As an analogy, to overcome physical illness, it is essential to recognize the nature of the disease and find its cause. Having seen the cause of the disease, we should proceed to remove it. We should strive toward the goal of attaining physical and mental well-being, free from illnesses. After having set the goal, we should rely on the actual medicine that will cure the disease. The fourth noble truth is the medicine. The first noble truth is the nature of the disease. The second noble truth is the cause of the disease. The third noble truth is the goal of well-being.

The Noble Truth of Suffering

The noble truth of suffering concerns the world as a container, containing sentient beings. The world is referred to as an impure world system that acts as a support. By "world" we mean the external environment like mountains, hills, and everything else. The Buddha said that the evolution of the external world system began from complete emptiness. In the beginning, there was nothing apart from emptiness, just space. Space somehow facilitated the attraction of wind energy, creating the mandala of wind. From this, the mandala of the water element was created. The element of water possesses a lot of potentials, and when the water element was then churned by the wind element, in the same way as butter is churned from milk, this gave rise to solid phenomenal existences. Gradually, the external world system evolved, and the external universe as a container was formed. After this, the evolution of sentient beings took place.

The Buddha also talked about the evolution of the four major and minor continents. In the center is Mount Meru surrounded by seven mountains, again surrounded by seven oceans. Further out, lay the salty sea surrounded by a ring of outermost mountains. The Buddha explained this in different ways; according to the Abhidharma, the sutra tradition of the world formation, and the tantric tradition on the world formation. The various presentations were given according to the audience. He also talked about the pure world and the impure world, depending on whether the mind of the listener was pure or not.

The color of the snow on the mountain is white, but a person who suffers from a certain disease will see it as yellow. The Buddha said that if different beings of the six different realms were to look at the water in a glass, they would perceive this water in different ways. Creatures of the hell realm would perceive the water as something hot. Creatures of the hungry ghost realm would see the glass of water as disgusting liquids such as puss and blood. Animals may perceive the water as their habitat. Human beings can regard water as something that quenches thirst. The asuras of the demi-god realm perceive water as a manifestation of weapons. Beings belonging to the god realm see water as nectar. Beings with the most perfect perspective will perceive the five elements as the five Buddha families, where the element of water corresponds to the female Buddha. As another example of the sutra teachings, the Buddha talks about a specific animal that perceives the element of fire as something that cleanses the body. We can find fish that dwell in cold water, and we can find fish that dwell in warm water. We cannot say that the water is absolutely warm or absolutely cold. The objective reality of the water is relative. In this way the root text talks at great length about how the world was formed.

The sentient beings who are the inhabitants of the world system are the beings of the six realms. There are six types of creatures in the six realms: gods, half-gods, humans, animals, hungry ghosts, and hell beings. There are also sentient beings that do not belong to the six categories of sentient beings; the sentient beings that experience the Bardo ("in between"), the interval between death, and future rebirth. The species that dwell in the *Bardo* possess only four aggregates. They do not possess a gross physical aggregate, but instead a subtle form. Sentient beings that are trapped in the Bardo possess five sense organs; they can smell, and they are able to pass through solid matter. Nothing can stop them, apart from the womb of the mother. The Bardo-being possesses miraculous powers that come from karma. On average, the time to remain in the Bardo is forty-nine days. The dwelling place and companions of the Bardo are changeable and uncertain.

The noble truth of suffering encompasses the external world as a container and the inner world of sentient beings belonging to the six realms, as well as the Bardo-beings. To understand the true nature of suffering, we need to recognize the four characteristics of suffering: impermanence, pain, emptiness and emptiness of self. If we know these four unique characteristics of suffering, we can understand the true nature of suffering.

The Noble Truth of the Source of Suffering

The second noble truth reveals the source of suffering. When we talk about the source of suffering, we understand it to mean ignorance with its accompanying emotional complications and karma.

Karma

Generally, we create karma through the door of the body, the door of the speech and the door of the mind. Karma created through these three doors has different degrees of strength.

We can accumulate karma in four different ways. The first one is "karmic results that are experienced in this very life." The next is "karmic consequences that will be experienced in the next life." The third is "experiencing the consequences of karma in later lives." The fourth is "the uncertainty of experiencing karmic consequences."

There are two forms of karma: "propelling karma" and "completion karma." Take for example birth in the human realm. The cause of birth in the human realm is due to propelling virtuous karma of past lives, but the suffering that many individuals experience is because of unwholesome completion karma. Sentient beings can also be born in the lower realms due to the accumulation of propelling karma in their past life. Nevertheless, these beings, such as animals, may also possess what is known as virtuous completion karma. For example, some animals have very good owners and are treated very well. There can also be the case of virtuous propelling karma together with virtuous completion karma, for example a sentient being born human and experiencing happiness and joy. There are also non-virtuous propelling karma and non-virtuous completion karma, for example beings in the hungry ghost realm and hell realm.

Virtuous and Non-Virtuous Acts

Within the working of karma, there are the ten virtuous acts and ten non-virtuous acts. I assume this to be a familiar topic. So, we will not discuss these here.

Emotions

Next are the emotions along with the emotional complications. These are the six root emotions and the twenty subsidiary emotional complexities. The noble truth of the origin of suffering constitutes the karmic and emotional patterns. This is something we should try to give up. This means giving up ignorance.

The Noble Truth of Cessation

The noble truth of cessation is twofold. The first is "one sided nirvanic peace." The second is "the nirvanic state that neither abides in the extreme of peace or pain." The last one is enlightenment.

One-sided nirvanic peace is also twofold: nirvana without remainder and nirvana with remainder. If the practitioner has removed the origin of suffering, but still possesses a physical body, this is called nirvana with remainder. Moggallana, one of the disciples of the Buddha, who was well known for his miraculous power, is a prime example of the attainment of nirvana with remainder; even if the sentient beings of the whole world were to oppose him, they would not be able to defeat him. But eventually he was killed by a non-Buddhist Tirtika. This happened because of the maturation of specific karmic effects from the past.

The Noble Truth of the Path

The noble truth of the path is something we should practice. The noble truth of the path consists of five spiritual paths. These are the path of accumulation, the path of linking, the path of seeing, the path of meditation, and the path of no more learning.

The path of accumulation should be understood as accumulation of merit and wisdom. If we have been able to complete this accumulation, we will be able to link to the path of seeing through the second path, the path of linking.

The primary practice on the path of accumulation is the practice of fourfold mindfulness. This is mindfulness of body, mindfulness of feelings, mindfulness of mind, and mindfulness of phenomena. The path of accumulation has a threefold subdivision, the greater path of accumulation, the middling path of accumulation, and the smaller path of accumulation. Fourfold mindfulness is practiced during the smaller path of accumulation. I am not going to elaborate on these classifications; it suffices to know that they exist. During the middling path of accumulation, we practice the fourfold perfect abandonment. During the greater path of accumulation, we practice the four miraculous feet.

The Path of Linking

The path of linking joins the path of accumulation with the path of seeing. The primary practice of the path of linking is shamatha and vipassana meditation. These practices are supported by faith, effort, and mindfulness, three of the five faculties associated with purification and enlightenment we discussed earlier.

The Path of Seeing

On the path of seeing, the individual gains insight into the ultimate truth. Someone who has arrived at the path of seeing starts traversing the ten bodhisattva levels. The first level is the ground of utter joyfulness which is another name for the path of seeing.

The Path of Meditation

The fourth spiritual path is the path of meditation. The path of meditation should be understood as familiarization. We must familiarize ourselves repeatedly through meditation; otherwise, our understanding will fade.

The Path of No more learning

The last path is the path of no more learning. This name signifies that the wisdom that realizes the ultimate truth has become non-dualistic. There is no gap between the wisdom that realizes the ultimate truth and the ultimate truth as an object. There is nothing more to learn. This is good news!

The four noble truths should be practiced as follows: the noble truth of suffering should be recognized, the noble truth of the origin of suffering should be abandoned, the noble truth of cessation should be actualized, and the noble truth of the path should be pursued.

Questions and Answers

Question: What are the four miraculous spiritual feet?
Answer: "Feet" should be understood as a cause. There are four causes that facilitate the attainment of miraculous

power. It is a metaphorical expression. It is not non-smelly feet. (Laughter.)

Question: In the sixth topic, where you talked about death and cessation of life force, you referred to three types of deaths. What was the third one, to do with karmic action? Can you elaborate on this?

Answer: We have accumulated karmic energy over many past lives; this propelled us to be born as human beings. When the force of that karmic energy is used up, we must leave the human realm. It is like shooting an arrow up into space; when there is no energy left to drive the arrow further up, it will fall.

Question: We see things around us, and we become aware of them. This takes some time, and when we perceive our surroundings they will already be in the past. Therefore, we can never experience the present. How does this relate to this analysis?

Answer: When we talk from the perspective of the relative truth, we should not sneak in the perspective of the ultimate truth. From the perspective of the ultimate truth, time does not exist. In the relative truth, time does exist. We must establish the law of time either on the relative or the ultimate level. The birth that happens in one instant is termed the present moment. This birth is followed by death in the next instant. This is termed future. This is a mental construction fabricated by the mind. Everything is mental constructions, constructed labels of the mind. Those who know me, know me as Khenpo Sangpo, but those who do not know me, cannot tell that I am Khenpo Sangpo, they will only know me by my general character of a human being. The law of interdependence is inconceivable. If we place a cup of hot water in front of us, we will refer to it as hot water. But if we place a small amount of tea in it, we will not see to it as water, but as tea. This is the power of dependent origination. Also, water is not something that is unchangeable. When the season of the winter comes about due to the law of dependent origination, the water freezes to ice and is solidified due to the water meeting certain causes and conditions. The water in a cup cannot dent our head when poured out, but frozen water can. Also, in general, different species perceive phenomena from different perspectives.

Question: Is it correct that in the absolute we see things as they really are, but in the relative we see things as we experience them?

Answer: On the ultimate level, we realize the ultimate truth. On the relative level, we interact conventionally with other people of society. When somebody who has recognized the ultimate truth interacts with people, his or her interaction will be tremendously beneficial for others.

The Vehicles of Spiritual Paths

The ninth topic deals with the classification of different vehicles. The meaning of the Sanskrit word yana should be understood as something able to carry. By relying on the spiritual path, we can lift ourselves up from pain and suffering to experience happiness and peace.

While we remain within the conditioned existence of samsara, the emotional patterns of desirous attachment are said to be comparable with an agitated ocean. On such an ocean a small boat can easily be lost. If our being is overpowered by the disturbed pattern of desirous attachment, our lives will be upturned.

A mind influenced by the presence of the emotional pattern of aggression is comparable to residing in the intense heat of fire. Such an individual is not able to experience peace and joy because the fire is constantly burning from without and within.

Pride and arrogance are comparable to a mountain top; its sharp peaks cannot retain the soothing rain. Similarly, a mind afflicted with the emotion of arrogance cannot keep worldly and spiritual qualities.

The emotional pattern of ignorance is comparable to dense darkness. If somebody tries to walk in the middle of the night, the individual will most likely deviate from the right path.

If we want to transcend the limitation of emotional complexes, we should study and meditate upon the classification of the different spiritual paths. No effort is needed to create more emotional complexities and stay in samsara, it will happen by itself. But to achieve the qualities of nirvana requires diligence and effort. For example, it does not require any effort to remain seated on the ground. But to be seated in mid-air requires a lot of effort. It is worth investing energy in terms of effort and diligence to achieve the spiritual goal of liberating ourselves from imprisonment in the cyclic existence of samsara and attaining the final state of nirvana.

The Yana of Humans and Gods

Generally, five yanas are presented. The first yana is the yana of humans and gods. The first yana prevents us from sinking into the three lower realms, and we are propelled to be born as human beings or gods. The practice of the first yana constitutes ascertaining the genuine conventional view by abandoning the ten unskillful non-virtuous actions, and instead practice the ten virtuous actions. The genuine conventional view was taught by one of the early kings of Tibet. He outlined the rules of ten non-skillful actions to be avoided, and how to practice the opposite of these.

The practice of this yana also leads to enlightenment. The decisive factor is motivation. If we wish to attain full enlightenment and practice the ten skillful actions with this aspiration, then the virtuous acts will become a cause for attaining full enlightenment. If we pursue the practice of ten virtuous actions and avoid the ten non-virtuous actions in order to be reborn as a human being or being of the god realm, then this is what will happen.

The Yana of Brahma

The yana of Brahma is the first realm of the seventeen form god realms. We must distinguish between the god realms of the first and the second yana; the first yana refers to the desirous god realm, the second yana refers to the form god realm. By practicing the four immeasurable thoughts the individual is capable of rebirth in the first realm of the form god realm. The four immeasurable thoughts are immeasurable love, immeasurable compassion, immeasurable rejoicing, and immeasurable equanimity. The first and second yanas are referred to as worldly yanas because these yanas can transcend the limitations of the cyclic existence of samsara.

The Shravaka-yana

Third is the yana of the listener, the shravaka-yana. The shravaka-student will initially approach a spiritual master, who is either fully or partly enlightened, and listen to discourses on the Four Noble Truths. They then try to internalize the meaning of the truths to attain the one-sided nirvana, liberation for themself alone.

The initial part of the practice is to undertake one of the individual vows of liberation. The practitioners of shravaka-yana claim that whoever practices this yana will be an *arya*, a noble being. They understand a noble person as someone who has developed a tremendous sense of satisfaction and reduced desire.

Those practitioners distance themselves from physical

and mental busyness and pursue the spiritual path of listening, contemplation, and meditation. They primarily meditate on the selflessness of the individual. They also pursue other spiritual training based on their understanding that all conditional existence has the characteristic of suffering, impermanence, selflessness, and emptiness. They strive to cut the root of the misconception of holding onto the reality of the self of the person. Thus, they can establish the emptiness of the self, and this is their goal. The vehicle of the shravaka-yana can free the individual practitioner, not only from lower realms but from all the six conditioned realms of samsara.

The Yana of the Pratyekabuddha

The next yana is the yana of the pratyekabuddha, the solitary Buddha. These practitioners do not depend on instruction from a spiritual master. They contemplate and meditate on the twelve links of dependent origination in the forward and reverse order. By such spiritual endeavor, they can attain realization as a solitary Buddha. This is called arhathood.

The view of the pratyekabuddha-yana is higher than the view of the shravaka-yana. The view of the shravaka-yana is the selflessness of the person. The pratyekabuddha has a full realization of the selflessness of the individual, but only a partial understanding of the emptiness of phenomena. We could say that only fifty percent of the selflessness of the phenomena has been realized as they do not recognize the emptiness of the perceiving mind.

The follower of the pratyekabuddha-yana develops a profound certainty about their view, the view of emptiness of the self and half of the emptiness phenomena. They deepen their realization by repeating their spiritual practice and ultimately attain the state of the solitary Buddha, or arhathood.

The Yana of the Bodhisattva

By relying on the spiritual practice of the bodhisattva-yana, the individual practitioner is freed from the extreme pain of samsara as well as from the ultimate peace of nirvana. This is full enlightenment.

The practice of the bodhisattva-yana is based on taking the bodhisattva vow. The view is the realization of the emptiness of the self of the person as well as the emptiness of phenomena. They practice the six transcendental virtuous actions, the six paramitas, which are generosity, ethics, patience, diligence, meditation, and wisdom. The result is perfect enlightenment.

Generosity

The first paramita is the transcendental virtue of generosity. But all forms of giving are not regarded as a transcendental virtue. Transcendental virtue should be understood concerning Buddhahood; all forms of giving and sharing that directly act as a cause for the individual to attain Buddhahood are transcendental giving. These are forms of giving that are embraced by the element of wisdom and cannot be impure or limited.

Impure acts of giving include impure receivers and impure objects that are given. Giving impure goods will seldom benefit either oneself or others. Giving somebody weapons or poison will not contribute toward peace for anyone. An impure receiver could be an individual or an organization. If we give a gift to an organization that directly or indirectly inflicts pain on sentient beings, such an organization is an impure receiver. Within this category of impure receivers, we can also include individuals who are addicted to drugs. They may buy more drugs and become more addicted as a result of being given these drugs. It is the same for alcoholics; if we give them money, they will end up drinking more.

It is therefore essential to employ transcendental wisdom in order to attain a decisive understanding of the practice of transcendental giving. To whom should we give, and to whom should we not? Will the giving provide temporary or long-lasting benefit, or not bring any benefit at all? After applying the element of wisdom, we should pursue the practice of giving.

The supreme element of wisdom is to embrace the act of giving with non-referential wisdom. The act of giving without a point of reference becomes ultimately transcendental. The view of non-reference is referred to as the three spheres: the emptiness of the existence of a separate giver, the emptiness of the receiver, and the emptiness of the act of giving. This ensures that there will not be any boundaries between oneself and others. If the practice of giving is not embraced by non-referential wisdom it may be contaminated by the presence of other emotional complications. This might cause us to regret our act of giving at a later stage or practice the act of giving with jealousy or competitiveness. But when the act of giving is embraced by non-referential wisdom there is no possibility of such pollution.

The paramita of generosity has three divisions: the gift of material objects, the gift of protection and fearlessness, and the gift of Dharma. The gift of material objects is giving things that will be helpful for the receivers and includes all kinds of material things. The gift of protection from fear includes the practice of releasing sentient beings that are going to be killed and protection of endangered wildlife. This also includes protection from fear of losing our material possessions, or fear of being separated from happiness. The gift of Dharma is regarded as a supreme gift because it is a gift of truth. It is not possible to give the truth of Dharma if we have developed a fanatical attachment to our spiritual tradition. Also, converting or brainwashing other people is not regarded as the genuine act of giving Dharma. If we are motivated by fame, prestige, or wealth, such sharing of Dharma does not belong to transcendental giving.

Moral Ethics

The next topic is the transcendental paramita of moral ethics. The Tibetan term for moral ethics means "in the manner that noble beings act." The paramita of moral ethics becomes transcendental if it is blessed by non-referential wisdom. Not all forms of moral ethics are necessarily transcendental in nature.

Genuinely generous conduct should be based on the practice of transcendental wisdom. If it is lacking, we will not be able to distinguish between proper and improper behavior. Some individuals claim that they are doing good, but what they do? is not only not beneficial it is just the opposite. This is a lack of transcendental wisdom.

There are different forms of the paramita of moral ethics: the moral ethics aimed at individual liberation, the moral ethics practiced by the bodhisattva, and the moral ethics undertaken by tantric practitioners. There are also other ways to classify the paramita of moral ethics; the moral ethics of gathering virtue, and the moral ethics of benefiting others.

The practice of moral ethics is one of the most important disciplines because this practice creates the very foundation for other practices. The Buddha said that if we lack the practice of moral ethics, we will not be able to accomplish even our own benefit, much less accomplish benefit for other sentient beings.

Patience

Next is the transcendental virtue of patience. The Buddha said that there is no greater ascetic practice than the practice of transcendental patience. Not all forms of patience necessarily belong to the category of the transcendental virtue of patience.

If we have developed aggression toward someone else, and then examines this aggression with transcendental wisdom, this is transcendental patience, because we observe the non-separation between ourselves as the developer of aggression and the object of aggression.

One can also practice transcendental patience while attending spiritual discourses. If a spiritual lecture is awfully long, we may experience physical discomforts such as hunger and thirst or mental fatigue. Practicing patience in these circumstances is a transcendental virtue.

When we pursue the spiritual path, we will come across many major and minor obstacles. If we can overcome these by practicing the transcendental virtue of patience, these obstacles will be transformed into causes that will lead us to enlightenment.

One should not follow a spiritual path merely because of tradition, thinking "This is my tradition; therefore, I have to adopt such and such a practice." Such spiritual practice will lack the necessary trust and faith, as well as lack investigation and analysis. Merely maintaining a tradition is a tremendous struggle. But if the pursuit of the spiritual path is based on investigation and analysis, we will develop a profound sense of trust and familiarity and be able to practice without a struggle.

The following story illustrates the transcendental virtue of patience that disregards pain. Long ago in Tibet, there was a man who was meditating on the slope of a hill outside Lhasa. Someone went to see him and asked him what he was doing. The man answered, "I am meditating on patience." The visitor said, "I am delighted that you are practicing the transcendental virtue of patience," and made an offering to express his gratitude. After a while, the newcomer departed and went to circumambulate a holy mountain, and the practitioner continued his practice of patience. After completing one circumambulation, the visitor came back to the practitioner and gave him a hard blow with his fist. This caused the so-called meditator to become extremely agitated. When the visitor saw the angry reaction of the meditator he said: "You could practice patience when I made an offering to you, but it seems you cannot practice patience when I strike you!" It is not possible to practice patience without an object of patience. In other words, there must be some form of adverse circumstances before we can practice patience.

There is also the patience that does not fear emptiness. The Buddha himself said that the teaching on emptiness is very risky. If someone views emptiness and grasps it in a wrong way due to lacking the necessary intelligence, they will experience a tremendous loss. If the teaching on emptiness is misunderstood, there is a real possibility of falling into the extreme view of nihilism and losing trust in the law of cause and effect. Someone who correctly understands the Buddha's teaching on emptiness develops trust in the law of cause and effect. In fact, trust in the law of cause and effect is evidence that the individual has properly understood the teaching of emptiness.

Many individuals fear the teaching of emptiness because they think that this will diminish their sense of self. We can reduce this fear by practicing the paramita of patience.

Effort

The fourth paramita is enthusiastic effort. But not all enthusiastic effort is necessarily a transcendental virtue. Some people are naturally diligent when performing negative actions, but negative effort is not transcendental diligence.

The transcendental virtue of effort delights in pursuing the spiritual path. However, only when this effort embraces non-referential wisdom will the act of effort become transcendental.

There are different types of transcendental effort. Armor-like effort protects the practitioner from opposing forces on the spiritual path and helps the practitioner to develop the courage to defeat these obstacles, even if the task is tremendous.

The second type of transcendental effort is that of respect and application. When the individual practitioner has undertaken a spiritual task, this is essential for developing a sense of respect for what they are doing.

The third type of transcendental effort is continued application, which is the repeated effort that is applied to all spiritual tasks the individual undertakes and includes the continual practice of all paramitas.

Meditation

Next is the fifth paramita of the transcendental virtue of meditation. The Tibetan term for meditation means stabilized mind. Just as a tree will be stable and can bear flowers and fruits if the roots develop in proportion to the tree itself, so one who is involved in the transcendental virtue of meditation is able to create a balanced mind that can serve as a foundation for all kinds of spiritual qualities. Meditation is essential to attain Buddhahood.

Again, there are different types of meditation. The first is meditative concentration that is employed by ordinary beings; we are all able to meditate on tranquility by doing shamatha meditation. Then there is the meditation called clear discerning meditation, an understanding of the ultimate truth. There is also a type of concentrative meditation that is called the meditation that delights the tathagatas. This is the practice of illusion-like meditation and indestructible meditation.

Wisdom

Next is the transcendental virtue of wisdom, the sixth and final paramita. The practice of the paramita of wisdom should permeate the rest of the five paramitas. If the preceding five paramitas are accompanied by the paramita of wisdom, this transcendental and virtuous practice will enable the individual to attain Buddhahood.

The other paramitas are like small streams and the paramita of wisdom is like a large river. The small streams are not able to reach the ocean by themselves but with the help of the large river they can. Similarly, if the other paramitas are mixed with the paramita of wisdom, the spiritual energy will flow to attain Buddhahood.

Questions and Answers

Question: Can you explain how the two terms for wisdom, "sherab" and "yeshe", are different?

Answer: The word "sherab" in Tibetan is usually translated into English as knowledge. "She" means knowledge, "rab" means tremendous. The term "yeshe" is usually translated as primordial wisdom, "ye" means primordial, "she" again means knowledge. In the final analysis both knowledge and primordial wisdom will reach the same goal. The difference lies in how we define the terms. Sherab can be understood as supreme knowledge, but supreme knowledge can be found on many levels, for example, the supreme knowing of hearing and listening, or the supreme wisdom that comes through contemplation and meditation. In a way, the wisdom that comes only from listening is less supreme compared to the wisdom that comes from meditation. Primordial wisdom is only enjoyed by fully enlightened beings. Supreme wisdom is enjoyed by people who are not enlightened.

Question: So, the sixth paramita is sherab?
Answer: Yes.

The Composite and Non-Composite

The tenth and final topic of The Gateway to Knowledge is the topic of composite and non-composite phenomena. Now everything is quite easy because we understand the preceding topics, so we do not need to exert a lot of effort. But it might also be that this final topic will serve as a foundation for additional topics.

Composite Phenomena

Composite phenomena are named thus because their arising depends on various causes and conditions.

The existence of the phenomenal external reality depends on many causes and conditions. There is no self as a separate entity, or whatever label we give it, for example, a supreme self, that causes the production of external existence.

Sentient beings possess the aggregates of body and mind. The physical existence of the body is created from the energy of the karma of the consciousness of past life together with the essential substances from the mother and father. The food we consume makes us grow a physical body. The manifestation of consciousness is said to be dependent on many causes and conditions. The preceding moment of consciousness creates the continuity of a subsequent moment of consciousness. In a wider perspective, the consciousness of the past life creates a momentum that ensures the continuation of consciousness into the future life. The teaching of the Buddha clearly states that the existence of body and mind, the physical and the non-physical, cannot be dependent on just one cause. It is important to bear in mind that they are the result of a multitude of causes and conditions.

We should not think that the ripened karmic energy of body and mind is totally virtuous or totally non-virtuous. We should describe it as neutral. It is categorized as neutral because both positive and negative karma can be created from the present body and mind. If the thoroughly ripened karma of our body and mind were either negative or positive, it would be impossible to change, and we would have to continue doing good or bad actions. But, since the present body and mind can be directed toward creating good or bad karma, we cannot say that thoroughly ripened karma is solely positive or negative.

A cause can either be positive or negative, having the potential to give rise to happiness or suffering. The natural consequence of practicing virtue is physical well-being. The practice of generosity leads to more profound wealth, like spiritual wealth and merit. Pure discipline acts as a cause for rebirth in the human or god realm.

On the contrary, the result of stinginess and greed is poverty. The criterion for poverty here is not material wealth but whether we have a profound sense of inner contentment or not. A person who is extremely rich can at the same time feel extremely poor.

The Buddha said that miserliness and greediness lead to the experience of the hungry ghost realm. The beings of the hungry ghost realm experience hunger, thirst, and poverty, even while surrounded by lots of food, drink, and material possessions, because they are not capable of utilizing these for themselves or others. They are impoverished despite being surrounded by wealth. Being born as a human being with a greedy mind can amount to being born in the hungry ghost realm because our mind is possessed by the quality of the hungry ghost realm. But even if our minds are captivated by miserliness, we will not necessarily be reborn in the hungry ghost realm

The opposite of patience is aggression and hatred. If someone is angry or full of hate, his or her physical manifestation will be transformed by these emotions. The emotion of anger is ugly, and the body becomes ugly by imitating the ugliness of the state of the mind.

We should reflect on how virtuous actions cause happiness, joy and peace, and how non-virtuous actions cause pain and misery.

The Six Categories of Causes

The Buddha explained that causes can be classified into six categories. The first category is termed acting causes. This is a general category that consists of all kinds of phenomenal experiences and existences other than resultant experiences. There are two subclasses of acting causes: effective acting causes and ineffective acting causes. Effective acting causes have the potential to support phenomenal experience. Ineffective acting causes cannot support resultant phenomenal existence, and therefore cannot harm phenomenal existence.

The second category is the co-emergent causes. The co-emergent causes are established in the present moment. Co-emergent causes should be understood as the support and the supported. In order words, co-emergent causes depend on two things. For example, if conceptual thought is inherent in our minds, a non-conceptual capacity must also be inherent. They depend on each other. If something exists, then the opposite also exists. Other examples of causes in this category are male and female, perceived objects and the perceiving mind, and day and night. In fact, all polarities are included in this category. The ancient example of the texts is two angular roof beams that support each other; take one away, and the other will also fall.

The third category is similar causes. The capacity of human beings to reproduce is an example of this. Generally, it should be understood as results that share similar qualities

223

with their causes.

In the past, Tibetans were prohibited by the communists from practicing the Dharma. Despite this, we could encounter many people who would do regular prayers, and therefore the authorities had appointed spies to report people who did spiritual practice. At that time, there was a practitioner who was reading a Dharma text when suddenly a spy burst into his house. Immediately, the practitioner hid the book behind his back. Not knowing what to say, the spy uttered, "Do you have children?" "Of course, I have children," the man said. The spy then said, "Are these children both boys and girls?" "Yes, they are both boys and girls, did you think they would be puppies and kittens?" Not knowing what to say, the spy left. The man's utterance is an example of the category of similar causes.

The fourth category of causes is the resembling causes. The difference between the third and the fourth category is that a similar cause pertains to the objective phenomena and the perceiving mind.

The fifth category is the all-pervasive causes. All-pervasive causes should be understood as conflicting emotions. As long as we remain unenlightened sentient beings our minds are filled with conflicting emotions. They can burst into our mindstream at any moment and crush us. Conflicting emotions are incredibly good at deceiving us and will not allow us to have a good rest, but drag us in all directions, until we are completely exhausted. If we want to be angry, we should not be angry toward the objective reality such as enemies or adverse circumstances, we should be angry at the presence of the emotional patterns themselves. It is good to do away with hatred, but we should focus on the emotion itself, not on the external objectivity that induces the anger.

The sixth category of causes is the fully matured causes. A fully matured cause is a positive, negative, or neutral resultant phenomenal experience caused by, respectively, positive, negative, or neutral actions performed in the immediate past or a past life.

Enlightened beings have said that all conditioned phenomena come into existence based on these six types of causes; it is not possible to find other forms of causes.

Non-Composite Phenomena

Non-composite phenomena are not brought about by any other phenomena or by the meeting of causes and conditions. When an individual practitioner can do away with emotional complications by utilizing the wisdom of discrimination, then this wisdom state of absence of emotional complications is a non-composite phenomenon known as "cessation by discrimination."

The second type of non-composite phenomenon, "cessation without using discriminating wisdom," should be understood as cessation of non-existence. For example, to realize the non-existence of the horn on the horse's head, we do not need to develop discriminating wisdom.

The third non-composite phenomenon is space. Space facilitates the unfolding, abiding, and exhaustion of phenomena. We cannot differentiate space in general, other than for example, to compare the space inside a cup with the space inside a vase.

The fourth non-composite phenomenon is suchness. Suchness should be understood as the true reality of all phenomena. This is emptiness. From the perspective of the nature of suchness itself, there is no difference, but we can classify phenomenal objects that act as a support for the genuine reality. Take for example a cup. The cup is the relative truth. The ultimate truth of the cup is emptiness of the cup. The cup acts as a support for the ultimate reality. We cannot talk about different classes of the emptiness of the cup, but we can talk about different types of cups. The Buddha differentiated between contaminated and uncontaminated suchness. When we remain unenlightened, our enlightened Buddha-nature is temporarily obscured by emotional complications. The genuine reality of the nature of mind that is temporarily obscured is referred to as contaminated suchness. The liberated and stainless mind of an enlightened being is uncontaminated suchness.

Advice on Meditation on Emptiness

Beginners should primarily meditate on non-affirming emptiness. Why? Because the problem for most people is that they grasp onto the solidity of reality. To lessen this conceptual clinging, it is suggested to meditate on emptiness. Then gradually, we should familiarize ourselves with the meditation practice that is referred to as "meditation on non-existence." Meditation on non-existence is not the ultimate meditation but is devised to counteract fixation on emptiness that we may develop in the first meditation. Having gone through the second stage of meditation, we can proceed toward the meditation that is known as "meditation on simplicity that is free from all kinds of mental constructs."

The Buddha himself stated that the purpose of the first stage of meditation is to lead the meditator to experience the meditation of simplicity free from all mental constructs. If the Buddha had revealed the meditation on simplicity directly, his audience would have been shocked. So, the Buddha skillfully created the stages of meditation that lead to the meditation on simplicity.

Once upon a time, a turtle that lived in the ocean befriended a turtle that lived in a well, and the ocean turtle would often come to visit the turtle in the well. One day, the turtle of the well asked the turtle of the ocean "How big is your well? Is it one third of my well?" "Oh, you cannot compare your well with my ocean," the ocean turtle answered. Then the turtle in the well said, "Then it must be two-thirds of my well!" The ocean turtle gave the same answer. Shocked, the turtle in the well asked, "Then it must be the same size as my well!" "It is beyond comparison," the ocean turtle answered. The turtle in the well retorted "It is inconceivable, one cannot conceive of a bigger well than mine." Then, to remove the delusion of the turtle in the well, the ocean turtle invited him to visit the ocean. It seems like the ocean turtle was a little bit stupid taking the turtle from the well directly to the ocean, but anyway, when the turtle from the well got to see the huge ocean, this gave him a massive shock that caused his head to explode, and he died.

The Buddha or the teacher skillfully guides the student to meditate on non-affirming emptiness, which then acts as a steppingstone for meditation on the simplicity free from conceptual elaboration. If the ocean turtle had been more skillful and intelligent, he would not have led the turtle from the well directly to the ocean, but perhaps to some small pond at first, then a bigger lake, and so on, until finally reaching the sea.

Because the Buddha was a very skillful and compassionate teacher, he first taught the Four Noble Truths to explain existence. He did not talk about emptiness but emphasized cause and effect. During the second sermon, the second turning of the wheel of Dharma, the Buddha talked about the emptiness of phenomenal existence. The teaching associated with the second turning of the wheel of Dharma is called The Yana of Non-Characteristics. This constitutes many volumes of texts that are categorized according to length. The shortest is the well-known Heart Sutra. The smallest volume contains eight thousand verses. The next contains twenty thousand verses. All these teachings are about emptiness, of non-existence. The final sermon is labeled "The turning of the wheel of Dharma that clearly differentiates things." Here the Buddha clearly defined existence and non-existence. In the third turning of the wheel of Dharma, he gave the ten teachings that reveal the presence of the Buddha-nature, thus preparing his followers for tantric practice.

If we become well versed in this final topic, we will be

able to overcome the naive view that the self was once bound but has now been set free.

Questions and Answers

Question: Can you explain how conflicting emotions evolve?

Answer: Take the emotional complication of hatred as an example. Anger arises because of three causes. The initial cause of anger is an inherent habitual tendency from a past life. The second cause of anger is encountering adverse circumstances, for example, an enemy. The third cause is inappropriate thinking. This is precisely why we should seek an appropriate environment to cultivate tranquility meditation; by distancing ourselves from adverse circumstances, meditation will be easy for the practitioner. This relates to the second cause. To overcome the first cause of inherent habitual tendency, we need to be persistent in meditation. The third cause, inappropriate mental thought, is like grasping onto the reality of permanence when in fact the reality of phenomena is impermanent. It is like gripping onto the reality of the existence of a self when in reality existence is selfless. If all these three causes are present, anger will be experienced by the individual. If one of the causes is lacking, the emotion of anger will not be experienced.

Question: I would like to know about how many vows we must observe in tantrayana.

Answer: The follower of the tantrayana must observe one hundred thousand million samayas. (Laughter.) Since the number is so huge, it is almost impossible to go through the list. Generally, the tantric samayas talk about the root samaya and the secondary samayas. Tantric teaching believes that the teacher is the root of all spiritual accomplishment. Therefore, you should strive toward taking good care of the lama. (Laughter.)

Respondent: Do you have any complaints? (Laughter.)

The subsidiary commitments are associated with the fellow Varjayana Sangha. If we transgress the root samaya, it is almost impossible to amend. But if the commitment toward the fellow practitioners is broken, it is amendable. But perhaps it is better to say that if samaya between practitioners is transgressed it cannot be amended. Otherwise, we might think that a transgression can be fixed later. We can talk a great deal about samaya and commitment connected to Vajrayana, but basically, it comes down to the samaya that pertains to body, speech, and mind. To maintain Vajrayana samaya is to regard all shapes as the union of appearance and emptiness, all sounds as the union of sound and emptiness, and all thoughts as coming from the union of awareness and concepts. This constitutes the simplest version of tantric samaya.

Final Words of the Teaching

There is not much point in talking a lot, so we will now conclude the final session of this course. I would like to pray for the success of your meditation practice. May you swiftly travel the spiritual path and attain Buddhahood, may you enjoy physical and mental well-being, and experience prosperity, auspiciousness, and everything that is good. I also hope to meet you all again in the future.

Commentary on Longchen Rabjams's Finding Rest in Meditation

Introduction

This commentary is based on a treatise written by the great Dzogchen master Longchen Rabjam, who is widely regarded as the most important Dzogchen practitioner in the history of Tibet. A great yogi of hidden practice, he exerted tremendous effort to realize enlightenment by purifying his own mind through spiritual practice. Many marvelous accounts exist of the spiritual manifestations that occurred when he undertook retreats in the very remotest parts of Tibet. He lived without any form of luxury and ate only very simple food. From his biography, we learn that he used only a sack to sleep in, and as a pillow to sit on. He completely renounced worldly life and attained enlightenment in a single lifetime. Among the many treatises that he wrote, *The Trilogy of Rest*, is comprised of *Finding Rest in the Nature of Mind*, *Finding Rest in Meditation*, and *Finding Rest in Illusion*. This commentary is based on the second book of this trilogy: *Finding Rest in Meditation*.

Usually, we are exhausted by our confusion; our body is tired, our mind is drained, and our speech is exhausted. Such exhaustion stems from our confusion about who we are on a profound level; this confusion must be eliminated by attaining genuine wisdom. Consequently, we seek rest by taking refuge and applying meditation to relieve the exhausting confusion. The difference between samsara and nirvana is not really that big; it is only a matter of confusion and non-confusion — recognizing the true nature of our mind or not recognizing the true nature of our mind.

The view of Dzogchen is the ground of our very being, our own true nature. There is no difference between the perception of emptiness in Dzogchen and the Madhyamika School's understanding of emptiness. The Buddha explained this emptiness as being "transcendental wisdom, inexpressible, inconceivable, and non-conveyable." Moreover, the view of Dzogchen knows no birth. It is not possible to locate the point in time when it came into being because its nature is like space; if there is no point of origination, we cannot find a point of abiding or a point of cessation. Thus, the ground of our being is free from origination, abiding, and cessation. It is unconditional.

The Dzogchen practitioner does not search for enlightenment elsewhere but looks for Buddhahood within him- or herself. If we forget that we are riding a horse and search for the horse in all directions of the world, we will never find it. Ultimate peace and harmony can only be found within ourselves because the treasure of complete happiness — harmony and peace — is buried deep within our own mind. Our joy does not depend on external factors; we can tap into the source of inner happiness to experience the genuine inner peace and satisfaction that is enjoyed by sublime beings like buddhas and bodhisattvas. Other than conditional and limited happiness, happiness cannot be given to us by a teacher, the Buddha, or any other individual. Consequently, the Buddha said we must work for our own salvation.

The mind, as the ground of our being, does not have an evil nature. Its nature is positive. The three fundamental qualities of the mind are emptiness, clarity, and compassion. Every living being is endowed with a mind that possesses such attributes. On this fundamental level, there is not the slightest difference between the mind of a fully enlightened person, a Buddha, and the mind of a completely confused sentient being.

The essence of mind is empty in the same way that space facilitates form. The emptiness of the mind offers us the possibility to experience samsara or nirvana. The mind is free from duality but can still manifest dualities. The mind is naturally free from the duality of happiness and sorrow; however, we dualistically experience happiness as opposed to misery, or misery as opposed to joy. The spacious sky is free from change, but we still experience day and night; a crystal is colorless, yet it still assumes the color of any object it is placed upon.

The clarity of mind can be compared to the illumination of heavenly objects such as the sun, and the stars. The luminosity of these objects is inseparable from the object itself. The rays of the sun are not separate from the sun. Likewise, the enlightened qualities attained by fully enlightened beings are present as a potential in the very ground of our own being. The clarity nature of the mind is self-aware, meaning we can be aware of this nature on a deep experiential level. If we understand this and meditate to attain realization of this view, we do not need to put in a lot of fabricated effort to attain enlightenment or escape the causes that lead to samsaric existence. The nature of our mind does not have to be corrected at all; it only has to be left as it is, observed as it is. It is completely perfect. If we try to intrude upon the nature of the mind with fabrications — if we do not leave it alone — it will be disturbed. Consequently, instead of improving it, this will deteriorate its manifest quality. In other words, our very effort will create difficulties.

Many masters have said that if we really want to understand the Dzogchen view of trekcho, we need to understand the Madhyamika view of emptiness. Without doing so, we run the risk of straying into "neither existence nor non-existence," which is the peak of the cyclic existence of samsara. This state of deep absorption can easily be confused with Dzogchen meditation.

Ordinarily, we sentient beings are under the influence of karma, rambling thoughts and emotions, and their corresponding miseries because of our fixation on the duality of the perceiver and the perceived object. When we encounter the six sensory objects as form, sound, smell, taste, and texture as well as mental phenomena through our senses, the six corresponding sensory consciousnesses arise. Visual consciousness arises upon eye contact and so on. If the sixth mental consciousness fixates upon the objects perceived by the five consciousnesses as independently existing experience — not triggered by the encounter with the corresponding objects, but instead existing by itself — this is what we mean by dualistic fixation of the perceiver of the perceived object. The result is grasping onto the self.

When the eye sense faculty looks at a visual form, it does so to satisfy this faculty. When our "I" encounters beautiful objects, it reacts with craving; when it meets repulsive objects, it reacts with aversion. The reactive emotions of craving and aversion contain the element of delusion. Together, craving, aversion, and delusion are the three root poisons that afflict our minds. Because of these emotions, we accumulate karma of body, speech, and mind. These karmic complexes act as the primary causes of the various forms of myriad limitations, shortcomings, and mistakes that we experience as suffering in samsaric cyclic existence.

In our ordinary situation, we seem to take refuge in the fictitious self. Our body and mind have been serving this self, not only in this life but since time without beginning up to this point. Yet it is not beneficial to serve this fictitious ego in this manner. Thus, as Dharma practitioners, we are not concerned about the well-being of this fictitious ego but focus instead on selflessness, trying to realize the emptiness of the self. To this end, we must gain realization of and take refuge in the wisdom that realizes the emptiness of the self.

It is challenging to cultivate loving-kindness and compassion with a strong sense of ego. The mind becomes so full of self that no room remains for these positive emotions to arise. On the other hand, the wisdom that realizes the emptiness of self coexists naturally with loving-kindness and compassion. As a bird with two wings can soar high in the blue sky, a spiritual practitioner endowed with the wisdom that realizes the emptiness of self, loving-kindness, and compassion can soar high in the exalted state of Buddhahood.

The Buddha gave two kinds of tantric teachings: teachings based on method — the development stage, and teachings based on wisdom — the completion stage. We use techniques based on the development stage to purify our impure perceptions of the environment and the sentient beings within. By practicing the completion stage, we try to remove the gross and subtle fixation on our self to remove even the last traces of belief in the inherent existence of things. Whether we meditate on a deity, our spiritual master, the buddhas and bodhisattvas, or whatever sublime beings we envision in our mind, it is essential to unify our practice with the completion practice — the wisdom aspect.

Ordinarily, sentient beings perceive apparent reality but do not realize actual reality. In apparent reality, we perceive the point of origination (birth), the point of abiding, and the point of cessation (death). This goes for all phenomena as well as for people. However, with the perception of actual reality, we transcend beyond these three concepts. In the ultimate truth, our body and mind, and the content of mind: thoughts and emotions, know no birth and, therefore, know no death. Something that knows no birth cannot go through a process of death. This is not like the concept of eternalism but is a kind of pervasiveness.

If phenomena appear to come from birth, we should employ analytical meditation and ask whether this birth has occurred from itself or from something else. If we gain insight into how birth occurs for one phenomenon, this will be equal to gaining insight into the birth of all phenomena. By gaining this insight, we meditate that outer and inner phenomena assume the nature of clean, clear empty space and allow our minds to rest within this space, without the barriers of origination, abiding, or cessation. The reason we dissolve everything into the expanse of space is not that we do not like outer and inner phenomena, but to lessen our fixation on the duality of these phenomena, which splits reality into pieces and creates complex afflictive emotions.

All these meditation techniques should be sealed by the practice of loving-kindness and compassion, and the generation of the altruistic mind of bodhicitta, as well as wisdom. Otherwise, our meditation technique will not have the flavor of the true Dharma and will not serve the purpose of liberating meditation. Instead, it will confine us to the higher planes of existence, leaving us unable to escape the cyclic existence of samsara.

The Preliminary Practices

The realization of the genuine nature of our mind cannot be attained through money, power, prestige, or fame. The ultimate reality of our mind cannot be achieved only by becoming very learned or knowledgeable in the Buddhist scriptures. One of the Buddha's disciples was very learned in the scriptures, but he was a failure when it came to the ultimate realization of the nature of his mind.

The inner quality of sentient beings is wonderful, but as this quality is not apparent, we cannot see it. When we are not able to see it, we cannot utilize it and are not able to attain the corresponding advantages of this beautiful quality. Our inner quality can be compared with a high-quality car; not using it correctly will create a risk for the driver as well as people on the streets. Our body, speech, and mind are beautiful mechanisms, but they must be appropriately used. Doing so guarantees us full enlightenment. However, if we use them incorrectly, tragedy will befall ourselves and others. Buddhadharma compares our physical human organism to a boat sailing on the samsaric ocean. We cannot cross to the other shore of nirvana without the boat. Lacking a human body, we will not be able to attain Buddhahood.

At present, our mind is like a dirty mirror. Since the nature of the mirror is clarity, the dirt is adventitious and can be removed. After removing the dirt from the mirror, the surface does not need to be improved by further cleaning — it is clean by nature, with an ability to reflect external objects. Likewise, since the stains on our mind are adventitious, they are removable, and we can realize the clean and transparent nature of our mind, capable of reflecting everything without fixation and grasping. To remove these stains, Longchen Rabjam's treatise *Finding Rest in Meditation* presents us with three preliminary practices: meditation on impermanence, cultivation of loving kindness and compassion, and Vajrasattva and guru yoga practice. These practices are referred to as the outer, special, and unique preliminary practices.

The progression of the preliminary practices is likened to a staircase. First, we practice meditation on impermanence, then meditation on loving-kindness, then Vajrasattva practice, and finally guru yoga. If we are beginners, then the preliminary practices are more important than the main ones. By stepping on each step of the staircase, we safely reach the top; however, if we try to jump over some steps, we are in danger of falling. Thus, progressive development is important.

Preparation for Meditation

We should seek a place that is free from external distraction and noise, where our mind can be peaceful and free from discursive thoughts and emotions. We should abstain from meditating in places that are inappropriate or pollute our minds with rambling thoughts and feelings. In general, it is advisable to find a quiet and beautiful place outside the city.

We must also practice the discipline of not harming other sentient beings, which is called the practice of love and compassion. We need to cultivate a practice of deep trust and joyful exertion. We need to develop renunciation with regards to the cyclic existence of samsara. We need to improve our intelligence and develop an expansive mind. We need to establish a bright outlook and a profound sense of devotion. Endowed with these spiritual qualities, we engage in the practice phases of listening, contemplating, and meditating. In this way, we acquire wisdom and purify our mind from conditioning and internal toxins, ensuring that we will be able to fulfill our spiritual goals.

Meditation on Impermanence

All composite phenomena are subject to change because of the law of impermanence. If we try to find the ultimate truth by relying on composite phenomena, our expectation will not be fulfilled. Sooner or later, we will feel frustrated when the impermanent nature of composite phenomena manifests itself. This will cause significant turbulence within our mind which manifests as discursive thoughts and emotions, and we will encounter many difficulties. Therefore, it is essential to understand that relative reality is impermanent. With this understanding, many difficulties simply vanish because we are viewing reality as it is. By observing our thoughts and emotions, we see that their nature is impermanent. Also, we can observe that our body is impermanent; it does not remain the same from one moment to the next, but continually changes — whether we are able to perceive it directly or not. Likewise, our friends and enemies are impermanent. By understanding that the nature of phenomena is impermanent — whether matter or consciousness — we see that samsaric phenomena and experience cannot transcend pervasive suffering.

The purpose of meditation on impermanence is to generate a profound sense of renunciation from the cyclic existence of samsara. However, many people misunderstand renunciation. Some think it means that we must separate ourselves from our family, our possessions, our work, our status in society, our identity, our property, and so on. This way of thinking is a source of misery. When the Buddha said that we should attain separation through the means of renunciation, he meant that we should achieve separation from the discursive thoughts and emotions of craving, aversion, and ignorance. We do not need to separate ourselves from our family in the name of spiritual renunciation. We do not need to separate ourselves from our children or our spouses and loved ones. What we need to separate ourselves from is unhealthy fixation on the people close to us. When we have separated ourselves from our craving, attachment, and fixation, we will instead cultivate love and compassion towards our family, our friends, and our loved ones, as well as ourselves. This will act as a powerful force to attain enlightenment.

The Four Ends of Impermanence

It is traditionally taught that all composite phenomena succumb to four endings: 1) the end of birth is death, 2) the end of meeting is parting, 3) the end of rising is falling, and 4) the end of gathering is dispersion. Without question, the end of birth is death. No historical account exists of anyone who has not experienced death.

As an example of separation, right now our families may be together, but ultimately, they will part. As another example, many organizations have numerous members, but those members will separate at some point in the future. We might only be able to stay together for a short time. Knowing that meeting will end in separation, we should value the time we are together as much as possible.

Individuals who have risen to a remarkably high status in society cannot maintain this status forever; the law of impermanence ensures that they will eventually lose their status. Therefore, we should not fixate upon high status as it will not last forever. This does not imply that we should not enjoy our high status. As long we have such status, we should use it to benefit ourselves and others. If we have not experienced a rise and fall in status, this is also fine. We can take delight in our low status, knowing that we are fortunate not to have attained a high status that we will eventually lose. A Tibetan expression says, "I would like to be elevated up to high status but staying low seems safer."

The fourth ending is that the end of accumulation is dispersion. Sooner or later accumulation of wealth and property will be scattered. Some are very skillful in accumulating wealth and material possessions, but eventually, what they have accumulated will disperse. Accumulating wealth or property is not necessarily a problem, but if we fixate on our property as everlasting and become unable to separate ourselves from it or use it for the benefit of ourselves or others, great misfortune will result. If we do not utilize our wealth for the benefit of ourselves and others, we will feel regret when the law of impermanence disperses our fortune. However, if we have gained the insight that accumulation ends with dispersion, we will be able to practice generosity, and our material possessions can be used to bring about benefit for ourselves and others.

We should also remember to practice spiritual generosity, giving loving kindness and compassion to other sentient beings. We should be generous with our speech, offering compliments and praise in a soft and gentle voice. We can also be generous with our physical expression by presenting ourselves with a beautiful physical appearance and generously share smiles to create peace and harmony in the minds of others. It is also essential to practice right livelihood. Wealth and possessions should be used for the benefit of those who are dependent on us—our family as well as those destitute of food, clothes, and shelter. It is important to give some of our accumulated wealth back to society.

In this way, all worldly composite phenomena come to an end. By gaining insight into the true nature of composite phenomena, we develop a genuine sense of renunciation to help us avoid fixating on phenomena as permanent. In addition, meditation on impermanence will urge us to practice the Dharma because we realize that the impermanence of death may come at any moment.

Subtle Impermanence

Subtle impermanence is more challenging to understand because it cannot be perceived with the five sense faculties or the five sense consciousnesses. Subtle impermanence is very pervasive and must be comprehended for us to be liberated from misery. It can only be detected with the sixth mental consciousness.

By not understanding subtle impermanence, we naively believe in the existence of an "I" and refer to "I," "me," and "mine" regarding our body and consciousness. We believe in a single physical existence and a single consciousness that does not go through any major or minor changes. Yet the reality is that everything is changing—on an apparent level as well as a subtle level. The Dharma explains that, in the single instant of a finger snap, our body and mind go through enormous changes that are not ordinarily detected. We think naively that we are the same person, but this is not true.

Fixating upon true existence is the extreme view of eternalism. This fixation is dissolved by meditation on subtle impermanence. Fixation can be compared to a piece of wood.

The fire of wisdom burns the wood of fixation to ashes; when the wood is burned out, the fire also extinguishes. Similarly, the wisdom of emptiness used to meditate on subtle impermanence will disappear into the expanse of reality once confusion has disappeared.

Generally, an ordinary person knows only two things — existence and non-existence, much like a small baby only knows its two parents. We cannot conceive the third category of reality without fabrication. This is the reality of simplicity, called togal in Tibetan. To liberate us from unrealistic fixation onto existence, the Buddha taught meditation on subtle emptiness as a technique of non-affirmative negation. Chandrakirti, one of the ancient Buddhist masters, said in one of his spiritual works, "If we become well accustomed to meditation on emptiness, this very experience will enable us to abandon our fixation on the true existence of phenomena. When we have negated fixation on the true existence of phenomena, there is a risk of fixating upon non-existence. To counteract this fixation as well, we should do non-conceptual meditation."

By lacking knowledge of the gross and subtle impermanence of phenomena, sentient beings become susceptible to many difficulties; however, instead of feeling pity for such sentient beings, we should generate love and compassion for those who suffer because of their ignorance regarding impermanence.

Bodhicitta: Loving Kindness and Compassion

We try to generate loving kindness and compassion towards all beings — especially those who do not understand impermanence. We also cultivate the notion that all sentient beings have been our mother in one of our past lives; therefore, we refer to sentient beings as "motherly sentient beings." We remind ourselves that our mothers have given us tremendous kindness, care, and affection many times. We generate a deep sense of love and try to develop a strong aspiration to repay their kindness by entering the practice of Dharma. By practicing loving kindness and compassion towards all motherly sentient beings, all notions of duality of friend and enemy disappear. The mind develops equanimity and becomes balanced, peaceful, calm, and serene. When we begin to develop the bodhicitta of loving kindness and compassion, our lives become very meaningful.

The word "bodhicitta" consists of two terms: "bodhi" and "citta." "Bodhi" consists of two words: "bo" and "dhi." "Bo" should be understood as perfect abandonment, meaning the state of Buddhahood that perfectly abandons the suffering referred to in the first noble truth and the causes of suffering explained in the second noble truth. "Dhi" refers to perfect realization. Thus, "bodhi" means the state of the Buddha endowed with the twofold wisdom that knows the multiplicity of phenomena, the mechanisms of karmic causation, and the ultimate nature of things. The term "citta" should be understood as mind or spirit. More simply, we can translate bodhicitta as altruism.

By giving rise to the precious attitude of bodhicitta, we distance ourselves from self-centeredness and the egoistic mind as well as from the cyclic existence of samsara. We come closer to the realization of ultimate truth: the state of nirvana. When we have given rise to bodhicitta, then whatever Dharma practice we undertake will be Mahayana practice. Without the precious attitude of bodhicitta, even presenting ourselves as profound practitioners of Dzogchen would be mere pretense and not real Dzogchen practice that brings about true benefit and transformation.

As soon as we manage to give rise to the genuine attitude of bodhicitta, we are promoted from the level of ordinary individuals to the status of a Bodhisattva, and our self-centered and egoistic mind transforms into a selfless mind. The selfless mind can be compared to infinite space. Within such space, all phenomenal appearances brought about by the four elements—earth, water, fire, and air—

manifest, abide, and dissolve without harming space in any way. Similarly, within the mind of an individual who has generated the positive attitude of bodhicitta, the manifestation of conflicting emotions and thoughts abides and ceases without leaving any negative traces in that mind.

The experience of the exalted state of mind of perfect abandonment and realization is attained when we attain enlightenment. Enlightenment is brought about by practicing compassion in union with wisdom. Compassion means that we wish all sentient beings to be liberated from suffering and the causes of suffering. Requesting and receiving Dharma teachings help us to increase our wisdom. Receiving teachings on the Dharma — and thoroughly analyzing and meditating on these teachings — is the general practice of the path of listening, contemplation, and meditation.

Vajrasattva Meditation and Guru Yoga

The final preliminary practice is two practices: meditation practice on Vajrasattva, the Buddha of purification, and undertaking guru yoga practice. These practices are unique to tantric Vajrayana Buddhism and are therefore called the unique preliminary practices.

In the practice of guru yoga, all phenomena — outer as well as inner — should be perceived as the emanation of our lama. We visualize that our spiritual master takes on the appearance of Padmasambhava in the sky in front of ourselves. In Tibet, Padmasambhava is known as Guru Rinpoche. We feel the deep presence of Padmasambhava and request him to bestow upon us the four empowerments. We combine the practice of Vajrasattva with guru yoga practice, by visualizing Vajrasattva as inseparable with our guru.

Some individuals claim that it is not necessary to perform the outer, special, and unique preliminary practices, but Longchen Rabjam states very clearly in his writings that

that is a mistaken approach. By relying on the practice of meditation on Vajrasattva, we can purify the obscurations of our body, speech, and mind. By building on the practice of guru yoga, we can achieve the ordinary and supreme spiritual accomplishments (Skt. siddhis). Ordinarily, we generate negative vibrations by perceiving things with a negative outlook. These negative vibrations radiate out into space. By practicing Vajrasattva meditation and guru yoga, we counteract this, and instead spread positive vibrations by cultivating a pure perception of the outer environment as the energy field of the buddhas, where sentient beings have been transformed into meditational deities.

In the practice of the Buddha Vajrasattva, we visualize our environment transformed into the pure land of the Buddha Vajrasattva and ourselves transformed into the body, speech, and mind of the Buddha Vajrasattva. We imagine that there is no separation between ourselves and the Buddha Vajrasattva. Other sentient beings in the energy field of Buddha Vajrasattva are visualized to become the various aspects of the fivefold Vajrasattva family.

To begin, we sit with our ordinary body on the floor in meditation posture. On the crown of our head, we visualize a white, fully blossomed lotus with one thousand petals. On top of the lotus, we imagine a full moon lying flat. On the top of this moon stands the seed syllable "HUNG," white in color, clean and clear, brightly illuminating and transparent, shining like the sun. We imagine that the syllable "HUNG" contains all the blessings and compassion from all the buddhas and bodhisattvas. We then offer a supplication prayer to this syllable by uttering, "Since time without beginning I have been wandering from realm to realm, experiencing all kinds of suffering and limitations. My mind has been dark with discursive thoughts, emotions, and defilements, but throughout this time you have not been there for me to take refuge." If we happen to be tormented by specific suffering or illnesses, we can bring these to mind as we focus on the seed syllable. This supplication reaches the Buddha Vajrasattva. He cannot bear our suffering and responds by transforming the seed syllable into a fully-fledged Vajrasattva with consort. The figures of Vajrasattva and his companion are dazzling white, like a snow mountain illuminated by the sun. We feel that we have never seen something like this before and that we are indeed in the presence of the Buddha Vajrasattva. At this point, note that our visualization should not be too substantial. Vajrasattva and his consort are vividly apparent but simultaneously intangible like a rainbow — like the union of emptiness and appearance.

We now visualize moon discs in the heart region of Vajrasattva and his consort, lying flat with a white seed syllable "HUNG" on top. The syllables are tiny as if written with the finest of brushes. Around the syllables circles the hundred syllable mantra. Initially, the mantra is still, but as we start to recite it, the syllables circle around faster and faster. The recitation of the mantra fulfills the offering of the supplication prayer and activates the spiritual mind of Vajrasattva. When the syllables are rotating very fast, they start to produce nectar — which we visualize as vividly as possible. While imagining this, we shift our focus to the face of Vajrasattva or the vajra and bell that he holds in his hands. Like rain falling from the sky, the hundred syllable mantra drips nectar down through the bodies of the male and female deities. From the point of their sexual union, the nectar enters the central channel at the crown of our head. The nectar then passes down through the crown chakra, filling up the body throughout the many channels that spread out from the throat chakra, heart chakra, and naval chakra, cleansing illnesses and evil influences from non-humans as well as negative karma and obscurations. The flow of the nectar pushes out all negative influences and suffering, and our bodies become entirely cleansed and purified. When the nectar pushes out all negativities, diseases, obscurations, and defilements, we visualize these as frightening animals — such as frogs, spiders, and snakes — which leave our body and fall to the ground. The ground then cracks open and swallows all these creatures, without any chance for them to return. At this moment, our whole being — thoroughly cleansed and transparent — becomes as if made of light, complete with the three channels, chakras, and subsidiary channels. At this moment, we should feel extremely blissful. We should believe that we have attained a deep level of physical and mental blissfulness through this process of purification. This visualization has proved to be greatly beneficial — even for people suffering from severe illnesses like cancer who visualize the tumors being washed away by the nectar.

Vajrasattva becomes very delighted and says, "Fortunate child, from this moment and onwards, all your defilements and negativities are completely purified," before melting into light. This light dissolves into us, and we become Vajrasattva with consort ourselves. In our heart, we visualize a moon disc with a blue seed syllable "HUNG" as if written with a single hair, encircled by the mantra OM BENZA SATTVA HUNG, with a white "OM" at the front (facing east), a yellow "BENZA" to the right (facing south), a red "SA" behind, and a green "TVA" to the left.

As we start to recite OM BENZA SATTVA HUNG, luminous light radiates from the seed syllable and the surrounding mantra in all directions as an offering to all buddhas and bodhisattvas residing in the ten directions throughout the universe. When we have made this offering, the light returns to our hearts with blessings from the buddhas and bodhisattvas. A second light then radiates out in all directions towards all sentient beings and the environment, transforming everything into the pure land of the buddha families.

By meditating in this manner, we will relate correctly to the outside world as well as the sentient beings who inhabit it. All forms are inseparable with emptiness, all sounds are inseparable with emptiness, and our thoughts — as awareness — are inseparable with emptiness. If we feel inspired to, we can sing the hundred syllable mantra and the six-syllable mantra with a melody.

Having spent some time visualizing Vajrasattva, we enter the dissolution stage. In this phase, the outer environment — previously transformed into the energy field of the five buddha families — now melts into light and dissolves into all sentient beings. Sentient beings also melt into light, which again dissolves into us as Vajrasattva. We, as Vajrasattva, then vanish into light, starting from our fingers and toes and gradually reaching the "HUNG" syllable in our heart surrounded by the six-syllable mantra. First, the mantra dissolves into light beginning with the "OM," then "BENZA," then "SA," and then "TVA." Finally, the "HUNG" syllable dissolves into light from the lower part upwards until only the very top part remains. Eventually, this also vanishes into the expanse of space.

We now rest our minds in the non-referential expanse of space for as long as we can. If conceptual thoughts start to stir, we alternate between resting in the expanse of emptiness and visualizing Vajrasattva. This time, we do not have to create the visualization of Vajrasattva in a very elaborate manner but can visualize the deity in a single instant.

At the end, we make a brief dedication of the merit we have gained by doing this practice and then rest.

The Actual Practices

Here we rely on three techniques that enable us to trigger experiences of blissfulness, luminosity, and non-conceptuality to realize the true nature of our mind. These techniques are based on meditation on the immaterial energy channels (Skt. nadi), energy currents (Skt. prana), and energy concentrations (Skt. bindu). Bindus comprise the purest substance of our nervous system and consciousness. They permeate throughout the network of channels in our body. We activate the already present bindu energy by generating the flame of wisdom in our hearts. By employing prana — the energy current — we experience the clarity aspect of our minds by carefully controlling our breath. The technique based on the nadi — the energy channels — has three stages: the stage of ejection, the stage of fixation, and the stage of purification. The purpose of this technique is to generate a state of non-conceptuality linked to the emptiness of the mind. While performing these techniques, it is essential to observe the wholesome motivation of bodhicitta. As always, if the motivation is healthy, then the practice will be beneficial; if the motivation is unwholesome, then the practice will be destructive and produce an adverse effect.

Generating bliss and luminosity and resting in the natural state of the mind have the favorable result of an experience of the union of bliss and emptiness, which is inseparable from luminosity. Thus, if we meditate not on misery, but on joy, we will be able to understand the third category of phenomena — that of neither existence nor non-existence. This state of freedom from all elaborations and mental formations is the true nature of who we really are.

The main practice gives rise to four different types of meditative experiences. The first experience is that whatever appearances we encounter provide us with a sense of bliss. The second experience is that we will not be separated from this bliss, day or night. The third meditative experience is that our mind will not be disturbed by discursive thoughts and emotions. Either these will not arise at all or, if they do, they will be powerless. The fourth meditative experience is that our intelligence will improve, and we will swiftly understand the meaning of Dharma. If these four meditative experiences unfold as we work with this meditation, it means that our meditation is working as it should. Through these methods, we can also gain spiritual powers, like the divine eye, clairvoyance, and many more.

Therefore, it is crucial to put effort into this practice. Without practice, the desired result will not come about. If we only talk about the food being placed in front of us, instead of eating it, our hunger will not disappear. Likewise, if we do not undertake the practice of Dharma, it will be difficult to abstain from discursive thoughts and emotions. When these are not purified, we will experience a polluted mind incapable of giving rise to genuine meditational experiences and spiritual realizations.

Dharmakaya, the formless body of the Buddha, is likened to space which facilitates all phenomenal appearances that consist of the four elements of earth, water, fire, and air. However, these appearances do not transcend beyond the nature of space itself. In the same way, the appearances of sambhogakaya and nirmanakaya do not transcend beyond the appearance of dharmakaya. These three kayas — these three realities of the Buddha — share the same essence, but they appear differently to beings according to their spiritual development. Ordinary people are only able to perceive the reality of the emanated form body of the Buddha. Individuals who have evolved to a very elevated spiritual state are able to commune with the enjoyment body of the Buddha. The dharmakaya reality of the Buddha is perceived and communed with directly by someone who has attained full and perfect enlightenment.

Space itself has neither shape nor color, but we can talk about its shape in relation to a tangible object, such as by referring to the space inside a room. In the sutras, the Buddha said that "Those who perceive me as form and sound do not truly perceive me" and "Those who perceive me in terms of form and sound have actually entered the wrong path." Therefore, the Dharma talks about seeing something that cannot be seen — something that defies all forms of defining characteristics. Such seeing is said to be supreme seeing.

Ordinary sentient beings may claim that they have seen space, but if they were asked how they did so, they would not be able to answer. Likewise, bodhisattvas may claim that they have seen the ultimate truth, but seeing the ultimate truth is seeing something that cannot be seen. There is nothing to see. We use the phrase "seeing the ultimate truth," but the ultimate truth can never be seen as an object because it does not have the characteristics of an object. It cannot be seen with the eyes or the mind. This perception is said to be true seeing. This objectless object—the true nature of our mind—cannot be perceived through the sense faculties, yet it can be experienced deep within us, like a mute person experiencing candy, unable to explain the sweet taste to others. If we look within ourselves, just by simply observing the natural mind without generating any mental fabrication, it is possible to observe the reality of our mind. The nature of this mind is the actual dharmakaya. We can experience it, but we cannot describe it.

Generating Inner Bliss

First, we assume the seven-point posture of Buddha Vairochana and visualize our body becoming transparent like a rainbow, vividly apparent without any solid substance. Inside our body there are the three primary energy channels: the blue central channel, the white right channel, and the red left channel. It is essential to assume a proper physical posture by straightening the spinal cord so that the three primary energy channels are also straightened. In this way, the energy will flow unobstructed and activate the bindu. When this happens, the mind becomes blissful, peaceful, and bright.

The lower end of the central channel descends to a point four finger widths beneath our navel. The left and right channels start from the nostrils and descend on each side of the central channel to join it at the point beneath the navel. The three primary channels symbolize the three kayas—the dharmakaya, the sambhogakaya, and the nirmanakaya, which respectively represent the formless body of the Buddha, the enjoyment body of the Buddha, and the emanated form body of the Buddha. The upper end of the central channel touches the apex of our crown.

At the area close to our navel, inside the central channel,

we visualize the Tibetan syllable "A" red in color and very warm. Inside the center of our crown chakra, we visualize the seed syllable "HAM" white in color. If you are not familiar with these syllables, you can visualize them as small spheres of colored light. The fire at the level of our navel shoots up through the central channel and melts the "HAM" in the crown chakra, causing nectar to drip down through the central channel. This nectar passes through the throat chakra, the heart chakra, and the navel chakra and permeates our body throughout the myriad subsidiary channels. The crown chakra has thirty-two channels facing downwards. The throat channels have sixteen channels facing upwards. The heart chakra has eight channels facing downwards. The navel chakra has sixty-four channels facing upwards.

We now visualize the seed syllable "VAM" — blue in color — at the level of our heart. As the nectar reaches the "VAM" syllable, it generates a profound sense of bliss before shrinking and vanishing into space. Then we rest our mind in the expanse of space, free from any reference points. At this point, our thoughts are free from any fabrications. We do not try to bring our mind back, and we don't try to send it away. Dwelling within the expanse of space in this way is called trekcho meditation — the meditation on the nature of mind.

Generating Inner Clarity

In the second main technique, we are introduced to the bright and luminous nature of mind. This practice focuses on the energy currents — namely, the prana.

As before, we assume the seven-point meditation posture of the Buddha Vairochana. We visualize that the lower ends of the right and left channels curve inwards and merge with the lower end of the central channel. The upper ends of the right and left channels end at the nostrils. The upper end of the central channel goes up to the apex of the crown. We then exhale the stale air three times quite forcefully from the nose and imagine any diseases and hindrances leaving us.

We now breathe in deeply, inhaling the pure energy of all external phenomena, the environment, and the sentient beings within. The air passes through our nostrils into the right and left channels and moves all the way down, where the air enters the central channel and then moves upwards. The air then reaches the heart chakra — the wisdom chakra of the five buddha families — and remains there as a pure energy sphere of round white light. To keep the energy sphere of light in place, we control the air below and above the heart chakra, but we should not strain ourselves too much holding our breath. When we feel uncomfortable, we gently release the breath and relax. As we do, we imagine that all the pure energy is released and spreads out throughout our body and further throughout the entire universe.

Non-conceptual Meditation

We do non-conceptual meditation to realize the nature of our own mind. Meditation on non-conceptuality is done in three stages. The first is called transference. The second is called focusing on space. The third is called purification.

Transference

Again, we assume the seven-point posture of the Buddha Vairochana and visualize the energy channels in the same way as the first and second primary techniques. In our heart center is a pure, bright ball of five-colored light that symbolizes the luminous nature of our own minds. We then start to exclaim "HA" twenty-one times on the out breath. There should be an interval of two or three seconds between each utterance. To give this more energy, we can place our upper palms in our lap and push down. With each shout, the ball of light rises gradually upwards through the central channel until it finally leaves the crown of our head and soars into space. We keep our attention on the ball as it travels upwards. After uttering "HA" twenty-one times, the ball of light becomes smaller and smaller, and ultimately vanishes into space. At this point, we allow our mind to rest free from concepts in the expanse of space, where there is no individual meditator, no object of meditation, and no action of meditation. The boundaries between subject, object, and action have been erased, and we attain the experience of totality. Merging with this universal totality, we allow our minds to rest.

If traces of concepts of subjects and objects appear while we attempt to dwell in the expanse of universal totality, this means our meditation has been interrupted. We must then re-enter the experience by starting this technique all over again.

Focusing on Space

Sitting outside, with the sun shining on our backs, we gaze unwaveringly into the vast clear blue sky in front of us. This triggers the experience of non-conceptual inner space, free from mental constructions, and our mind naturally becomes calm and composed. Simply looking directly at this internal space gives us a deep experience of primordial awareness. While doing this, we breathe very gently, without excessive sound. If we are unable to remain in this inner space, we should start again by focusing on the sky.

When we look at a tangible object with our eyes, this triggers the reactive emotions of craving or aversion; however, when we merely look into the middle of space, this does not trigger any reactive emotions in our minds because we do not experience any craving or aversion towards space. This is because space cannot be owned.

This technique is also termed the threefold sky, referring to the meditation on outer space, inner space, and deep primordial space. This meditation is found in the sutra teaching of the Buddha called The Compendium of the Buddha. This technique of focusing on space was also taught by Kamalashila, one of the early Indian masters who came to Tibet.

Purification

Again, we start by focusing our minds on the expanse of space. While gazing deep into space, in a state free from wavering thoughts, we visualize that the animate and inanimate world, the environment and its inhabitants, and ourselves all transform into pure, clear empty space. Our channels, energy currents, and chakras also take on the nature of empty space. This process is comparable with the way clouds dissolve in the sky. We then rest our mind in this openness of empty space, without division between outer, inner, and innermost space. We become entirely free from all barriers and experience the wholeness of reality. All duality is exhausted, and we only experience primordial purity.

We do not dissolve the outer environment and the sentient beings in it because they are impure, but to prevent them from triggering discursive thoughts and emotions within ourselves.

The expression "primordial purity" signifies that our minds have been pure from the very beginning. This purity is not made by us or anyone else. The nature of water is pure, but it still can be polluted by adventitious phenomena. We can restore the original purity of the water by removing these adventitious phenomena. In the same way, the obscurations that hinder us from recognizing primordial purity are temporary phenomena that can be removed. If the nature of our mind was aversion, then aversion would express itself or underlie all situations. This is not the case. Likewise, the nature of the mind is not craving, or else we would be craving all the time.

Meditative Experiences of Non-Conceptual Meditation

The first meditative experience is that gross, dualistic conceptions are removed from the mind of the meditator. This process is like the border between subject and object becoming thinner. The second meditative experience is that the non-conceptual state of mind does not easily leave us; we can abide in it for days. The third meditative experience is that the five root defilements begin to become pacified and the mind becomes very gentle. In fact, the mind goes through such a transformation that makes it impossible to give rise to any defilements. The fourth meditative experience is that we perceive the nature of manifold phenomenal appearances to be like space, without any point of origination. Whatever has no point of origination, will not have a point of cessation, and a vast experience unfolds without any concepts of birth, abiding, or cessation.

Questions and Answers

Questions Concerning Impermanence and Causation

Question: If you are a fully enlightened being, how can you perceive other beings?

Answer: The state of Buddhahood is the state of the dharmakaya. The dharmakaya creates the sambhogakaya, and the sambhogakaya creates the nirmanakaya. The dharmakaya is the formless body of the Buddha. It is like the vast expanse of empty space. From this expanse arises the sambhogakaya that emanates the nirmanakaya body of the Buddha. Thus, the Buddha is not actually the creator of the sambhogakaya and the energy field of nirmanakaya. The manifestation of the three kayas and the energy field of various Buddhas come about not by anybody creating them, but from many causes and conditions. Perhaps "create" is not a good word to use. When we say create, it makes us think of a creator who can do magic without regard for the law of causes and conditions.

Question: What is the difference between self-creating and causes and conditions?

Answer: According to the Buddhadharma, the reality of the self comes into existence because of causes and conditions. Our belief in a self is very naive. We believe that there is a kind of separate, independent self that exists by and of itself. Yet Buddhadharma says that no such self exists — that such a self is a mere fabrication, whether philosophically or naively. If we obtain this insight, we realize that the self is a mere label. However, what is the basis of this label? It is our own psychophysical being. If we believe in the self, this will give rise to a belief in others, causing the actual reality to become split in two. If the interaction between self and others is pleasant, we react with craving. If it is unpleasant, we respond with aversion. If we express a negative emotional complex such as craving or aversion, we perform harmful karmic activity that will hurt others. In this way, we pollute our minds with reactive emotions and karmic creations. The evolution of fundamental ignorance culminates in the fully-fledged experience of samsara.

With the two root poisons of craving and aversion present, the element of ignorance is also strongly present. Ignorance is very strongly present in a mind that fixates on the self as real. Lacking wisdom, the totality is split into two — subject and others — and from the interaction between these, emotional complexes form that evolve into karmic complexes, which causes samsara to solidify. Thus, the root of the cyclic existence of samsara is the fundamentally ignorant mind that takes on the actual reality of the self. Therefore, the meditation on selflessness is one of the most essential meditations in Buddhadharma.

When we perceive a visual form, then who sees it? Ordinarily, we believe that "I am the perceiver." But if there is no self to see it, then who does? For example, when the eye sense faculty, which is based in the eye organ, contacts a visual object, it triggers the experience of visual form in the visual consciousness. We say that visual consciousness arises from the meeting between the eye sense faculty and the visual object. Without this meeting, the visual consciousness would not be triggered, and there would be no experience. So, who is the perceiver? There is no perceiver as a self. Still, ordinarily, we think that deep inside ourselves something called a self exists as the independent and separate owner of all experience. The Buddhadharma explains that, without this sense of self, we still function perfectly well as everything is experienced as a result of many causes and conditions.

When we see the universal spiritual law discovered by the Buddha—that is, the law of interdependency—everything becomes important. Not only our self, but also others become important. For the first time, we see and experience, not intellectually but personally, that everything is intimately linked together; therefore, we give importance to others. It becomes effortless to develop loving kindness and compassion towards others because we regard others as ourselves—without much difference between ourselves and others.

For example, if a very egotistical person somehow manages to accumulate a significant amount of money, his or her ego will grow, thinking, "I am such a successful and important person." But where does the money come from? It comes from society—perhaps from a lot of people. Often, the egotistical person thinks that he or she does not need anybody else, that he or she managed to accumulate all this money by him or herself. But how could he or she have made all that money without the existence of others? It is not possible.

If we lessen the egotistical mind, we will be more willing to distribute some portion of our wealth back to society. Buddhadharma tells us that just by eating one mouthful of food innumerable sentient beings have been involved in producing that food. Therefore, when we eat, it is vital to remind ourselves that our food came about due to the meeting of many causes and conditions and through the participation of many individuals before it somehow ended up on our plate, where we now also participate in the chain of events. Therefore, we generate loving kindness and compassion towards all sentient beings that have worked so hard to produce this food necessary for our survival. Undoubtedly, the law of interdependent connectedness that the Buddha discovered is fundamental.

Question: Can you explain subtle impermanence?

Answer: In the smallest of instant, there occurs a change in the body on the physical and mental level. Usually, we are not able to detect this form of subtle difference. Intellectually, we might have knowledge of it, but since we do not experience it on a personal level, we do not believe in it with confidence. Consequently, we react strongly to physical and mental sensations. Our reactions arise because we do not understand the subtle impermanence of sensations. Like the Buddha said in the sutras, ordinary individuals are not able to perceive subtle impermanence. Sublime beings, however, can do so, and this enables them to leave misery behind. The Buddha gave the following example. If we place a strand of a hair on the palm of our hand, we will not feel it. But if a hair enters our eye, it will cause a strong sensation. Likewise, ordinary sentient beings are not able to detect the misery of all-pervasive suffering due to their ignorance of subtle impermanence. Yet buddhas and bodhisattvas are so sensitive that they experience all-pervasive suffering just as a hair feels when it falls into our eye. Ordinary beings, like us, are occupied with escaping gross misery. Sublime beings are concerned with escaping subtle suffering.

Question: Who created the three realms?

Answer: According to the Buddhadharma, the creator of the three realms is the self. Nothing exists in these realms that is not created by the self—even sentient beings are created by the self. If we are liberated from the grip of the self, we are not a sentient being but a bodhisattva or a buddha. This is attaining the totality. One of the spiritual laws discovered by the Buddha is that of selflessness. Some opponents of Buddhism expounded that there is a small "I" and a supreme "I". Buddhadharma says explicitly that believing in such a self is mere fabrication; it does not accord with reality. Buddhadharma says that believing in the reality of a true self is the source of all suffering. Even in a family, problems come about because of intense fixation on the existence of a true self. Also, between two people, disputes occur because of fixation on a self that does not want to be threatened by others. Conflicts between two parties in general — whether between two persons, people in a family, different religious organizations, nations, or society in general — come about from grasping onto the true existence of the self.

Question: How does this relate to the Buddha-nature?

Answer: The Buddha-nature is found in the core of selflessness.

Respondent: How does the Buddha-nature come to be?

Answer: The Buddha-nature has not come into existence. The Buddha-nature is the all-pervasive reality, free from birth and death.

Question: If everything is created by the self, and if we do not have a self — only Buddha-nature — how can things exist?

Answer: We must distinguish between the relative self and ultimate selflessness. The apparent reality of the relative self experiences certain outer and inner phenomena. Belief in the reality of the relative self is the actual creator of everything. For example, many dream appearances unfold to a person who is sleeping, and he or she perceives these to exist vividly. Now let us say that next to the dreaming person is another person who is completely awake. For the person who is awake, the dream experiences are not real, but mere projection by the dreamer. If the person who is dreaming wakes up, all the dream appearances will vanish. This is like attaining full enlightenment. The Buddha-nature is there when we are fast asleep and when we are awake. It is said that Buddha-nature is the ground for both samsara and nirvana. When the Buddha-nature is not recognized by self-awareness, this lack of awareness gives rise to the experience of samsara; but when it is identified by self-awareness, this gives rise to the experience of nirvana.

Questions Concerning Vajrasattva Meditation

Question: What is the purpose of Vajrasattva meditation?
Answer: The reason for using this technique is that beginners are not able to instantly dissolve their discursive thoughts and emotions. By applying the development stage of tantric meditation, we attempt to purify our impure perceptions, which have been habitually cultivated over many lifetimes. This purification works for our past life, our present life, and our future life as well. It is like a circle.

Question: What is the purpose of visualizing ourselves as Vajrasattva and receiving the light from the five Buddha families?
Answer: The purpose is to create a pure perception of the environment and the sentient beings within it. We transform our environment into the energy field of Vajrasattva, sentient beings into the five Buddha families of Vajrasattva, and view the environment as a Buddha realm containing buddhas. This does not mean that all sentient beings become a copy of Vajrasattva, but that they attain the

enlightened spiritual state of Vajrasattva. The deepest level of our mind is already enlightened with the buddha potential, which is nothing more than Buddha Vajrasattva. When we visualize Vajrasattva, the embodiment of all enlightened beings, we are not actually fabricating something that does not correspond to the deepest reality of being. There is a very intimate relationship between the visualization of Vajrasattva and our own buddha potential. It is not a superstitious concept.

Question: I find the visualization of the sexual union confusing. Can you explain?

Answer: The nature of mind has two basic qualities. The essence of mind is empty, the nature of mind is clarity, and the indivisibility of these two is pervasive compassion. The union of male and female Vajrasattva symbolizes the union of emptiness and appearance. Emptiness is the ultimate truth; appearance is the relative truth. We can find emptiness within appearance, and appearance within emptiness. In the Hinayana teachings of the Buddha, the Dharma says that monks should abandon relationships with women. This refers to ordained Sangha members, and monks do meditation techniques to generate a sense of repulsiveness towards women to prevent them from being sexually attracted. Certain individuals might come to the wrong conclusion, though — that women are bad or inferior, thereby devaluating women. To rectify this, the tantric teaching of the Buddha say that one should not scold or abandon women. In fact, in certain tantric teachings, practitioners use physical sexual union to achieve enlightenment.

Question: Can the depicted sexual union also mean the inner female and male side of ourselves?

Answer: Yes. It is not necessary to rely on an external sexual partner in order to attain enlightenment. We can rely on the inner sexual partner. As human beings, we are a union of male and female sexual energies. We attain enlightenment when we strike a balance between these energies.

If visualizing the deity in union with a sexual partner triggers our passion, we should not do this form of visualization. We should visualize a single deity. Remember, the purpose of all these techniques is to overcome the three root defilements of craving, aversion, and delusion, not to increase them. Certain people will benefit a lot from this technique; but if it does not benefit us, it does not mean that the technique is totally useless. It may be useless to some, but not to others. This is the reason the Buddha taught many different techniques. We can choose between Vajrasattva being in union or alone.

Question: Would it make it easier for us to do this practice if we receive Vajrasattva initiation?

Answer: Yes, the practice will certainly be more fruitful for someone who has received Vajrasattva initiation. If we want to practice Dzogchen, we will have to begin from the very beginning. We must travel in a progressive manner. Patrul Rinpoche's book *The Words of My Perfect Teacher* reveals the gradual path that we follow in the Nyingma tradition.

Questions Concerning the Actual Practice

Question: If we do not have a very deep understanding of karma, is it still okay to do this meditation?

Answer: Without depending on relative truth, we cannot meditate on absolute truth. We must study relative truth first. Read about what is meant by impermanence and karma. Then you will be prepared to explore the ultimate truth of emptiness.

Question: Is there a connection between bliss and love?

Answer: Supreme bliss certainly has a deep connection with genuine love. However, if it is not a supreme bliss, then it relates to passion. Sensual pleasures or sensual bliss is just mere bliss, not supreme bliss.

Question: What is the quality of the energy that we draw in from the outside world? Is it positive or negative?

Answer: It is positive. It is energy that will lengthen our life and create physical and mental well-being—energies that will create prosperity and harmony.

Question: Are we born with the obscurations that prevent us from experiencing primordial purity?

Answer: These obscurations can come from past lives or from this present life.

Question: What if we feel unwell while we hold our breath?

Answer: We should not strain ourselves too much. If we strain ourselves, we could cause harm instead of good. The heart center is extremely sensitive. Focusing too hard or holding our breath forcefully can cause tension in this area. So be gentle. If we begin to feel slightly uncomfortable, release the breath. After we have released the breath, we can do the second part, where the light spreads out from the ball of light into our body through the channels, completely illuminating our body.

Question: What is the purpose of the transference meditation?

Answer: If we meditate like this, we will be able to experience the fruition of shamatha, which is the experience of mental and physical suppleness. When we experience the fruition of shamatha, we will be able to use our mind for whatever purpose in the most effective way. We will be able to engage in virtuous projects without resistance from our mind.

Question: Some people claim they can see others' auras.

What do you think about this?

Answer: According to the Buddhadharma, our body is made of light. Our whole body is made of light because the building blocks of the body are simply vibrations of light. This is the view of tantric Buddhism. Tantric Buddhism says that we can attain a rainbow body when we depart from this life simply because the nature of the body is light. This light is inseparable from our own mind. It is perfectly fine to try out this meditation technique without believing in it. If we meditate properly, we will achieve the intended fruition, and faith will arise.

Question: Is there a danger of increasing the ego if we practice this by ourselves at home?

Answer: We should not focus on temporal meditative experiences. The ultimate purpose of meditation is to experience full enlightenment. Beautiful, but temporary, experiences are just a by-product of meditation; we should not take them to be the ultimate result. We should focus on attaining full enlightenment, free from all fixations.

Question: Where is the "I" when the light sphere disappears into emptiness?

Answer: Actually, to begin with, there is no "I" at all. This is the Buddhist view. The "I" is a fictitious phenomenon. The self only exists on an apparent level. To purify our confusion concerning this self, we do this meditation.

Question: Does the observer disappear when the concept of the mind disappears?

Answer: Actually, it is not that easy to enter the experience of the non-conceptual mind. Even if we manage to do so, it is difficult to sustain the experience for an extended period. So, we do not need to worry about entering this state; it will not make us disappear. It is a natural reaction to fear the expanse of emptiness, but if we enter into this expanse, we will experience that it is a lovely state to be in. When the ball of light vanishes into the expanse of space, allow our mind to rest within that expanse, free from the three conceptions — the conception of a meditator, the notion of an object of meditation, and a conception of performing meditation.

View, Meditation and Action in Mahayana and Vajrayana

View, Meditation and Action in Mahayana

I have visited your center several times since 2000, which has given us the opportunity to teach and listen to the discourses of the holy Dharma together. It has been about nine years since I could visit you, so I am pleased that today we again can meet and participate in this discourse of the Dharma.

Often, teachers give teachings by following scripture or texts, but today I would like to provide oral instruction based on my personal experiences of Dharma practice from the age of seven up until now, at the age of forty-five. It is my own experience that it brings about a more significant benefit to those receiving the teachings when I expound the Dharma spontaneously in this manner.

The Uniqueness of the Buddhist view

Within the Buddhist teachings, the understanding of the threefold "view, meditation, and action" is fundamental. Of these, the view concerning the four seals distinguishes Buddhist from non-Buddhist spiritual views. There is Buddhist meditation and non-Buddhist meditation. The criteria for determining whether meditation can be said to be Buddhist meditation is whether it acts as an antidote to negative self-grasping. What actually binds us to the suffering of the wheel of samsara is not the self but grasping to the self.

Action, as Buddhist behavior, should not fall into extremes, for example, excessive indulgence in sensory gratification or pleasures, or excessive or extreme practices in the name of religion or spirituality, like asceticism.

Fruition is the result of having transcended, or overcome, karma and afflictions, and this is the third noble truth which marks the difference between the Buddhist and non-Buddhist view. On the bases of "ground, path, and fruition," or "view, meditation, and action," we must progress along the path of Dharma to reach fruition.

It is fundamentally important to cultivate pure vision because our actions ensue from the beliefs that we adopt, which leads us to accumulate either afflictions or non-afflictions. Therefore, the view is so important.

There is also the mundane path, and by following the mundane path, we can attain mundane fruition. Likewise, there is the transcendental path, or the path of Dharma, by which we can achieve the transcendental fruition of the Dharma. When we attain a deeper understanding of the fundamental view, we can experience realization. This experience of realization can become a powerful remedy against the karmas we accumulate in our mind.

So, if we possess a sound view, we will naturally possess a good character and become a good person. The view is the support that acts as fertile ground. Based on this fertile ground, we can get a good fruition. Cultivating an excellent spiritual view gives birth to positive thoughts. This is like when we cultivate something on fertile ground, we will attain positive fruition.

Our belief determines our wishes and actions. If we want happiness in all areas of life, we engage in various activities to attain this happiness. When someone loves their children, they want their children to have all the joy they can get. But we can easily believe that our happiness comes from some external objects, and then engage in activities to accumulate these objects to achieve satisfaction. But it is not possible for us to achieve ultimate happiness from all these external objects, either now or in the future. To attain ultimate pleasure, we need to engage in spiritual practices. This is the only way.

The view of Buddhism can be described as the view of dependent arising. This is because there is a dependence between the inner mind of the person and outer objects. We can use this mutual dependence to give rise to happiness.

If we want to have a good life, we need to rely on the practice of meditation. To have good meditation, we need a correct view. Without correct view, our meditation will not produce the right results. If our meditation does not progress, we will not be able to maintain ethical conduct. If our behavior is not good, we will not be able to achieve any good results on our spiritual path.

The basis of the view is the realization of emptiness. Even if we do not fully understand emptiness, if we only have some idea of what it is, this will benefit our life. There are two levels of emptiness, emptiness on the gross level, which is the explanation of impermanence, and subtle emptiness. The teachings on impermanence are the most important subject as far as Dharma practice is concerned.

Impermanence

In our lives, we may encounter three kinds of obstacles: inner, outer, and secret obstacles, but if we keep impermanence in mind, these obstacles will be reduced as time goes on. For example, in Norway, we do not experience dangerous outer obstacles like earthquakes, or any difficulty with housing or food, but although these external obstacles are not present, we still encounter inner and secret obstacles, which seem to be commonplace.

When we are born as sentient beings, there will always be obstacles. Based on the afflictive thoughts that we experience; we will still encounter obstacles due to wrong ideas. For example, when we see people around us, we can experience negative thoughts, and hearing things can produce negative thoughts in our mind. These things can happen when we are having conversations, eating or socializing. We can experience a lot of feelings that arise in our mind, and they induce afflictions, which leads us to engage in different kinds of karma.

Generally, we have five senses and five sense-consciousnesses. Based on these, we encounter different kinds of objects. There are different kinds of practitioners: competent practitioners, and not so good practitioners. Good practitioners will not engage in hope and fear, and do not experience such obstacles. Sometimes I tell my students that we have two eyes and two ears, so we can listen and see, and if we can also reduce the activities of our speech, by observing and listening, we can increase our wisdom.

The subtle impermanence refers to dharmata, the ultimate nature. To understand this, we need to practice meditation. The primary practice should be meditation on the fact that no matter what happens, we will still have to face death. Generally, it is said that the end of meeting is parting, the end of living is dying, and the end of having a high status is the loss of status. We need to contemplate this, and when this becomes a part of our path, we will gain certainty. When we have confidence in this fact, then even if somebody is not treating us well, we will not become so angry, and if somebody does treat us very well, we will become less attached. Gradually, as we practice like this, we will reach the state beyond hope and fear, distance ourselves from our afflictions, and come nearer and nearer to enlightenment.

We should think about the four extremes, which are: 1) the end of meeting is parting, 2) the end of living is dying, 3) the end of accumulation is loss, and 4) the end of high status is to lose status. If we think that we can live forever, without having to confront the losses of the four extremes we will continue to suffer.

The four extremes are the natural rules of the phenomena of our lives, and no one can do anything about this; the Buddha could not do anything about this, neither could other powerful beings of high status. If we are not paying attention to this, we are not following these rules in our lives. Say for example we think that we want to love somebody forever, and we are not following these rules, then we will have to face the consequences of losing what we have been attached to.

So, the subtle impermanence of Dharmata is the impermanence of our mind, body and objects, and the primary purpose of practice is to realize this. For example, when we engage in the practice of meditation, we can think of it like breathing. When we breathe in, we can imagine being born, when we breathe out, we can imagine ourselves dying. Or, when we go to sleep, we can think of this as a state of dying; when we dream, we can think of this as arriving in the bardo; and when we wake up, we can think of this as a state of entering the next life. Because, when we pass away, although this life and body have ceased, our mind will continue. This is what our practice must be; it must happen at the level of the mind.

Because the end of living is dying, we need to practice properly in this life to benefit ourselves. In general, in Dharma practice, our intent is most important. All phenomena are conditioned, and the most important phenomenon is our motivation. Dharma practice depends a lot on our ability to transform our purpose. If we can change our aim, we will be able to establish good Dharma practice.

Karma and Afflictions as Causes of Suffering

The first of the four seals of Dharma is that all phenomena are impermanent. The second seal is that all contaminated phenomena, karma, and afflictions, cause suffering. The purpose of Dharma practice is to be able to master karma and afflictions. If our mind and body are under the control of karma and afflictions, then they will follow their influence. So, it is imperative not to allow our mind and body to come under the control of karma and afflictions. If we can free our mind and body from these two forces, they will achieve freedom.

Cessation is the elimination of karma and afflictions. There is no other state of cessation than this. Here, cessation is referring to the third of the Four Noble Truths, the cessation of suffering, which is achieving nirvana or liberation.

The Buddha did not say that the nature of mind and body is suffering. He also did not say that their quality is that of the afflictions. He said that if the body and mind are under the influence of afflictions, then there will be suffering. In the practice of Dharma, body and mind are like a vessel, and they become the nature of the path. When enlightenment has been achieved, body and mind display their nature as the cause of enlightenment. For example, in the practice of Dzogchen, when we attain rainbow body, the body itself transforms into the light of the rainbow body. If the nature of the body was afflictions, then it could not become a rainbow body. The nature of the mind is Buddha-nature. This is the big difference between Sutrayana and Vajrayana.

The Emptiness of the Five Aggregates

Referring to the four seals of Dharma, the first is that all phenomena are impermanent, the second is that all contaminated phenomena are suffering, and the third is the explanation of emptiness, which is the lack of individual identity, or lack of self.

In the teachings of the Dharma, all phenomena are categorized into the five aggregates. When we say, "all phenomena," we are referring to the five aggregates. The five aggregates are the aggregate of form, or the body, the aggregate of feeling, the aggregate of perception, the aggregate of mental formations and the aggregate of consciousness. Clinging to these leads to rebirth in samsara. When we say "emptiness," it means that the five aggregates are empty, meaning that they lack identity or self.

Generally, when we use the word "emptiness," this refers to the lack of identity of phenomena, and when we use the term "lack of self" it refers to the lack of self of the individual. These are the two types of identity. When the feeling of self-grasping, or the "I", increases, this increases our afflictions, and this also increases the two types of identity. Because of this, suffering increases. So, the root of all of samsara is the clinging to self. Consequently, the lack of clinging to self is nothing other than the state of Buddhahood.

We, who are born in this world, believe that there is a truly existing self. This clinging to the self takes two forms: clinging to the "I" and clinging to the mind. The first is the cause of the other. The first is the clinging to the self of the individual. Based on this, we cling to the phenomena that surround this self: my house, my property, and whatever we call my phenomena. This "mine" can also refer to the identity of the phenomena.

To eliminate clinging to the body, we can establish the emptiness of the body. We can do this by understanding the body as the result of causes and conditions. By considering dependent arising, the body is recognized as a product of causes and conditions.

The Heart Sutra states that "Form is emptiness, emptiness is form. Form is not other than emptiness, emptiness is not other than form." If we can examine and understand the meaning of this, it would be beneficial for our spiritual practice.

In general, it is quite difficult to realize the understanding of emptiness. We can first examine gross emptiness, which is impermanence. We can see that all phenomena are impermanent. Because of this impermanence, phenomena cannot abide by themselves. They do not exist independently, and all phenomena are nothing but impermanent. If we can examine like this, we can see that phenomena are not independently existing. We need to study this properly.

For example, we can examine our body by thinking about yesterday's body and today's body. Asking ourselves whether these bodies are the same or different. We can also do this concerning our feelings. If we are happy today, while we were suffering yesterday, we can ask whether these feelings are the same or different. Also, we don't know whether we will suffer or be happy tomorrow.

When we examine the nature of our body in this way, we arrive at the conclusion that the nature of our body is inexpressible and inconceivable. Further, if yesterday's and today's body are the same, then we cannot grow old. If yesterday's body is different from today's body, then cause and effect will not be able to function, because if we did something bad with yesterday's body, then today's body will not be able to experience the effect. On the other hand, it is difficult to accept that yesterday's body and today's body are not the same, that they do not have the same continuum. Because if we did something nice yesterday, the body of today would experience the effect. If we examine the nature of the body in this way, we will find that it is beyond being the same or different.

In the teachings of the sutras, it says that there is no arising and there is no ceasing, there is no permanence, there is no creation. This is true for every single entity. It can be understood with the body as an example, but it is also true for all other phenomena, even a grain of rice. By understanding one phenomenon, we can understand the nature of all phenomena.

If we consider the fact that there is no coming or going, then according to the nature of reality as explained in the scriptures, the body of yesterday cannot transform into the body of today. We cannot really understand the nature of yesterday's body, because it is gone, and we cannot understand the body of tomorrow, because it is not here yet, but if we know the nature of our current body, we will be able to understand the nature of the body as it is.

This process is an excellent way to practice the first of the

Four Mindfulnesses, the mindfulness of the body, the others being mindfulness of feelings, phenomena, and mind. For myself, I often receive tasty food from people, as well as good things to treat the body with, but the fact is that this is not really what the body needs. The body needs to receive love and compassion. When we increase our wisdom, we will naturally experience wellbeing. It is said in the scriptures of the sutras that the three higher pieces of training are discipline, concentration, and wisdom, and if we can train well in these, we will experience unsurpassable bliss.

To understand the meaning of emptiness, we need to examine the nature of our body. We need to see if there is anything that can abide permanently. Is there a permanent abiding entity in the body? We also need to check if there is an independently existing self. Is there anything that lives all by itself, like God? Within our aggregates, no single entity can function independently, without depending on anything else, like a God. When we examine the aggregates or the five faculties, like seeing, hearing, smelling, and so forth, we need to check whether they can exist without relying on something else. We will find that there is nothing in the body that can exist independent of some other part of the body. There are two kinds of meditation, analytical meditation, and resting meditation. Examining in this way is called analytical meditation.

I would also like to explain two terms, emptiness and lack of self, or identity. Let us examine the body as before by considering feeling, the second aggregate. There are three main categories of feelings: happiness, suffering, and neutral feelings. We can see that when we examine the three kinds of emotions we experience, none of these experiences are able to abide permanently. Feelings fluctuate from happiness to suffering, to neutral and so on. Although we want to stay happy, there is no way we can be continuously happy, because feelings are impermanent. Feeling, the second of the aggregates, therefore, does not have a fixed identity. It does not exist inherently.

Among the five aggregates, the aggregates of feeling and perception, the second and third aggregate, are the most essential aggregates to examine. This is because we go about our daily life while engaging in the aggregate of feeling. It is our feelings that motivate us in our daily life. The aggregate of perception motivates us when we engage in the higher tenants of the philosophical teachings and practices. Different people practicing different religions such as Christianity, Buddhism, and Islam, have a different perception of things. So, it is essential to analyze these two aggregates.

Understanding and Cultivating the View

Again, it is essential to understand the nature of impermanence. For example, when we are being treated well by others or experience a pleasant situation, we should not think that this person or condition will be able to give us permanent happiness, because if we at some later point receive negative treatment, we will feel unhappy. We should therefore not fall into the habit of clinging to whatever happiness or suffering we experience. If we were guests checking into a five-star hotel, we would still have to check out very soon. It is not permanent happiness and the guests that check-in know this very well. Similarly, if we were to check into a bad hotel, we would not feel so depressed, because it does not belong to us, it is just temporary accommodation. If we can see ourselves as a guest passing by, we will not be so attached to whatever happens in our lives.

It is important to know that our view is affected by the way we think. We are currently explaining the emptiness of three kinds of subjects. The first is the five aggregates, the second is formation, or karma, and the third one is mind, or consciousness. When we examine these three, we need to know that they all are empty, that they lack an independent self. So, what we need to do is to understand that the nature of the five aggregates is empty and that they have no independent self.

We usually think in terms of my body, my mind, my feelings, as well as my thoughts. It seems that we accept that there is an entity, something that is independent of these things, as a genuinely existing "I", or self. It is one hundred percent certain that all of us believe that this "I" exists among these five aggregates and that we do everything for the sake of this "I". Even the beginning of samsara or nirvana comes down to this "I".

When we think about all this, it seems that the "I" is the creator of this world. Everyone has this "I" in their mind or brain somewhere, and we are carried away by this "I". The Buddha said that this "I" is the great demon, and that there is no greater demon in the three realms of samsara other than this "I". It is this "I" that controls everything, that everything else is dependent on. Like the king who has the authority over everything, the "I" has the authority over all other phenomena.

When the Buddha taught the emptiness of this identity, the arhats fainted. Therefore, this topic may feel a little dangerous. If we do not feel any fear while listening to the explanations of emptiness, it can be because we do not understand it, that our ignorance obscures it. When we do appreciate it, we can sometimes perceive it as dangerous. If we contemplate this by ourselves, we can feel lonely, or even afraid. Some people will experience these things, but not everybody.

In many religions or philosophical systems, the self is examined, but the Buddha taught that the self does not exist. Even if we are not able to understand that the self does not exist, it is also beneficial if we can reduce this feeling of self by whatever method we choose.

We are always saying, my body, my mind, my things, my car, my properties, but this increases the clinging to the self. It would be good if we could reduce clinging to the self through our various activities, such as when we talk. If we can reduce our usage of the terms "I" and "mine," it will help reduce clinging to self, because the more we use these words, the more it increases our attachment to the "I". So, it would be good if we can be mindful and reduce these. The "I", or self, is the root of samsara and nirvana, and it would be good if we could understand that there is no such thing as an "I" that is independent of the five aggregates. This is what we mean when we say that all phenomena are empty or lack identity or self.

The Buddha taught that the ultimate result of spiritual Dharma practice is nirvana. This is the highest level we can achieve in our life. The state of nirvana is also called peace, or the state of pacification. There are many people on this planet, but very few who work towards achieving the ultimate result of nirvana. To achieve this, we need to engage in practice. For example, if we just smell food, we will not become full. In the same way, we cannot achieve the result from the Dharma by just listening. If we just listen and fail to put it into practice, it becomes a fraudulent practice. We call this wrong learning and wrong contemplation.

Of the three, practice, learning and meditation, meditation is the most important. The Tibetan word for meditation, "gom," means cultivation, not just meditation. So, cultivation should be performed in our daily lives. It is not just something we recite or do while we sit on the meditation cushion. We need to apply it in our daily lives. The basis of the practice, the view, is something we need to apply in our daily life.

The view is the basis of the practice. Most people, being intelligent, can do the necessary things to get what they want, but it is quite rare to find someone who has the pure intellect to achieve the freedom from suffering in samsara. Therefore, it is crucial to establish a pure mind.

To cultivate the right view, we need to engage in the Middle Way. To accomplish a high view, we need to manage subtle karma. For example, some lamas claim to have achieved the realization of emptiness but go around sleeping with many women, drinking a lot, hoarding wealth, and wallowing in luxury. These actions are not signs of realization of emptiness. This is a wrong way of going about realizing emptiness. This is falling into the extreme view of thinking that karma does not matter. Such lamas, who have accumulated many wicked deeds, may believe that it is good that everything is empty, that they do not have to worry, and they can do anything they like, thinking that emptiness is very comfortable. For myself, if I were to act like these lamas, and explain emptiness in this way, then I could probably get a lot of followers and students, but this would not be the right thing to do. This is also stated by Guru Rinpoche. He said that the understanding of the view should be like a bird descending from the sky. When the bird flies down, it can clearly see everything on the ground. It knows where it is going. All the subtleties of karma exist, always. Also, when the bird wants to fly up into the sky, it takes an effort to do that. We should therefore still be mindful of karma, and always engage in the accumulation of virtuous deeds to purify the mind.

It is therefore critical to understand the right view, and we need to engage in learning and contemplation to appreciate the view correctly. To understand the view, we need to rely on wisdom from learning and reflection. When we achieve this wisdom, we will be able to make natural progress in meditation.

The wisdom of contemplation is the actual experience of the path. We cannot fully realize the view properly by only relying on knowledge from learning. We also need the skills of contemplation and meditation. Through these, we can recognize the proper view.

As my own teacher once said, we should not treat the practice of learning like eating food, putting it into our mouth and defecating it out later. Then we will just lose it. When we engage in the practice of learning, if we do not follow it up with the practice of contemplation and cultivation of meditation, we will not experience any benefit when we meet obstacles.

This concludes the explanation of the view.

Questions and Answers

Question: You have been talking about the ego, that it should be suppressed somehow, reduced but not suppressed, somehow transformed, as I understand it. Is it right that in Buddhism the ego should be reduced, but not suppressed and pushed away, or somehow transformed?

Answer: The primary objective is to reduce the clinging to the self. This is what we want to cut so that we can realize the wisdom of the non-existing self. It is not the self itself. When we recognize that the self does not exist, then we have achieved the first bhumi, and become a bodhisattva. Then we can make friends with Chenrezig!

Question: My question is about clarification on the right view, and its relationship with what we value as right. I have noticed in my life, when I have some great interest... for example, I recently started fixing some rust on my car, and after that, for the first time in my life, I noticed rust on other vehicles around me. So, my view, or perception, seems to be very related to my value system. My question is about the relationship between value and right view.

Answer: Compared to the rust of the mind, the rust of the car is quite insignificant. When our minds get rusty, we are in trouble. There is a strong relationship between the correct view and the view we hold in our daily life. For example, when we have the right view through the practice of true meditation, we will have a balanced mind. And with this mind, whatever we do in our daily life, such as sleeping, can be done very well and properly, and we can also take better care of the people around us. We will have more loving kindness and compassion for the people around us.

We can see examples of having the right view and understanding in our daily lives. For example, a doctor, who gains a correct understanding of an illness after examining the patient´s body, can prescribe proper medicine and treatment. This example also applies to our own practice. If we observe and understand the mistakes and confusion of our mind, we can gain a correct view, and be able to engage in the right practice of purification of the mind.

Questioner: Maybe I did not formulate my question so well. Of course, these things are perfectly accurate. I think my question is: Are the words "value" and "view" almost the same? If I have a right or correct value system, will I then also view things correctly? This is perhaps a question about language. Because when I hear that we must have the right view, I do not have a good understanding of this or intuitive feeling for what the view is. For example, I think I should value the right things in this room, like for example paying attention to Rinpoche, and value him. But if I pay attention to a lovely girl, if I have the wrong values, then my experience here would be something superficial.

Answer: The view is connected to wisdom, or we could use the synonym perception. When we perceive something, our perception can see its value. In other words, our view can appreciate our value. In that way, the value is influenced by the view, by the right view or perception. So, when we attain the right view regarding karmic causations, we become afraid of engaging in the karmic causes that result in unpleasant experiences. We are not afraid of the consequences themselves but fearful of the causes that lead to consequences. We will know that there will be no consequences if we stop generating causes. So, the right view prevents us from engaging in the wrong causes.

Most ordinary people are afraid of consequences, but they are not scared of causes. For example, people are generally not scared of the resultant disease that is caused by anger. Ordinary people can become outraged and react with tremendous anger repeatedly, then this anger can create stress and tension and can be the cause of certain deceases. But ordinary people are not afraid of the actual cause of the resultant disease.

Let us compare the practice of love and compassion with anger. When people get angry, we can see that their facial expression changes. Their face becomes red and unpleasant looking. On the other hand, when we practice love and compassion, then even if our facial expression might not become as peaceful as that of a bodhisattva, it will undoubtedly look at lot better. In general, we can see that our habituation with anger is strong, and our habituation with bodhicitta and compassion is exceedingly small.

Question: Thank you for the teachings so far. My question is related to what you said at the outset of the lecture, that you would speak freely from your experience of thirty-five years of overcoming the clinging to the "I", or self. Can you say if there have been any experiences in your life where you think there has been a change or development in your relationship to the clinging to the "I"? Are there any episodes that you can share with us?

Answer: In the East, I spend approximately six to seven hours every day merely listening to other people. And it is very tiring. I give my precious time for the sake of others. This does not mean that I do not cherish my valuable time. This happens by the blessing of the Dharma. Also, back in Tibet, I was the abbot of Samye Monastery. If I were to cling to that position and hold onto it, I would, spiritually speaking, become powerful as far as status is concerned. By giving all these things up, the natural expression of altruism comes about from the practice and blessing of the Dharma. When I encounter difficulty or get exhausted and tired after listening to others for six or seven hours every day, I do not become angry. Neither do I react with dislike.

Ideally, the physician or doctor should spend as much time as possible with the patient. When the patient is cured, the doctor takes delight in it. A spiritual teacher, as a physician, spends a lot of time with the patient if it is needed to help that person. This is also an integral part of this practice.

In a relationship, like between two lovers, it is critical to introduce the quality of patience. This will further enhance their loving relationship. The quality of patience is essential. It should be patience based on the wisdom of the view.

Meditation

We have talked about the realization or understanding of the view, which is the emptiness or lack of identity or self. This explanation of emptiness, and lack of inherent self, or identity, belongs to the Four Seals of Dharma. We need to be certain of these Four Seals, without feeling any doubt.

This view is the basis for all practices, and if we can develop the right view, then our actions of body, speech, and mind will improve, and we will also achieve better results. The view involves understanding the right path towards enlightenment. And once we know this, we will arrive at a firm decision of what to do in our practice. This includes what we must do regarding our practice, from the moment we wake up, until the moment we fall asleep. Once we know what to do, we will be able to complete the accumulation of merit and wisdom.

Now, we shall talk about the second topic, meditation. Meditation means to habituate, to become habituated to the practice of Dharma, to become habituated to the view. The purpose of engaging in meditation is to be able to master our mind. If we do not engage in practice here and now, we will not have much mastery or control over our mind, body, and speech.

When we try to practice shamatha meditation, the practice of calm abiding, we may not be able to focus on the object of meditation, our mind being distracted towards the objects of the five senses. Therefore, it is stated in the sutras that our mind is like a monkey. This is illustrated by the example of a monkey inside a building, the windows representing our five senses. The monkey continually jumps between these windows, always reaching out, not being able to settle down in the house. During the practice of shamatha, we need to control the five senses, seeing, talking, hearing, touching, and smelling. It is crucial to monitor the activities of our senses because our mind will engage in activities through these.

More systematically, we classify our senses in the eighteen elements or the five aggregates. The eighteen elements, or dhatus, consist of the six sense objects, the six sense faculties, and the six sense consciousnesses. When there is a form that appears to one of these elements, for example, a form appearing to the eye element, then the mind starts to engage in this object. The idea here is to stop this from happening.

One of the methods to do this is to try to block the five senses from engaging in their respective objects, so that the monkey in the house will not lose itself to each of these individual objects. Once this happens, there is a possibility that due to the force of habituation, the monkey will be able to stay inside the house. It is said that there is nothing that the mind cannot become habituated to if we give it enough time. Until we have achieved the level of shamatha, the ninth level of meditative concentration, it is a challenge to block the gross level of consciousness from going out to its respective objects.

The mind is such that it is difficult to prevent it from doing something. Mental activity is an ongoing process. When people look at their mobile phones, the mind is very concentrated because it has a job. The mind can engage in this gross kind of concentration. It is not a particularly good concentration, but it is doing something single-pointedly.

That is why chanting mantras as a basis for meditation, or meditating on deities or the breath, is something we initially feel is difficult. There is resistance. This is because the mind has become so used to being very friendly with our afflictions. But after a while, if we keep meditating, our mind will gradually let go of the afflictions, and it becomes easier and easier. If we keep on engaging in virtuous practice, like offering mandalas and doing prostrations, then over time, it will become easier and easier for the mind to settle down on its own.

This is also the case when I ask monks to do the preliminaries of Dzogchen, the ngöndro practices, completing one hundred thousand prostrations and so on. Some of them experience a lot of difficulties after they have accumulated a few thousand. Because of laziness, they are not able to do a lot of these practices. In the same way, I have a student in Asia, who struggles to meditate for half an hour, because his mind cannot remain concentrated on an object for so long. But when he goes to the casino, he can concentrate single-pointedly for twenty-four hours. This is because he has a strong propensity towards bad things. Therefore, it is said that we should not fall into the habit of harmful activities.

As already mentioned, when we use the word "meditate" here, it means to habituate ourselves to positive activities and qualities. It does not just mean to sit somewhere comfortably or sit in a meditation posture like a Buddha statue. It means to habituate ourselves in our daily life with good activities and qualities.

The Noble Eightfold Path

In general, the Buddha's teachings are very extensive and vast, but we should remember to practice the Dharma when using the three doors of body, speech, and mind. The noble eightfold path is an exceptionally good teaching for this.

The noble eightfold path here means the eight paths of the noble ones, the Aryas, the eight noble paths practiced by enlightened beings. The opposite of this can be found in the ordinary world, by ordinary beings, called the eight wrong paths. Our job is mainly to not engage in a wrong path, and instead, practice the right path. If we can walk the eightfold path of the Aryas, we too can become Aryas, noble beings. On the other hand, if we are engaging in a wrong path, then we are just ordinary beings.

In brief, the purpose of the noble eightfold path is for us to achieve the state of the noble ones. The objective is mainly to create happiness. If we engage in the wrong path, we are going to encounter suffering. Since we are all looking for happiness, we should join the eightfold path of the Aryas.

Some of us may expect to be able to practice Mahamudra or Dzogchen, the experience of the inseparability of samsara and nirvana. But if we are not able to engage in the eightfold path, then we will not be able to participate correctly in the practices of Mahamudra or Dzogchen or achieve any results from these. Most Buddhists know about the eightfold path, but also, most Buddhists are not familiar with the realization of this path, and therefore cannot attain the results.

When we talk about afflictions, we mean the polluted part of the mind. The purpose of meditation is to act as a remedy for afflictions. Otherwise, there would not be any point to cultivating meditation. What we should do is to examine whether the mind is separable from the afflictions. Some people may think that the mind and the afflictions do not have the same nature. If the mind and afflictions are of the same nature, they cannot be separated. But if they are different, they are separable.

For example, it is said that the mind is like an ocean and the afflictions are like waves. Waves rise from the ocean, but also go back to the sea, so they are the same thing. No matter how many waves or afflictions there are, they have the same nature as the ocean. Another example is that the mind and the afflictions are like water and dirt in that water. In this case, the water and the dirt are two different things. These two examples give us different perspectives.

The mind rises from the karmic winds, but if we leave it

alone, the karmic winds will settle down, and the mind will be clear. However, the mind seems to be unable to do without the afflictions. It is like the fact that we have to eat food to survive. It seems like the afflictions cannot leave the mind alone. When we look at it in this way, the afflictions are like temporary events that can be removed.

The mind and the afflictions can also be explained by the example of the sky and a rainbow. A rainbow is not the same nature as the sky. The mind is like the sky, without any color or shape, but many kinds of colors and rainbows can appear in the air. These are equivalent to the different types of afflictions that can arise in mind. By understanding it this way, we can see that the rainbow is not separable from the sky, there is no such thing as a rainbow without a sky.

When we look at the mind using these examples, we can understand the nature of mind. From my own point of view, I think we can say that the mind and the afflictions have the same nature. This is because the mind is necessary for the afflictions to arise. It is also within the mind that the afflictions subside. But in the same way that the rainbow cannot affect space, the afflictions cannot affect the mind.

It is especially important to understand the nature of mind through these various examples. When we practice meditation, we need to use these examples to introduce ourselves to the nature of the mind.

According to the teachings of sutra, we must abandon negative thoughts, and we must habituate our mind to positive qualities and beliefs. The afflictions are abandoned in stages from the first up to the seventh bhumi. Cognitive obscurations are discarded from the eighth up to the tenth bhumi.

In the sutra explanations, the view is realized by abandoning the obscurations. In addition to be able to leave the afflictions and obscurations to realize the view, we can also abandon them through the accumulation of merit, the purification of the mind, and the blessings of the guru.

The main thing here is that we need to practice meditation to habituate ourselves to the eightfold path of the noble ones. This practice is based on being mindful of the three doors of body, speech, and mind. There is no way to separate the eightfold path from the three doors. If we can make this a part of our daily life, we will surely succeed in the practice of the noble eightfold path.

The first of the eightfold path is correct view. We have already talked about this. The second is correct thought. Once we have managed to develop a correct view, we will be able to have right ideas.

We are experiencing suffering here and now because our body, speech, and mind are controlled by wrong view, which causes wrong thoughts, which again cause pain. What do we mean when we talk about right thoughts? Correct thinking means to believe in cause and effect, in karma, and have faith in the three jewels and the right view.

The third of the noble eightfold path is correct speech. Correct speech is critical because speech is compelling. The first two of the noble eightfold path are practices that involve the mind. Our speech affects the world around us to a great extent. If we engage in right speech, we will benefit ourselves and others, but if we engage in wrong speech, we will harm ourselves and others. This is the power of speech. News and information are very influential. If they are given with right speech, they will affect many people lives in the right way. If they are not, they can harm many people. When I am in Taiwan, it is evident that the news is not quality news. The news usually talks a lot about bad things, and it affects the people there quite severely. So, we can see how the media influences us. Also, education is based on speech.

So, it is vital to have correct speech in our daily lives. But also, consider that the Buddha taught that we can in fact lie to protect others, but we cannot engage in lying for the benefit of ourselves. Imagine a robber who is looking for someone specific he wants to rob, with the plan to take that person's life and money. When he asks us where he can find that person, if we tell the truth, the person can be harmed or killed so this will be harmful speech. But if we lie, we will save that person's life. Consider also, in our daily lives, when someone asks us whether they look good or not. Sometimes they will be happy if we lie a little. Perhaps you have asked such a question yourself?

The fourth of the noble eightfold path is right action. Sometimes we find that some people think that their life is not going very well. This is based on the actions we take in our daily lives. If we continue doing right actions, our lives will improve gradually, even if we cannot see the small changes directly. This is a potent approach.

When I stay in Asia, many students come to me because their lives are not going well. They have various problems, perhaps feeling that harmful spirits are making trouble for them, that they get trouble from the authorities and such things. Sometimes they also talk about the "feng shui" not being right. But when I examine, it looks like they have wrong views, and based on these wrong views, they have wrong thoughts, resulting in wrong actions. Because of this, they have a lot of problems in their lives. But sometimes, when I try to tell them that, it is tough for them to accept this, making the situation difficult. It would be easier to explain to them that their problems are due to other causes and conditions, instead of telling them that it is their own fault. Because, when telling them that it is their own fault, they cannot accept it because of strong clinging to the self. So, the main thing we need to do in our spiritual practice is to subdue the clinging to the self. To do this, we have to train the mind.

If we believe that we can entrust our happiness to somebody else, another external authority, we will never be able to achieve true happiness. We can gain temporary satisfaction, but not true happiness. This is like the saying in the *Guide to the Bodhisattva's Way of Life*, "We cannot cover the world with leather, but if we cover our feet with leather, we can protect ourselves."

The fifth of the noble eightfold path is right livelihood. When we talk about right livelihood, it means not having a wrong livelihood such as a butcher. A right livelihood should not harm others or the environment.

I have a student in Canada, who is a quite wealthy person, who told me that he could make a good deal by shipping a vast amount of meat to foreign countries, earning tens of thousands of dollars, but I advised him that this is a wrong kind of livelihood, and he accepted the advice.

In our daily life, we should not separate from the principle of right livelihood. It is important what kind of job we do. I do not know what kind of work every one of you has, but whatever job it is, it is essential to choose a position that does not harm others or the environment.

The sixth of the noble eightfold path is right effort. There are different kinds of effort. For example, it is difficult to muster the effort to do the right actions. On the other hand, it is quite easy to find the effort to engage in wrong activities.

Right effort means to have an interest in good qualities. Some people always procrastinate and postpone doing the right things, doing something wrong today, while planning to do something right tomorrow. Some people feel they need to take immediate revenge when they are poorly treated by others. If they are not able to do so the same day, or as soon as possible, they lose sleep. On the other hand, the practices of generosity, prostrations or beneficial practices, can easily be postponed until the next day, without any need for immediate action.

When we engage in right effort, it is essential that it is done with the middle way approach, as taught in the scriptures. Our effort should neither be too tight nor too lose.

The seventh of the noble eightfold path is correct mindfulness. In the *Guide to the Bodhisattva's Way of Life* it is taught that to have a good Dharma practice, both mindfulness and awareness are essential. We should continually examine the three doors of body, speech, and mind, and check whether we have fallen under the force of afflictions and whether we are accumulating adverse or virtuous actions.

When we do this examination, we should examine ourselves, not others. For example, a wife should not scrutinize what her husband is doing, and the husband should not investigate what his wife is doing. The same applies between partners and lovers. However, we tend to examine people who are the most important to us. In Dharma practice, we need to understand that it is more important to study ourselves. Practicing mindfulness should be like carrying a mirror in front of us, twenty-four hours a day, looking at ourselves. Many women carry a mirror with them to examine their faces, but in our case, the mirror is for reflecting the mind. So, mindfulness and awareness are most important for practicing the Dharma.

The final and eighth element of the noble eightfold path is right concentration. Concentration refers to meditation, and meditation in this case also means cultivation. We talk about three kinds of meditation or cultivation, analytical meditation, resting meditation, and meditation on what appears to the mind.

The practice of meditation on what appears to the mind is when we focus on an object, for example, a lamp, and place our mind on it. This is also what we do when we meditate on a deity, or whatever aspect of a deity we recall. This is a practice that most people can do.

Analytical meditation involves the practice of analyzing the reality of objects, firstly, how they appear conventionally, and secondly, achieving a valid cognition of how they appear ultimately. Once the analytical meditation has been developed to the point where we have achieved certainty in the valid cognition of the object, we can abide in that certainty. This is resting meditation.

We can use these three methods of meditation alternatingly in various situations. For example, when the mind harbors different thoughts of this and that, and we can recognize the multiple thoughts that appear to the mind, we can also call this recognition meditation for what appears to the mind. We can also analyze where our ideas come from, where they abide, and where they go. When we examine like this, this will be analytical meditation. If we analyze whether our ideas come from various sources, like an object, a condition, or a faculty, then this is also analytical meditation. Once we can achieve certainty, for example, that thoughts are magical illusions of the mind, arriving at the understanding that they have no inherent existence, we can rest upon this fact with resting meditation.

So again, the word meditation means to put ourselves in the process of habituation, and here we are talking about habituating ourselves to the noble eightfold path. If we do this in our daily life, then after some time, we will be able to realize the path of Dharma. Then our karmic afflictions will slowly reduce over time.

As far as meditation and action are concerned, we should neither fall into the extreme of being involved in the hedonistic pleasure of the senses nor asceticism, enduring extreme hardships in the name of spiritual practice. For example, if all our energy is spent on a luxurious housing, beautiful clothing, high-quality cars and so on, then this is the extreme of hedonistic pleasure and is wrong conduct. Mind you, if we already have these things in our life, then it is a different matter, but spending a lot of time to pursue these things is wrong. The main thing is that we should not dedicate a large part of our lives to run after possessions and money.

Regarding the extreme of asceticism, as an example from the past, the Tirthakas, Hindus of India, endured long periods under the sun, surrounding themselves with fires in the four directions. Observing these hardships under the hot sun, they think that they will achieve enlightenment. The Buddha said that this is not the right path. Some people also propitiate deities by inserting metal objects through their cheeks and beating themselves with a whip. These are extreme conduct, and are wrong. There are also Tibetans who practice extreme behavior. They bind their finger with string so that it becomes blue, and then they light it up like an offering lamp. This is also a wrong practice.

In brief, the conduct of the noble eightfold path should follow the middle way approach. We should also form relationships with friends and the society based on the middle way approach. Also, the relationship between the guru and the student should be based on the path of the middle way. Sometimes, if the relationship is too close, there is a danger of developing a wrong view. There is the example of the monk who served and followed the Buddha for twenty years. He was very close to the Buddha. Still, he developed a wrong view after all those years, without any progress on the path.

Our conduct is an essential factor in our daily lives when we are among different people and friends and in different cultures. We should conduct ourselves in a balanced way, neither too tight nor too loose.

In brief, to develop the right view, we should meditate by habituating ourselves to the noble eightfold path. Conduct should be done in a balanced manner. If we do this, we can achieve experience and realization along the path of the Dharma. We can produce the temporary result of happiness, as well as ultimate satisfaction. Temporary happiness here refers to a good life and rebirth as a human or god, a good financial situation, good health, and freedom from illness. Ultimate happiness refers to enlightenment as a Buddha.

This covers a brief explanation of the view, meditation, and conduct, as well as the result. Our understanding of Dharma should not be left as something we have just written down. We should not just leave it as words. When we have understood the meaning of Dharma, we will always be able to remove the superimposition of doubts that we have in our mind regarding Dharma. Through the power of learning the

Dharma, through the wisdom of learning, we can achieve a peaceful mind, and through the force of the wisdom of meditation, we can eliminate the obscurations and afflictions. Patrul Rinpoche has said that if we do not develop these qualities, then we could meditate in caves or mountains for a hundred years without any result. Such meditation would be fruitless.

Questions and Answers

Question: Meditating up in the mountains, you can feel remarkably close to nature. I do not quite understand what you are saying.

Answer: If the afflictions are eliminated, then that will be correct meditation. In a quiet place, we do not have the objects that stir up the afflictions in our mind, so our mind becomes peaceful. But if our afflictions are not eliminated, once we leave those places, they will still be stirred again by these objects. When the mind is again affected by afflictions, meditation has not been effective.

Questioner: Why is it not effective?

Answer: Because the meditation is not done in the right way.

Questioner: Yes, but in the mountains, you can also feel very natural, close to your inner nature. I have difficulties in seeing quite what you mean.

Answer: Actually, animals also feel closer to nature, but they are not achieving realization. Sometimes humans, who feel like they do not get along with others, want to stay alone like that, but because they have not understood the nature of mind, they cannot achieve realization.

Questioner: But how about Milarepa? Did he not stay in an isolated place?

Answer: Of course, the general idea is that we should stay in an isolated, quiet place for meditation, but we need to have the right understanding while doing so. If Milarepa had not had the benefit of Marpa's instructions on how to practice, he would not have been able to achieve realization.

Questioner: But through practicing the Dharma, he could get close to something high up in the mountains.

Answer: We should observe that Milarepa put in a great deal of effort, although he suffered a lot under Marpa, he practiced extremely hard and understood that he really had to apply Marpa's instructions. It is true that through his efforts he was able to achieve Buddhahood. If he had not had all those conditions, as well as right understanding and applying all this effort, then just staying in those places would not have given the same result. This advice I was referring to from Patrul Rinpoche was meant for students who had made long retreats, maybe three or even ten years long, and who felt immensely proud. But this is a wrong view, and not a sign of realization. Practice is not meant to be a way to showoff to others. The purpose of Dharma practice is to serve as a method to tame the mind.

Question: My question is regarding the right effort. I often feel resistance. Although I know that it will be good for me and maybe for others, I do not like to start doing it. This is also the same for sitting. I know it is good to do it, but then I feel this resistance. I have heard other teachers say that right effort should have an element of joyfulness. Maybe you could say something about how resistance and joyfulness relate to each other?

Answer: This seems to be a problem for most people. The main thing here is that it is also important to have the right wisdom, to understand the purity of the three elements of agent, action, and object. When we do something, we should try to avoid expectation and hope for certain things. Our mind harbors all kinds of thoughts, right thoughts, and incorrect thoughts. These are usually at war with each other. If we have more incorrect ideas, which is often the case, then the right thoughts will typically loose, and we will get all these problems that we were talking about. What we need to have is more correct thoughts, so that they can win the war. It is said that we must have the right wisdom to overcome affliction.

The way of doing this is to pay homage to the three jewels. One of the three jewels is the jewel of Sangha, our companions that give us positive support. It helps us a lot to spend more time in company with friends that support us on our spiritual path. It is a beneficial thing to do.

I am quite a lazy person. Although I like to exercise, and I sometimes do a little boxing, it is hard for me to learn languages. With this, I can be very lazy. I remember, ten years ago, Aksel paid for me to receive English tuition from an Australian man who came to Karma Tashi Ling, but I did not want to learn. So, I think this is difficult for me. Sometimes we can be lazy, so we must fight. I still hope that I will learn more English in the future. In 2001 I had this intention, but still, I have not learned much today, seventeen years later. I think around 2005, I was in London, where I had been invited to Sogyal Rinpoche's center, but I did not have a translator, so I tried to say something. They were very interested in what I had to say, and I wanted to say something, but it was difficult. When I am thinking in Tibetan and translating into English, it is difficult for me. Perhaps they understood something of what I said because they seemed happy with my efforts.

I am now forty-five years old, and I have experienced a lot of obstacles. But I believe that if I can face my obstacles, I will gain a lot of power. I do not have any fear. Before, when I was in prison in Tibet for thirty-five days, it was tough, but I was not angry, I had no fear and was not depressed, and did not react with aversion to those who imprisoned me. Also, I think I am a fortunate person. My master is an excellent practitioner. He has taught me a lot of things, so I guess it has been effortless for me to face life. I feel I have a happy life. In general, I would say I have encountered a lot of obstacles, but despite that I am glad and feel lucky.

Accepting Obstacles on the Path

Every one of us encounters the suffering of birth, old age, illness, and death, even if that person happens to be the Buddha. But in the case of the Buddha, he did not suffer when he encountered the river of birth, old age, illness, and death. We are not exempt from this process, but if we apply the Dharma, then the frustration that ensues from birth, old age, illness, and death can be hugely reduced or even overcome. In Tibet, we say that if two people are riding horses, one a competent rider, the other not knowing a single thing about horse riding, and both of them fall off their horses, the suffering experienced by these two people will vary. The pain experienced by the competent rider will be much less than that of the inexperienced rider.

We should accept everything. I think this is especially important. Sometimes we do not accept the suffering we experience, but we recognize the good things that we, for example, get from a friend. If a friend gives us trouble, we do not want to accept this.

As long as we are unenlightened and live among people, it will be unrealistic to expect only happiness and good things from others. It is the nature of sentient beings to inflict pain as well as joy occasionally. If everybody could expect both good and bad, this would be more in line with reality. Then we would, to a certain extent, be able to overcome the frustration that arises from our interactions with others.

Before, when I was young, in Tibet, I learned about good and bad emotions from my teacher, and about jealousy. I remember that it was difficult to understand jealousy because I had never experienced it. I knew I sometimes had attachments, and sometimes felt a little bit angry, or experienced ignorance. These things I knew. But as far as I could remember, I had have never known jealousy.

Desire repeatedly occurs, throughout day and night. There is for example desire for good food, better accommodation, and so forth. A desire to associate with people we like, and a desire to keep away from people we do not like. According to my personal experience, the emotion of anger visits me very seldom compared to desire. The negative emotion of ignorance is very pervasive. Like the oil that permeates a sesame seed. Therefore, it is crucial to identify spiritual ignorance. Being aware like this, we should see the importance of overcoming discursive thoughts and emotions. We try to overcome them as much as possible by resorting to various antidotes or methods.

Our existence is conditioned by desire; as human beings, we find ourselves in the desire realm. If we have not divorced ourselves from the negative emotion of desire, we will encounter difficulties with money, as well as a lack of money.

I had one student in Malaysia. In the beginning, he was rather poor, materially speaking. He then approached me and asked for advice, which he got and followed. He managed to establish a business and did quite well in his ventures. Later he married, had a child, became wealthy, got a job, got everything. But then, because of the negative emotion of desire, which is never satisfied, he had an affair with another woman, while being married to his own wife. This caused a lot of problems. Within ten years, so many changes had occurred in the life of this person, and all these changes were mainly caused by desire and attachment.

One Western ideals is to assert full freedom. But according to Buddhism, if we give free rein to our discursive thoughts and emotions, this is not total freedom. In Buddhism, freedom is instead to provide freedom to our mind, so that our mind can experience the emotional positivity of loving-kindness, compassion, harmony, and peace.

When teaching or meditation sessions become exceedingly long, we can experience physical pain or exhaustion. Therefore, it is good to alternate, for example, to offer prostrations between teaching sessions. This will ease the body and mind from being depressed.

In China, there is a mental asylum where they have a program, in which each patient must do one hundred and eight prostrations. They have termed it "The Wonderful One Hundred and Eight Prostrations," because of the benefit of doing so. This program is introduced without being connected to any religion. All the patients in the asylum practice this and experience practical benefit.

Question: I have a question about compassion. In observing myself, and I think also for members of my Sangha, I feel that many of us often have sympathy for others. I have known Lama Changchub for some years, and I think that Lama Changchub has a very unsentimental form of compassion, while I myself, and perhaps other members of the Sangha? tend to feel good when we feel sad for others. It seems that my sadness is something that looks like compassion. When I meet people, and they are in a difficult situation, I feel sorry for them, and I do things for them, but this makes them helpless. But Lama Changchub never does that, his compassion seems much purer because he never takes away self-reliance. How do I recognize foolish compassion in myself, how can my compassion be more like Lama Changchub's non-sentimental compassion?

Answer: Many people are naturally sympathetic and compassionate from the early morning. They want to make others happy. It can be very tiring to engage in this kind of sympathetic compassion, to want to be a nice person by making other people happy all the time. If we work to make others happy all the time, then we will experience frustrated compassion, because it is impossible to maintain such sympathetic compassion. If we spend time with a person who is not desperately trying to please others or make them happy but have a compassionate quality, not too apparent, the fragrance of such a relationship will transfer to us, and we will also become compassionate. That is the meaning of going for refuge to the Sangha. When we realize that a teacher or another Sangha member possesses such unsentimental compassion, that also says something about the person who witnesses it, about his or her spiritual sensitivity.

I can speak a little from my personal experience. There is no human being that is mistaken about everything, just as there is no human who is entirely unmistaken, free from all faults. Theoretically and intellectually, we know the right path as far as the noble eightfold path is concerned. And we also would like to work on and pursue this path. But since our interests or level of willpower are different, we are not always able to effectively pursue this, although we have the intention to do so. Therefore, it is vital to strengthen our willpower, so that we can stay away from the wrong path and practice the right path.

The value of human existence is determined by whether we possess compassion and wisdom. If our human life is blessed by both compassion and wisdom, then our presence becomes extremely valuable. But if the dual quality of compassion and wisdom is missing, then our existence will not be as useful as it could be.

The Taiwanese ex-president has now been in jail for something like ten years. Without compassion and wisdom, then even if we have power and money, we can end up in prison in the future. Also, in Malaysia, the current president has big problems. We are not presidents, but if we lack compassion and wisdom, our lives can turn exceedingly difficult. So, I think we should practice compassion and wisdom in our daily lives. It is crucial that we use this practice to face our lives. Sometimes we can chant or meditate, or do some different practice, and this can help our mind develop wisdom and compassion in the right away.

For example, the reason for wearing monastic robes is that they act as a support for abandoning discursive thoughts and emotions. If we, as monastics, were to engage in something that is negative and wrong, the monastic robes will help discourage us from doing that. It is a little bit like the uniform of the police.

For example, you are sitting down there listening to me up here, sitting on my elevated seat. This happens because you value how I embody compassion and wisdom. It is not because I have some worldly power.

It is essential to rely on an excellent teacher. If we relate to a bad teacher, this bad teacher might display himself as a divine being during the day, but as a devil during the night. It is like the locomotive of the train that pulls all the wagons behind. We need to make sure we are being led in the right direction.

So, I wish that every day will be happy and relaxed. Do not overthink things. Accept everything in your life. Go through all the activities you need to, and make sure that they come as close to the right path as possible. If you enter onto and welcome forth the right path, you may experience difficulties in the beginning. But when you pursue it further, you can be sure that you will become increasingly more peaceful and happier.

We have been talking about the path as view, meditation, and conduct. It is also possible to speak of the path as ground, path, and fruition. We are now going to talk about both ways. On top of this, we are going to talk about the three higher trainings: wisdom, concentration, and conduct, or discipline. Some of these things are similar. For example, in "view, meditation, and conduct," "view" is the same as "wisdom" in "wisdom, concentration, and conduct." In general, all topics of the Dharma are related.

When we try to rest in the view of emptiness, we need to understand the basis of what is empty, so we need to understand the five aggregates. If we, for example, are going to shoot an arrow, we need to know where to aim. We need to see where the target is, otherwise, we cannot hit it. In the same way, when we try to understand emptiness, we need to understand what is empty. That which is empty is the five aggregates.

If we do not understand the five aggregates, we cannot understand emptiness. So, among all possible phenomena, if we can understand what the five aggregates are, then we can understand ourselves. If we do not understand the five aggregates, we cannot understand ourselves. If we know where we came from, where we are now, and where are we going, then we will know the five aggregates.

We need to understand the nature of things so that we can be liberated from ignorance. If we do not understand this, we will not be free from ignorance. This is the difference between samsara and nirvana, the distinction of having woken up from sleep or not. If we want to wake up from ignorance, we need to know the truth of samsara and nirvana. If we are going to understand the meaning of Dharma, it is essential to have a good foundation for the Dharma. If we do not have a sound basis for the Dharma, then the process of learning and contemplation will not work correctly.

If you go through the teaching I gave previously on *The Gateway to Knowledge*, you can get some good information and understanding from it. It will be good for the body and mind. At the time, it was current knowledge given from what I had learned at the monastic university in Tibet. It was unpolluted knowledge. However, I am still fresh, there is not much change. When we eat clean, unpolluted food, we feel healthy. In the same way, the lucid explanations that were given at that time will also be beneficial.

These days most of us like to have delicious food, whether it is healthy for us or not. But the most delicious food is often not so healthy. Some food is healthy, but we do not feel like eating it. In the same way, when good lamas give precise teachings according to what the Buddha taught, the instructions may not be so easy to digest and understand, so we do not feel like listening to them, or we get bored. Other lamas may instead make things more pleasant by somewhat downplaying the teachings, to make them more interesting to listen to.

There are also cases of certain lamas, who act strangely and seem to be able to get a large gathering of students. There is a Chinese saying that goes, "When lamas are acting very strangely, they tend to get a lot of followers." For example, talking about a lot of miraculous powers in order to get more students.

When the lama is going to talk about the nature of the Dharma, he must use reasoning, logic, and analysis. The students also must engage in the process of analysis and logical thinking. This is quite difficult for most students. There are just a few students who are inclined to do this.

Whatever process we are engaged in, whether it is learning, contemplation or meditation, there is a saying that the body should be rested, and the mind should stay relaxed in the present, within the confines of the body. This instruction is very meaningful in Tibetan, although I am unsure of how the translation is sounding, whether the full meaning is conveyed.

When I first came to Norway, I would sometimes try to tell something which was supposed to be a funny joke, but when it was translated, nobody was laughing, and then I would say something quite reasonable, and people would be laughing! We all have different feelings, different views, and different cultures. So, things can appear differently to each of us.

Despite all this, the ultimate meaning, the teaching of the Buddha does not change throughout the ages. This is unlike culture and fashion that in fact do change over the generations. For example, clothing worn one thousand years ago would be considered very strange if worn today. Since the ultimate meaning the Buddha taught does not change, it can be explained today and brings the same experience as in the past. Therefore, it is imperative to rely on the ultimate meaning.

The Aggregate of Form—Seeing that All is Empty

All compounded phenomena are impermanent. This is always the case, no matter what. All that is contaminated has the nature of suffering, it has always been like this, and will always be so. These truths are the first and second of the Four Seals. The third seal is that nirvana is peace. This fact is guaranteed and signed by the Buddha himself.

Through the process of learning and contemplation, we can examine what the Buddha taught, to see whether or not it is true. When we do such an examination, we need to use the intellect. When we study and investigate, we need to know how to do so.

For example, the Heart Sutra teaches the topic of emptiness, and it is taught that "Form is emptiness, emptiness is form, form is not other than emptiness, emptiness is not other than form." The bases of what is empty is the five aggregates. So, we need to know the nature of the five aggregates. If we cannot understand the five aggregates, we will not be able to engage in a correct meditation practice. If we understand the five aggregates, we will achieve a proper experience of shamatha and vipassana. When we engage in Dharma practice, we need to do so without any mistakes or error. If we do make some errors here and there, we will fall back into samsara.

In the Heart Sutra, the Buddha taught that "there is no eye, no ear, no nose, no tongue", and so forth for all the sense-elements. But in our daily life, we think that there is an eye, an ear, a nose, and so forth, which is the opposite of what the Buddha taught. Therefore, we should look and examine for ourselves whether we have more attachment to what exists, or if we have more attachment to the things that do not exist. It is a high probability that we have an attachment to what seems to be, and this is reason the Buddha taught non-existence.

To understand the five aggregates, it is best first to recognize the first aggregate, of form. Here, the word "aggregate" means a collection of many things. When we engage in learning, contemplation, and meditation, we study the nature of the aggregates by contemplating that they are empty, that form is empty. This will show that things are dependent on each other. Emptiness is the essence of dependent origination. Because of this essence, this nature of emptiness, anything is possible, anything can happen.

If something is not empty, then nothing is possible, and nothing can happen. For example, the mirror has no shape or color by itself, but if we put something in front of it, we can see what appears to be colors and shapes in the mirror.

A form is defined formally as something that it is possible to be in contact with something else, and as something that can be examined by consciousness. A form has these two qualities. For example, take our own body; we can touch our body, we can see our body, and we can feel it, so it is a good object for examination. When we examine our body, we can gain certainty that it is empty, and we will understand that this is the nature of all other phenomena. It is therefore essential to start with our own body. This is the meaning of the saying that states that understanding the nature of one thing leads to the understanding of the nature of other things.

The body acts as a basis for the suffering that we experience. For example, it can serve as a basis for attachment, causing us to suffer afflictions. Therefore, it is essential to examine the nature of the body. The body is a basis of something that can be affected or harmed by other conditions.

The Tibetan word for form and body is the same. The body is formed by particles that have come together to constitute what we call a body. When we divide up the concept of a body, we can find the five sense elements. The five sense elements correspond to the five objects. There is also the imperceptible form. The imperceptible form is not the same kind of form as other forms, because it can only be conceived of by the sixth mental consciousness. Therefore, it is listed as the last type of form.

All the forms just mentioned are empty. Due to their emptiness, interdependent arising can occur, or we can say that because they have arisen interdependently, their nature is empty. The concept of dependently arising phenomena belongs to the conventional reality of truth, and the idea of emptiness belongs to the ultimate reality of truth. Together they form what we call the same nature with different aspects. It is a bit like making comparisons. For example, when we compare two people with their child, they become its parents.

How do we compare a person with realization with one who does not have it? A person with realization can see an object, for example, a flower. A person who is not realized will see the same object. The objects are the same, and they appear to be the same. The difference is that the person who has realization will not have any attachment to the object. It is the same object, but it will act as a cause in different ways, the object can cause the non-realized person to fall into samsara, while the other person does not. The person without realization will experience attachment to the flower, like being bound to the object, and then falling into the samsaric path. A person who has realization, whatever object they encounter, a flower or anything, is free. Because their mind experiences no attachment, they are not bound by any purpose wherever they go; they can have an open state of mind. It is a crucial point of practice, whether we have attachment or not.

There are two types of attachment, clinging to attributes and dualistic perception. Attachment as dualistic perception can be to perceive subjects and objects, to perceive good and evil, that kind of thing.

For example, when the faculty of an ordinary person meets an object, in the first instant there will be no conceptualization, then dualistic perception sets in, and once that happens, there will be attachment to the object. This process is caused by underlying ignorance. If we are not free from attachment, aversion, and ignorance, then whichever object we encounter, we will certainly experience clinging to perceptions of subject and object.

For example, when we think that we see a beautiful flower, there is an attachment. When we feel that we do not like the color of this flower, there is an aversion, and we start a process of rejection. There is an underlying affliction of ignorance, as we do not know that the nature of the flower is empty, we do not understand that the appearance of the flower is interdependent. We cling to what does not exist.

Are we looking at the flower, or is the flower looking at us? Is it the case that the flower comes to us, or is our eye consciousness going to the flower? Is it the color that is perceived by a human, or is it the color that is seen by an animal? The Buddha taught that there are six types of sentient beings and that they have different faculties. So what perception is correct? The actual reality is the reality of interdependent arising.

When we practice the Dharma, each of us has this kind of attachment with different types of clinging. We need to be free from attachment and clinging. Once we are free from them, we will be able to realize the actual reality of things.

For example, when we look at someone over there, we ourselves become what is over there for the other person. In this case, we can see that there is nothing that is unchanging. Seeing that all things are like that, we can understand that form is empty and experience realization. Have you had any experience of thinking about things in this manner? If you see a handsome man or beautiful woman, you can perhaps think like that.

If we were to employ the logical reasoning of middle way philosophy, this would be quite tedious. Even though they are exceptionally good reasonings to gain understanding, those who are lazy do not like to employ such reasoning. Lazy people can, for example, engage in the meditations in the higher levels of meditative absorption like "infinite space," "nothingness" or "neither perception nor non-perception."

Those states are very peaceful and happy. For such people, the view of the Chinese monk Hashang may be very appropriate and useful. It is somewhat similar to Dzogchen trekcho practice. There are many kinds of laziness. Some people are physically inactive. Some people are very lazy when it comes to talking. Some people are lazy when it comes to thinking.

In my case, when it comes to learning new things, I am quite lazy. But I am not physically lazy. For example, when I am in the Dharma center, I keep it clean. I am quite hard working when it comes to keeping things fresh. I also take good care of the plants and flowers in the Dharma center. I have three cats, and I also take care of them.

The Emptiness of the Indivisible Particle

Let us go back to the aggregate of form. The aggregate of form comprises the five sense elements of the eyes, ear, tongue, and so forth, having the corresponding sense objects of taste, smell, and form. As I mentioned before, there is also the imperceptible form. The imperceptible form is considered the form which arises when we take vows. It is considered a form because it is subject to harm. For example, if vows are not kept properly, they will be harmed. If the vows are broken, the body and mind will be subjected to harm, because it will lead to rebirth in the lower realm as hell beings, animals, and so forth.

There are also objects of the sixth consciousness. An example of these phenomena is the indivisible particle. It is the building block of all the forms in the three realms. The indivisible particle is not perceptible with our eye faculty, and therefore it is categorized as a phenomenon of the sixth consciousness, the consciousness of the ayatana. That form can only be perceived in proper meditation. For the practitioners of the Hinayana vehicle, this indivisible particle is the ultimate reality. For them, this indivisible particle is not empty. It exists genuinely. Although they might have an attachment to this indivisible particle, they will not be bound to samsara. It is because of this fact that Hinayana practitioners, the arhats, have realized the lack of inherent existence of phenomena. On the other hand, the Mahayana teaches that the indivisible particle does not exist within the three times, that it is beyond past, present, and future, and that it does not have any spatial direction, and this is why it is called indivisible. When we teach this form of emptiness, this is a Mahayana teaching.

In the Hinayana vehicle, it is not taught that form is emptiness. They accept that gross form is empty but believe that the indivisible particle actually exists. The approach of the Hinayana vehicle is a bit like the example of the house. The house itself represents form; the darkness inside represents ignorance. If the darkness obscures a rope inside the house, then, because of the darkness of ignorance, the rope may be misapprehended for a snake. But if we realize that the rope is a rope and not a snake, then we can be free from the darkness.

Similarly, the five aggregates are without a self. Identity has been superimposed on them. Once we realize that there exists no "I" among the five aggregates, then liberation can be achieved. We do not have to go to the extent of realizing that the five aggregates are also empty. That is not necessary for liberation.

Causal Form

To complete our discussion about form, we shall now mention the causal forms. They are the four elements of earth, fire, water, and wind. Our body is none other than the four elements that come from the father and mother, who give birth to the body. Flesh and bones constitute the earth element. Blood is the water element. The body is composed of seventy percent of water. The warmth in our body is the fire element. The breathing of our body and its movements are the wind element. These elements are called the four great elements because everything that is comprised of particles is nothing other than these four elements. When we understand that form is emptiness, we will realize that all other forms also made up of these four elements are similarly empty.

The Aggregate of Feeling—Going Beyond Hope and Fear

Now, consider the aggregate of feeling. The root of feeling is affliction. For example, we go about doing things to achieve happiness, and we also take measures to avoid things we fear. There is also the suffering of not being able to achieve what we want, and the fear of losing something we have already got. Even though we do not want to experience suffering, when any of these things happen, we will do just that.

I think that if we want happiness, we should also want suffering. Happiness and suffering are inseparable from each other. So, once we realize the nature of happiness, we will also realize the nature of suffering.

For example, if we look at how time works, when the day is gone, the night arrives, and when the night is gone, the day will arise. Suffering and happiness work in a similar way. If sometime in the future we experience happiness, suffering will be waiting for us, but later still, happiness will reappear.

Now, if we realize the basis, the sources of these two, then neither of these things will happen to us. The cause of these two is clinging, clinging to the experiences of happiness and suffering. If we can practice adequately, we can arrive at a mental state where we accept that both things will occur. It is possible for us to reach a state free from hope and fear, where all our feelings are like guests that come and go. If we cling to hope and fear, we will experience a diversity of problems. If we do not, neither of these feelings will bring us problems.

For example, I have some students in Asia who are

mothers, and who are very worried when their own children stumble and fall, but they do not react when other children fall. They have too much attachment to their own children. Both incidents are the same. Both mothers have a thread of devotion to their child. A strong reaction of "mine" provokes a different response to a similar event.

When we practice the Heart Sutra, and we experience happiness or wellbeing, we should look at the nature of that feeling, and understand that this happiness or bliss is empty, that happiness is bliss, and bliss is emptiness. Also, if a pleasant feeling arises in general, we should try to look at it in the same manner. If we engage in our practice in this way, then there is a possibility of achieving liberation in its own place, that the mind can be liberated within itself.

We need to do constant practice to understand that the body is empty, that the nature of the body is emptiness, and that emptiness forms the body.

The Heart Sutra says that "Form is emptiness, emptiness is form, form is not other than emptiness, emptiness is not other than form," going through the faculties one after the other in a repetitive way. What we need to do is to penetrate deep into the meaning of "Form is emptiness, emptiness is form" and be able to abide in this state of realization. If we, for example, are circumambulating the stupa, doing "kora," our mind can contemplate that form is emptiness, and emptiness is form, and we can try to get some certainty and abide in this while we do kora. We never know, before doing kora we are sentient beings, but we might end up as enlightened beings when we finish!.

The Aggregate of Perception—The Minister of the "I"

The third aggregate, the aggregate of perception, is a

tough one. It is tough because it is quite difficult for us to change our opinion. For example, those who adhere to specific religious or philosophical schools will mostly hold onto their perception. Usually, they do not want to change it. In general, individuals have their opinions of the people around them and the environment and do not want to change that. It is because of this people do not achieve liberation. It seems that perception is harder than diamond. It is so difficult to change. Because it is so difficult to change, it gives us problems. It also produces suffering in our body and mind.

Therefore, it is essential to learn about the aggregate of perception. The aggregate of perception is awfully close to the "I," or self. The "I" is like the king, and the perception is like the king's minister. The perception is doing the work for the "I." This is why the Buddha taught that we need to abandon wrong views. This can be related to freedom from elaboration. The view is like the rays of the sun. The sunrays do not have any wish to shine on any specific place or through any certain windows, or upon good or bad people. If somebody is liberated from clinging, that person can be like the wind, able to go wherever he or she likes.

The nature of the aggregate of perception is the apprehension of signs or attributes. The Buddha gave many different teachings because people have different viewpoints, he gave different kinds of teachings to bring freedom from different kinds of opinions. The Buddha did not provide different types of instructions to create a big group of followers. He also did not teach for the sake of politics. Neither did he teach to get power. The Buddha gave these teachings because every sentient being suffers from different kinds of illnesses, and it is to cure these illnesses that he gave different lessons. As an analogy, we should use the correct medicine to cure a certain disease.

When we meditate, we may experience that on certain occasions anger or resentment arises in our mind. When this happens, it would be good to meditate on love and compassion. For example, if attachment or desire appears in our mind, we should contemplate or meditate on the unpleasantness of the body or the object. For myself, I must say that "ugly" is a strange concept.

When we feel that ignorance prevails in our mind, we should contemplate dependent arising. When we recognize that we have strong pride, we should examine the six elements, constituting the five forces of earth, water, and so forth, as well as the element of the mind, a total of six. For example, the Dalai Lama has pointed out that the people in each of the four directions are all made of the same elements. So, what makes us so unique? Everybody is made of the same elements, the same substances, so there is no difference. The cars in Germany and Japan are the same, they consist of the same material, even if the color and shapes are different.

Releasing Thoughts and Concepts in Meditation

If we recognize that we have many strong thoughts and concepts, it would be good to meditate on our breath. When we do this, we can count the breaths to calm the thoughts, for example by counting from one to ten. We put our attention on the nostrils and start counting. This practice involves keeping our focus there, without forgetting to count the breaths.

There is also another method where we place our consciousness on the out-breath, letting the mind follow the out-breath all the way out, down to the soles of the feet. On the in-breath, the mind then follows the breath all the way up to the nostrils and in. There are these methods, as well as several others, to practice shamatha meditation, to appease the thoughts. It is also greatly beneficial to calm thoughts if we practice some yoga. When we continue to practice shamatha in this manner, then after some time, we will experience a light body and mind. This experience is called pliancy or workability of body and mind.

In brief, if we have the right perception, it will help us to achieve the state of enlightenment. On the other hand, if we have wrong perception, it will cause us to fall into samsaric states. If we can recognize the nature of perception, then we can remain happy whether we are alone or in the company of others. When we are in the company of others, we will be able to make others happy.

If we have a strong attachment to an object, we will end up arguing with others who do not like that object. They will make us unhappy, and we will make them miserable. More generally, we can see that there are a lot of arguments and disagreements in the world and that these stem from different perceptions. We can see this happening between countries, and between different races and religions. It even happens between husbands and wives, and among friends. All these disagreements occur for the sake of defending our perceptions.

When we can abandon clinging to our perceptions, it will soften up our character; the more we can surrender and reduce this clinging, the softer the character. To do this, we can apply the statement in the Heart Sutra, "Form is emptiness," to perceptions, giving "Emptiness is not other than perception, perception is none other than emptiness."

The Aggregate of Formation—The Innumerable

Now we have come to the fourth aggregate, the aggregate of formation. In general, the aggregate of formation refers to karma, or action. There is also the non-associated formation. The feature of the non-associated formation is that it is neither the nature of the mind nor is it the nature of form. So, it is not something that truly exists. All the fifty-one mental factors are also included in the aggregates of formation. Both virtuous and non-virtuous thoughts belong to the aggregate of formation.

When we look at the various thoughts we have, we can see that some have a virtuous nature, and some have a non-virtuous nature. This is not unusual. The enumeration of mental factors is infinite, but the Buddha summarized them into fifty-one mental factors as a brief explanation.

There are fourteen types of non-associated formation. For example, when someone has attained the state of Buddhahood, but actually we cannot say that it is something that has been attained. For example, it is said that the state of not seeing anything is the best type of seeing. And in the same way, that non-attaining is the best form of attaining. As another example, the statement that everybody has the same worth is a phenomenon that is existing as a form.

By contemplating in the same manner as before, we can observe that the nature of thoughts is emptiness, that emptiness is not other than thoughts and thoughts are not other than emptiness.

Mind you, the practice of meditating on emptiness that we do here is a practice of meditating on something that is non-existent. It is not like when a tiger is coming at us, and we start to meditate frenetically, "There is no tiger, there is no tiger." If we do that, we will end up being eaten by the tiger. Clearly, this does not work. It has to be a practice where we realize what is real, determine the actual case of the situation, and meditate on that.

The Aggregate of Consciousness

The last aggregate is the aggregate of consciousness. To understand the aggregate of consciousness, we need to understand the mind. Mind and consciousness are synonyms.

The five sense consciousnesses together with the mental consciousness make six. On top of these six, there is the afflicted mind. Then there is the sub-consciousness, or the alaya consciousness, giving a total of eight. Sometimes, in addition to these eight consciousnesses, we also talk about the immediately preceding consciousness.

The first to the fifth consciousnesses are called the five

doors to the five faculties. In general, the five sense consciousnesses are directed outwards. They do not recognize the inner mind, because they are non-conceptual. They are only able to recognize what is happening on the outside and cannot know what is happening on the inside. If we are only able to perceive the outside, we cannot abandon the afflictions and negative karma. For example, you can see me, but can you perceive yourself? If you happen to see me as good looking, then you might have positive thoughts, but if I do not appear nice to you, you might have negative thoughts. But you cannot perceive your own self.

Another example is the crane, the bird with long legs, standing in muddy water, when it bends its long neck down into the water to see a frog. The frog sees the legs of the crane, and it might tell the crane that its legs are filthy. But the whole body of the frog itself is foul.

Because our consciousness is directed outward, we can easily perceive if somebody stinks, but it is difficult to detect our own odor. The power of the nose does not seem to reach the armpit. Sometimes, we do not listen very well to what we are saying, but we hear very well what others say. Because of this, we tend to talk about the faults of others, but hardly about our own. If we were talking about our own faults even twenty percent of the time, that would be quite good. It is not easy to experience our own body, but if we can achieve a certain level of meditative stability, then we would experience bodily bliss and physical wellbeing. Instead, we often try to dress up nicely to make others feel good.

Because of all this, we end up placing our hope for happiness on external things. We try to do things to achieve happiness and wellbeing by, for example, wearing nice clothing or nice items based on the expectation of others. In a romantic relationship, we try to adorn the relationship with nice things to make each other happy. So, we end up relying on external things for happiness. If we instead can find meaning within ourselves, through meditative stabilization, then we can experience joy from within.

Our challenge is that the five sense consciousnesses are always looking outward, and we quickly end up projecting our hopes and expectations on external things. It is a fact that we cannot always get happiness from these five senses. We cannot always perceive sweet smells, we cannot always see pleasing forms, we cannot always have good tastes, and we cannot always live in good houses or wear nice, comfortable clothing. It is not possible for us to always encounter such conditions. But if we were to change the flow of our inner conceptual mind, then due to the power of this conceptual mind, we would be able to influence the five sense consciousnesses through practice. When we do that, because of the changes that take place in the conceptual consciousness, then we would be able to make good use of our five sense consciousnesses, instead of just following them. Otherwise, we will be in a situation where our five sense consciousnesses are forever going outwards, making contact with whatever objects are over there, and then send signals to the mind that the mental consciousness makes judgments about, like "this is good" or "that is bad."

The five sense consciousnesses are not able to do anything else other than going back and forth as messengers, bringing signals back and forth. So, we can see, among all these consciousnesses, it is the mental consciousness that is the most important. I have heard of meditation systems where they block all the five sense consciousnesses. But if we do this, we will have trouble. In Tibetan Buddhism, there are no meditation methods where we block off the five sense consciousnesses.

The mental consciousness has two aspects, conceptual and non-conceptual. Then there is the afflicted mind, the seventh consciousness. The focal object of the seventh consciousness is the alaya consciousness. The nature of the afflicted mind is to perceive an "I" or self and generate clinging to this self. This clinging is the pride of being "I." This is ignorance. The afflicted mind has these four features, seeing the "I," clinging to the "I," taking pride in the "I," and the underlying ignorance. The afflicted mind is always present. It is present while we have not achieved the first bhumi. Most likely, we all have this afflicted mentality. We can see that we have this concept of the "I," because we do have pride in ourselves, and there is ongoing ignorance.

Feeling Well off

We may think that we are extraordinarily rich. This is contrary to how realized beings such as Milarepa experience wealth. When people looked at Milarepa, they believed that he was totally destitute. However, Milarepa felt that he was wealthy. The reason for the difference in perception is that Milarepa had contentment, and others did not. Therefore, he thought that he was always rich. One of the qualities of the afflicted mind is the desire of the self. This desire will never be satisfied.

Some scientists say that if everybody on the planet would be as well off as the wealthy Europeans, then there would not be sufficient energy and resources to sustain everybody on this planet. We would have to move to another place, like the moon or something. We can see that in the past there were fights and wars for the sake of land and resources. Similarly, in the future, there might be fights and battles over this, which perhaps might even escalate to outer space. In the future, maybe it is possible that we discover a new planet. Then we would quarrel over who owns that planet. Whoever discovers it will lay claim to it and think that they own it because they were there first.

One of the most critical things in Dharma practice is to have little desire and be content. Also, we should try to be humble, have a pure mind, and not be too ambitious. If we are too eager, we will end up bringing harm to others.

The Subconscious

We will now talk about the eight consciousnesses, the alaya, or the subconscious. The alaya consciousness can be explained as the basis for samsara and nirvana. The reason is that for samsara to be produced, there needs to be a seed, or cause. The seeds of samsara are placed in the alaya consciousness. To achieve the state of enlightenment, we need to gather the two accumulations of merit and wisdom. Those two accumulations are also placed in the alaya consciousness, and they are placed stably; they cannot be lost or destroyed.

When the potential for a habit is stored in the alaya consciousness, it will be extremely hard to change. For this reason, it is challenging to eliminate the obscurations. In Tibetan, the literal translation of the alaya consciousness is two syllables meaning "all" and "base." The word "all" is used because it includes everything else. "Base" is used because it is the support for everything. For example, the basis for the four elements is space. Similarly, the basis for samsara and nirvana is the alaya consciousness. Therefore, it is called the basis for all. The nature of the alaya consciousness is such that it is neither virtuous nor non-virtuous. The quality of the alaya consciousness is neutral. Because of this nature, it is possible to accumulate both virtue and non-virtue.

The Continuity of the Aggregates—The Nature of Dependent Arising

We have now gone through the eight consciousnesses that are the fifth aggregate. If we analyze the nature of the five aggregates further regarding karmic cause and effect, we can see that the aggregates of the previous life become the five aggregates of this life. And the aggregates of this life become the cause for the aggregates of the next life.

Because we are unable to see the aggregates of the

previous life, some of us do not believe in the existence of previous lives. Also, we are not able to perceive the aggregates of a future life. This is because the aggregates of the previous life have ceased, so we are not able to see them, and the aggregates of the future life have not yet arisen. Therefore, some of us do not accept reincarnation, while others do.

Once, in the past, in Beijing, China, a Tibetan lama met Mao Zedong. Chairman Mao told him that he did not believe in the existence of past life, because he could not see it, so the lama replied to him, "Do you believe in tomorrow?" "Yes, I do," answered Chairman Mao. "But you can't see it, so why do you believe in it?" answered the lama. Consequently, Chairman Mao was forced to admit he had a good point.

If the continuity of the aggregates of the past could not extend to today, we could not have the present aggregates. If the present aggregates could not continue, then the future aggregates would not be able to exist.

Other than these explanations that I have given, there is also an explanation of the five aggregates in the sutras, on how the aggregates move in the various phases, in the bardo between lives, into the womb, and then onto the next life.

One example of how the aggregates move from one life to another is as follows: If I were to recite "OM MANI PADME HUNG" to somebody who previously did not know it, and he or she listened to the sound, then he or she could learn it and be able to say it themselves. It may look like the form has moved from me to another person, but there is no movement. If there were an actual movement, I would end up forgetting or losing my ability to say the mantra myself, but clearly, it does not work that way. Instead, it functions in the manner of cause and effect. Based on the cause of the sound that I indicated, the other person gets the result of understanding it. In general, it is difficult for sentient beings to understand how cause and effect works. Therefore, it is good to contemplate this occasionally.

A butter lamp is another example to illustrate this topic. Consider a series of butter lamps, where each lamp is used to light the next, one after each other. It is not the case that the flame moves from one to the other. The lamp in front is the cause of the next one to be lit.

If we analyze in this way and gain understanding, we do not have to be afraid that one day we will lose the continuity of our aggregates and die. They will continue as a cause from one place to another. We should prepare to make a sound basis for the new aggregates in the next life, like preparing a lot of good butter lamps in advance to ensure the stable continuity of the bright flame. However, it is not possible for the aggregates to cease. If the aggregates do reach cessation, that would be the cessation of nirvana.

The third example is the example of a mirror. When we stand in front of a mirror, although our form appears in the mirror, our form does not actually move or transfer itself into the mirror. If that were so, we would lose our form. It is not like we see in the movies, where people can teleport themselves from one place to another.

The nature of dependent arising is very amazing. It is the nature of becoming into existence. For example, when I make a phone call from Norway to Tibet, does my voice arrive in Tibet or not? If we look carefully, this can only happen when there are all sorts of causes and conditions coming together. All the details are inconceivable.

We can also analyze by using the example of planting a seed, and observing it growing into a tree or plant. Does the seed transfer itself into the shape of a plant or not? We should ask this kind of questions to ourselves, and when we think about and contemplate it, there is a chance to understand the ultimate truth.

Our life is such that sometimes we also ask questions that are not beneficial. This can be questions like, "I tried this and that to impress this beautiful girl or handsome boy, but why does she or he still not like me?" We often ask ourselves questions like this, but we should instead ask ourselves questions that are more beneficial. Also, we might wonder and ask questions like why some people have this or that item and are rich, and why am I not. Or we may sometimes wonder why am I being inflicted by this or that illness? Why not other people… why me? Again, these are not particularly useful questions.

When we see somebody consume something sour, like a lemon, saliva will also start to flow in our own mouth. But it is the other person that eats it, not us. So how does this generate a similar experience? There is also the example of a voice that leaves the mouth and creates an echo in some locations. How does it happen? How can the sound that goes from the mouth come back? The reason for these kinds of occurrences is that based on previous aggregates of forms, and so forth, the future aggregate arises.

There is also the example of the magnifying glass. We can ask how the magnifying glass functions, how it can direct the fire from the sun to a spot to burn something. The continuity of the five aggregates is possible because of the combination of afflictions, karma, and consciousness. This is like the magnifying glass, using the sun to generate fire in the grass. We cannot tell if the fire arises from the sun, the grass, or the magnifying glass.

All these examples are various methods that help us to understand the nature of dependent arising. The Buddha gave eight cases to explain the function of dependent arising. I think I can come up with a ninth example. If I were to yawn, then another person seeing that will also start yawning. (A little joke.)

As we have seen, it is not the case that the aggregates flow from one place to another. It is because of the condition of the previous aggregates that the current or future aggregates exist. The Buddha said that those who are wise should know this.

In brief, this is how we can understand that the nature of the five aggregates is emptiness. And because of emptiness, we can have the five aggregates. In the famous saying, "Form is emptiness, emptiness is form, emptiness is not other than form, form is not other than emptiness," the first one, "Form is emptiness," acts as a negation, negating the arising of self. Form can arise from four possibilities, from itself, from other, from both or neither. This is all explained in the philosophy of the Middle Way, by asking questions like "Does something arise from itself? Does something arise from another?"

We have now talked about the nature of the five aggregates, how they arise, and how they move from one state to another. The critical point here is to understand that although it appears that they arise, the fact is that there is no arising, and although they seem to cease, there is no ceasing.

Existence and Non-Existence

We usually accept existence or non-existence. One of the reasonings that is used in the Middle Way philosophy is the example of planting a seed. When we plant a seed of a tree or plant, we can get much fruit. We can ask, at the time of planting the seed, is the fruit already present within the seed? If the fruit is already present, there is no need for the tree to bear fruit again. If the fruit is not present, it is not possible to bear fruit, because the fruit does not exist. The fruit cannot both exist and not exist at the same time.

If we say that something does not exist and that it still somehow can exist at the same time, then we should be able to have flowers growing in the sky, but this is not possible. There is also the example that there cannot be hair on the back of a tortoise. These are the types of analogies that are presented in the philosophical school of the Middle Way. If we do not engage in reasoning like this, we cannot achieve the realization of emptiness. In the same way, we use analysis for the three other possibilities, to conclude that the self cannot arise from itself, from another, from both or neither.

The purpose of the first line of the Heart Sutra, "Form is emptiness," serves to liberate us from the view of permanent existence. The second line, "Emptiness is form," frees us from clinging to nihilism. The third one, "Emptiness is not other than form," serves to liberate us from the view of both permanent existence and nihilism. The last line, "Form is not other than emptiness," serves to free us from any other possible views other than the views of permanence and nihilism.

We also need to analyze from different perspectives. Some yogis like Milarepa probably had a lot of potential accumulated from practicing in their past lives. In their previous life they may not have achieved realization, but in this life, as the continuation of their last journey, having met with a good guru and put in good effort, and also due to various causes and conditions, they achieved realization.

In the same way, as Guru Rinpoche said, there are different types of people with different faculties, some with lesser faculties may be weak or dull-minded, but through their strong faith in the guru, they can achieve realization. There are also those of extremely high intelligence, and through that, they can achieve realization. But Guru Rinpoche said it is quite difficult for those who are in between, who are neither highly intelligent nor dull. It seems likely that most people belong to the intermediate category. Therefore, not many people achieve enlightenment.

Questions and Answers

Question: You explained about the eight consciousnesses, the five sense consciousnesses, the mind consciousness, the afflicted consciousness, and the alaya consciousness. These are all the ordinary consciousnesses, the deluded consciousnesses. My question is, is rigpa outside of this, and how can I recognize rigpa?

Answer: We can conceive our own mind. We have this cognitive ability that can be aware of whatever might be. This is the natural clarity of the mind. This is what is commonly called rigpa, but your question might have been about rigpa in the context of Dzogchen. In this case, one way of explaining it is that at enlightenment, the alaya goes through a transformation where it transforms into wisdom itself, that is the actual rigpa. The current state of the sub-consciousness is that it is contaminated by ignorance, and once the transformation is free from ignorance, then it becomes rigpa, or wisdom. When we talk about the tathgatagarba, Buddha-nature, the difference between samsara and nirvana is whether we can recognize the Buddha-nature or not. There exists a debate on whether the mind-consciousness and rigpa are of the same nature or not; there are all sorts of discussions on this topic. According to the explanation of Dzogchen, all phenomena of samsara and nirvana are complete within the mind itself. Therefore, it is like being in the state of enlightenment. It is like the sun shining in the sky, free from clouds. But if we want to receive a simple explanation, we could say that consciousness transforms into wisdom.

Norway is a perfect place for meditation. Sometimes, when I am in Shanghai, which is a huge city, full of people, I get stressed. Also, I am building a Dharma center there. It cost a lot of money, and many students there are doing business to help. So, I experience stress. Also, in Tibet, I have a monastery, there is one school for the monks, and another school for laypeople. I have had to face a lot of obstacles. But also, I am delighted when I get good food. All Tibetans like food, and so do the Chinese. Some people give me different cars, like Lexus and BMW. But all these things sometimes give me a lot of stress. Maybe it would have been better without them, without the monastery, without the schools, without the cars, without the houses, without the centers. Sometimes I think like this. I remember being incredibly happy before, in Tibet. At that time, I did not have anything, and life was very peaceful. But now, with four centers in Taiwan and three centers in Malaysia, I also enjoy a different kind of life. It is hard work every day. Maybe you get your weekends off. I do not have free time on weekends, Saturdays and Sundays are always terribly busy, because a lot of people come to see me.

In Asia, people are very hospitable. Some people that visit the center in Malaysia stay until midnight! And after that, they go out to a restaurant for a meal, perhaps going to bed at 2 am. I usually go to bed around eleven pm, but sometimes it is too noisy to sleep, because it is like a party at the center, with people talking and laughing. I do not know what they are talking about, but they sound incredibly happy. The reason people stay up late in Malaysia is that it is extremely hot. We cannot go outside in the daytime, but nighttime is wonderfully peaceful, and the temperature is pleasant. Therefore, many sleep during the day, and use the night to go out and enjoy themselves or have a party. Also, we have big pujas. One time in Taiwan, we had a puja with about one thousand eight hundred people. In Malaysia, we also have such big pujas.

I now speak Mandarin very well. Because of this, I can help a lot of people. They can understand the Buddha-dharma and support themselves, their family and business. It is also helpful for love. Dharma is helpful for everything, you know. Dharma can assist us in all aspects of our life, not only enlightenment. Love, when not selfish, will become much better between husband and wife. Also, business grows better when it is unselfish. By increasing compassion and wisdom, the Dharma can be of help for everything. Only thinking about enlightenment can make the Dharma seem extremely far away. The Dharma is something that should be practiced within the context of our daily lives, and this also becomes the process in which enlightenment takes place. Because enlightenment is free from suffering, free from bad karma, free from bad emotions, and free from ignorance, life is peaceful, I think.

Sometimes people tell me, "I don't like this world. I do not like human beings. I want to go to a pure land." I reply to them "if we think like that, maybe Amitabha will not accept us because our mind is too impure and we will end up polluting the pure land. Instead, if we one day choose to think that everybody is perfect and the world is a lovely place, that could be the actual pure land."

For example, we will not start to argue and fight with a small child if it does something wrong. In the same way, it is a matter of how much wisdom and love we have for others. Someone, who knows how to accommodate others can be called a bodhisattva. If we cannot assist others, it is not possible to be a bodhisattva. Some people may think a certain person is no good, and want to stay away from them, but it is not bodhisattva conduct to want to be away from people. Bodhisattvas do not stay away from people.

Daily Practice

We have the aspiration prayer, "May I always have bodhicitta, and never be separated from bodhicitta," but at times it seems that we are praying, "May we never be separated from money," "May we never be separated from our partners," or "May we never be separated from power." Even if we want to practice being a bodhisattva and pray, "May all sentient being be free from suffering," and so on, we sometimes get angry and lose bodhicitta. We suddenly may want to beat other people, with a face that resembles a wrathful deity. This is not good.

In the morning when we get up, we should pray and take refuge in the Buddha, Dharma, and Sangha. We can say, I hope that I can help people today and that I can help myself. Just like this, the Buddha, Dharma, and Sangha will give me power, good energy and karma, and supreme wisdom and compassion, so that I can face everything today without anger, without attachment, without any other harmful emotions. If we can pray like this in the morning, there will be a lot of auspiciousness in our life. I say the day can be "Tashi delek!"

At the end of the day, when we lay down to sleep, we can think about what we did today. If we did something bad, we can get up and perhaps do a hundred prostrations. Then we can sleep. If we have done good things, we can get up and give ourselves some ice cream! We can reward ourselves like this sometimes.

If we always think about what we have done, good or bad, we can change and improve. If we are willing to change, then we can improve. If we do not want to change, then we cannot develop our mind, our speech, or our physical actions. I think it is vital to be patient in order to be successful. If we cannot be patient, we will not achieve anything in our lives.

From when I was seven until I was twenty-three, my master taught me many things. At that time, I did not have good house or good clothes. Sometimes I got good food. Sometimes I got bad food. Many times, mice were eating my rice, noodles, and tsampa, and leaving their droppings behind. It was a difficult time. We did not have any fruit. We did not have any vegetables or meat. Sometimes we only had tsampa. I remember one friend who did not have warm clothes. Fortunately, my parents had given me a genuinely nice sweater for the winter, but I thought he must have been freezing. My master started teaching at 7 o'clock in the morning in the big house, and it was extremely cold. There was no electricity, no heating, no cushions, we just sat on the floor—very, very cold. I was looking at my friend shivering with cold, so I gave my sweater to him. Perhaps not quite like Milarepa, but still similar. It was nice.

Even if I experience a lot of obstacles, I do not have any fear. I think I will have an easy life. The Buddha went through six years of suffering austerity. Although it was not quite the same, I would say that maybe I went through sixteen years. My master did not want us to leave the monastery, meaning I could not go to Kandze city, which was my birthplace. If I had gone back home, I would have been more comfortable. But the road was in bad condition. From Kandze to Dzogchen Monastery took about two days at that time. Today it takes only two and a half hours by car. Now, the road is excellent. There has been a huge change.

Now in Dzogchen Monastery, everything is nice and

beautiful. But twenty years ago, it was tough. I think that if we want to practice, we should be patient. Then things will happen in our life.

Having a peaceful mind is important. If we practice very well, we can be very peaceful when we die. We can think of it as a beautiful ending, saying goodbye, wishing everybody good luck, without crying. My father had an outstanding practice. He was not a monk, but he practiced all the time for twenty years, in the morning and the night, every day. He was very compassionate. When he died, he had no tears. He only said to me, "Oh, I am ill, Sangpo, I am extremely ill, maybe I will die, I am ready to die, but I am still not dying. It is extraordinary!" When he did die, his body remained warm for three or four days. Many lamas saw his face. It was very peaceful. There was no bad smell. His body was brought to Dzogchen Monastery. My master came out of retreat to perform phowa for my father. I think he had a wonderful life.

Today we are here together. Karma has connected us with the Dharma. Not power, not money, not romance. We are here to learn the Dharma. Meditation is important. What we do in our daily life is more important than formal practice. Be kind, and always try to awaken your mind. Thank you!

Commentary on Patrul Rinpoche's teaching on Hitting the Essence in Three Words

Introduction

All beings of the three planes of existence pursue happiness. Still, we often seek this by means and methods that produce suffering. On the other hand, the Buddhist techniques that we use to find true happiness, and to abandon causes and conditions that induce pain, are valid. In Buddhism, we regard the means and methods that are propounded by these teachings as an excellent means to overcome frustration and attain genuine happiness.

If we cultivate the spirit of bodhicitta, or awakening, then this will suffice on this path. But if we lack that, we are missing something spiritually significant. If we separate from the precious mind of bodhicitta, it will be like a bad seed, not being able to sprout, and we will not be able to experience ultimate peace and happiness. Cultivating the precious mind of bodhicitta is essential in the beginning, in the middle, as well as in the end. Therefore, at the very outset of this session, when we are about to listen to this Dharma discourse, we should start by generating the precious mind of bodhicitta.

The theme that we are going to delve into is "view, meditation, and action" in Vajrayana. The immediate transmission of the lineage of this specific teaching goes back to my principal root guru, Padmasambhava. I have not only received Vajrayana teachings on these specific instructions but most of the other Vajrayana teaching instructions also. Therefore, the transmission goes back to my principal root guru. It is good to have gotten the transmission of all the Vajrayana teachings from a single master. It is rather easy to develop a sacred outlook when having a specific master.

Through fortune, I came across this excellent teacher, who is not only knowledgeable about the teachings but also put these teachings into concrete practice. He does not do wrong things. Therefore, it is effortless to develop a pure perception, and so develop devotion towards him. Since I have been his student and got all the Vajrayana transmissions, I will follow in his footsteps. My behavior will not be unruly or undisciplined. Therefore, you can trust me. You do not need to fear that you will lose your feeling of spiritual connectedness with me.

When it comes to sharing or distributing Vajrayana transmissions, it is easy to do this just by talking or reading. It is also easy to bestow Vajrayana empowerments. But it is somewhat challenging to elucidate the Vajrayana instructions given. Most teachers merely transfer Vajrayana transmissions through reading oral translations and bestow empowerments. There are fewer Vajrayana masters who can expound the hidden inner meaning by giving liberating instructions and ripening empowerments. This is important to help the student progress.

If we have not completed the preliminary practices, we are not given the advanced form of the Vajrayana instructions. So today is an exceptional case. I think that you are excellent students, so I trust that you are perfect vessels into which the precious Vajrayana instructions can be poured. Also, Karma Tashi Ling is not a new Buddhist center. It is rather old. Many of you have come to Karma Tashi Ling and received preliminary instructions. You have therefore, to some extent, laid a sound foundation to be suitable vessels. Consequently, I can impart the transmission of the Vajrayana instructions today. I will base this teaching on the original teachings given by the learned master Garab Dorje, which was elucidated by Patrul Rinpoche.

There are many distinguishing factors of the vehicles of Sutrayana and Vajrayana. However, when Vajrayana teachings are being presented, it is taught that this vehicle is potent, the reason being that Vajrayana contains many skillful means to trigger a spiritual awakening. Another distinctive feature of the Vajrayana is that we can attain spiritual awakening without exhausting ourselves by going through spiritual asceticism. Generally, Vajrayana transmissions are given to the student that has exceptional intelligence. Let us suppose that we belong to this category of students.

Homage to the Master

In the very beginning of the root text, the author pays tribute to his spiritual guide. The reason being that in the Vajrayana path, the lama is regarded as the embodiment of all the three jewels and all Buddhas and bodhisattvas. The lama is also viewed as the embodiment of the three kayas or bodies of the Buddha. The development of pure perception or sacred outlook of all phenomena depends on our spiritual guru. Therefore, Patrul Rinpoche, in his commentary, establishes the validity of the Vajrayana view, meditation, and conduct by citing the names of his three gurus, saying that the view is the Dzogchen master Longchen Rabjam. The name Longchen Rabjam means "infinite expanse." Infinite expanse, or dimension, suggests that the multitude of appearances of the relative truth is contained within the expanse of the dharmata, the ultimate reality.

There is an expression in Vajrayana, which states that all appearances are the mental proliferation or projections of our subjective mind. Because of this, if we modify our mind, we can also change outward appearances. Through the attainment of the realization of the nature of our mind, we can also attain the understanding of the nature of all phenomena.

In Vajrayana, another expression states that knowing one thing liberates all. "One thing" refers to understanding the nature of our mind through hearing, listening, contemplation, and meditation. It is said to be like a self-sufficient king because if we realize the quality of our mind, this is sufficient for understanding the nature of everything. The nature of mind is not confined to certain specific beings. It permeates equally every living being.

When we talk about view, there is a viewer and whatever is being viewed. In this case, what is being observed is the intrinsically abiding Buddha-nature. We all have the reality of the Buddha-nature. But not everybody is capable of seeing their own Buddha-nature. The reason it is so difficult to see our own Buddha-nature is that we are conditioned to view objects in a dualistic manner. But it is not possible to consider the Buddha-nature in a dualistic way.

At this stage, the crucial thing is to attain a precise understanding of Buddha-nature as emptiness, or primordial purity. This emptiness is none other than the ultimate nature of the Buddha, the dharmakaya. The Buddha-nature is also sometimes referred to as primordial purity. This primordial purity or emptiness is not a constructed emptiness; it is an intrinsic emptiness from the very beginningless beginning. That is why it is called primordial purity or emptiness.

This spiritual dimension of intrinsic emptiness is the natural state of the dharmakaya, the ultimate reality of the Buddha. The ultimate nature of the Buddha, the dharmakaya, defies the duality of attainment and non-attainment. The question of obtaining the final state of dharmakaya is inapplicable, and the question of not achieving the ultimate state of dharmakaya is likewise irrelevant. The essence of Buddha-nature is empty. However, its nature abides as clarity or luminosity. It is not one-sidedly empty. It is co-existent with clarity and radiance.

Likewise, the transparent nature of our mind is sambhogakaya, which is the enjoyment body of the Buddha. These spiritual qualities of the mind do not decrease nor increase. They are as they are. Ordinary, unenlightened sentient beings possess these two qualities of the Buddha. As an example, a regular light that is constructed by people, being a composite phenomenon, is subject to decrease. However, the light that comes from something that is uncreated knows no decrease or increase. For example, the sun is naturally radiating light, but this light knows no decrease nor increase. The natural clarity of the mind is the natural expressivity of the essential emptiness of the mind. Clarity and emptiness are not different things. Emptiness expresses the aspect of clear-light.

The third nature of our mind is the all-pervasive compassionate mind. This is represented by the third body of the Buddha, the nirmanakaya, the emanated form of the Buddha. The word for compassion in Tibetan is "tok-je." "Tok" generally refers to our mind, "je" means lord. It can be understood as the king of the mind, which is none other than the compassionate mind. In this context, the all-pervasive compassionate mind is entirely different from the compassionate mind we develop on the lower levels of the Buddhist path. Here, the all-pervasive compassionate mind recognizes the oneness of each and everything, the unity of all diversity. Therefore, this mind knows no limit. Hence it is said to be infinite.

The reason it is called infinite all-pervasive compassion is that it transcends dualistic perception of subject and object. Ordinarily, we experience the positive emotion of love and compassion. But for us, this positive emotion is mostly sentimental or romantic love and compassion, which is rooted in dualistic perception. A dualistic positive feeling that is rooted in dualistic understanding will, in the end, lead to frustration, whereas an emotional positivity of love and compassion that is not based on dualistic perception will not evolve into frustration. However, we are entirely unaware even of this third quality of the Buddha-nature of our mind. We only know ordinary love and compassion, and so forth, which are based on dualistic perception. Therefore, we are not able to liberate ourselves from fixation of dualistic perception. Thus, the spiritual qualities of our own Buddha-nature are deeply hidden, like a treasure within the depth of our being, but we are not able to acknowledge or recognize them.

Generally, human beings like to divide things up to classify things. We love to attain something that is significant and of high value, but we lose ourselves in the many nonessential things that prevent us from achieving what is most significant. For example, we all inhabit the same planet Earth, but human beings have succeeded in dividing the globe into many countries with borders. This division into many nations is the working of our dualistic mind, but from the nature of the earth itself, there are no dividing factors. The Earth is one.

In these instructions, we are first told how to establish a valid view, and then how to combine it with a continued meditation practice. The view is said to be Longchen Rabjam, the infinite expanse, or infinite spiritual dimension. This view needs to be sustained through continued meditation. Therefore, meditation is said to be Khyentse Öser, rays of wisdom and compassion.

Applying this view in meditation reveals insight, making the meditation become vipassana meditation. From this understanding of the view comes the light of compassion. This compassionate practice is the practice of shamatha, which is tranquility meditation. Insight meditation, or vipassana meditation, can be understood as something that is very stable, steady and balanced. When we practice the union of vipassana and shamatha, our meditation will be luminous and clear as the light of the sun, and at the same time very steady, stable, and balanced.

In the Vajrayana pith instructions, we talk about sustaining the nature of awareness. This means that we should remain in the understanding of the original view and not forget it. The clarity and stability of the mind are intrinsic to the nature of the mind. It is essential to understand that. Therefore, if we exert extra effort into making the mind clear and stable, such an attempt will instead distance us from our intrinsic clarity and stability.

The third of part "view, meditation, and action" is action. The action is Gyalwe Nyugu, who is another master. Gyalwe Nyugu means the sprout of the Victorious Ones, referring to the Bodhisattvas. It points to the actions of the bodhisattvas. These actions are summarized as the six paramitas. Ordinarily, the six paramitas are practiced based on the Sutrayana, but since these instructions pertain to the Vajrayana, tantric Buddhism, the six paramitas should be exercised without hope or fear about how we conduct our life. Ordinarily, hope and fear induce us to create emotional negativity as well as karmic actions.

So, when we practice the six paramitas without hope and fear, they become the genuine six paramitas and can be called transcendental virtues. But if we practice the six paramitas with hope and fear, then they do not become transcendental virtues. If we practice the six paramitas, without this transcendental insight, but with dualistic hope and fear, we will be stuck on this shore of samsara, and not be able to transcend to the other shore. But if we instead practice the six paramitas in a non-dualistic manner, we will be liberated from this shore and transcend to the other side.

Take the first paramitas, the practice of generosity, or giving, as an example. If we give something to somebody with hope or strings attached, perhaps hoping that the person will complement our gift, or anticipate something in return in the future, then this giving is not transcendental, it is not a pure gift. An impure mind contaminates it. Even if we were to offer something to the Buddha as a gift, anticipating blessings from the Buddha, this would not become a transcendental virtue.

The reason we may do this is that hope and fear are deeply rooted in the grasping of the self. Whatever we do, worldly or spiritual, if our conduct is rooted in hope and fear, which again are rooted in self-grasping, then it will become a cause for plunging us into samsara. It will not become a cause for liberating us from samsara.

Direct Introduction to Rigpa Nature

If we were to practice the synthesis of view, meditation, and action, as expounded in Dzogchen teachings, without self-grasping, we would attain supreme enlightenment without any difficulty. There is no question about it. Even if we fail to achieve supreme enlightenment, which is the ideal spiritual goal of those who follow this path, we will still experience happiness and a contented mind. Clinging to the self will decrease, and hope and fear will diminish as well. Our life will become very peaceful, and we will be harmonious and happy.

Threefold "view, meditation, and action," is introduced through three words or statements. The first is "Direct Introduction to rigpa nature." This is the definitive meaning of the Dharma. The second statement relates to the practice of meditation, and reads, "Decide upon one thing, and one thing only." This is meditation. The third concerns the action that brings about fruition, the statement reading, "Gain confidence directly in the liberation of rising thoughts."

These instructions are very succinct and very profound. They start with how to practice the view. We are instructed first to relax and release our mind as a preliminary meditation on the view. Not only should we relax our mind, but we should also relax our body and speech as well. The reason we should first relax our mind is to let go of discursive thoughts that are projected onto outward appearances. The coarse aspect of rambling thoughts generated towards physical appearances induces us to create karma. This karma gives rise to frustrations. Then we will get trapped in the wheel of samsara, and wander around experiencing a lack of independence, under the power of afflictive emotions and polluted karma. It is like a dog being led on a leash by the owner, our mind being like the dog. I use the example of a dog here, because I see a lot of dogs in Norway, walking with their owners on a leash, not being free. Perhaps we can use this example to understand how our mind can follow bad emotions and karmas. The Buddha told us plainly that the mind is emptiness, but usually, we are attached, creating "I" and "other," creating fractions.

According to these teachings, good positive thoughts, as well as negative thoughts, are the natural expression of the essential emptiness of the mind itself. Therefore, even if there are no "good" or "bad" thoughts, we like to divide up thoughts and categorize them into good and bad. Then we want to get rid of the evil thoughts and cultivate good thoughts. When we meditate, we usually welcome good ideas but reject the bad. This is not a good practice for our meditation. If we do this, we do not understand the Dzogchen view. Understanding the view is especially important.

The view is an infinite expanse, or endless dimension, which facilitates everything, good and bad. Without understanding this infinite expanse, we divide things up into different boxes, and then we react to them to generate further discursive thoughts and afflictive emotions, leading to the creation of karma. Therefore, without a proper understanding of the view, we are not able to meditate, because there is nothing to meditate on. To understand the view, we need to be properly introduced to it and recognize it. During meditation, we then abide in view, which knows no limitation, being of infinite dimension. When we lack a proper understanding of the view, our conduct will not contribute towards enhancement of the meditation.

The line that starts with "First, relax and release your mind" points towards the practice of shamatha, or tranquility meditation. Tranquility meditation helps us to prevent the mind from being drawn in by external appearances. The next line, "Neither scattered nor concentrated, without thoughts" points towards the practice of vipassana. The next, "While resting in this even state at ease" points towards the unity of shamatha and vipassana.

Whether we are engaging in shamatha or vipassana meditation, participating in stillness or insight, whether in meditation or post-meditation, whatever thought or emotions come across our mind, whatever appearances we perceive, we should never forget that all of these appearances, thoughts, and feelings are the natural expression of our dharmakaya mind. This is quite important. First, we relax and release our mind. Then we release all proliferations and mental engagements in discursive thoughts, emotions, and objective appearances.

When we manage to relax our mind and release all discursive thoughts, then, while we are enjoying the relaxation of the mind, devoid of rambling thoughts and emotions, we simply let the mind rest in that infinite state, devoid of conceptual constructions or fabrications. Do not react to any of this, do not construct any thoughts or emotions or concepts, but if they arise on their own, view them as the natural expression of the emptiness of the mind of dharmakaya. While in this state, we should suspend all kinds of all conceptual constructions and elaborations and relax our mind within that non-conceptual state.

When we relax and release our mind in this meditative state, we may occasionally sound a shattering "P'ET!" The "P'ET" should be very brief, but powerful. It is like somebody striking our head with a big piece of wood, and we become unconscious. We can say that we render the conscious mind into the sub-conscious mind or render the discursive mind into the mind that does not entertain conceptual thinking. It is like a powerful knock-out that defeats our opponent. With one powerful P'ET we overpower the discursive chattering mind. The purpose is to silence the verbose, chattering mind for a moment.

The mantric syllable P'ET contains a lot of blessing, and it is also a key instruction. In the root text, it is said to be amazing. In Tibetan, "E MA HO!" means fantastic or incredible. It is wonderful because we can temporarily suspend the chattering discursive mind, the mind that obsessively chatters and engages in rambling thoughts. This sound is made up of two letters, "pha" and "ta." The first letter, "pha," is the syllable of withdrawing. Therefore, it is the syllable of skillful means. The second letter, "ta," is the syllable of severance, of cutting through. Thus, the sound of this letter is connected to wisdom. So, if we properly sound the mantric syllable P'ET, the result is that we will be able to create a gap between the rambling thoughts in our mind. This is a beautiful thing. When we are transported to that state of mind, we experience a dimension of the mind free from obsessive discursive thoughts. This experience is emptiness, but not a dull emptiness. It is a vivid emptiness that is free from all kinds of obstructions. When we experience this spiritual dimension, we feel the sensation of everything being penetratingly transparent, crystal clear, without any obstacles. This experience of penetrating transparency is beyond vocal expression and conception. We may attempt to describe it, but it is primarily beyond conceptual thoughts. Our understanding cannot figure out what this experience is.

Guided Meditation

Let us now take the opportunity to meditate for a moment. I will guide you through the meditation. Initially, relax your body as well as your mind. Do not try to project your thoughts, and do not withdraw them either. If ideas are already there, do not try to push them back. If you learn the art of neither projecting nor suppressing thoughts, you will gradually learn to experience the thoughtless state of mind, where there are no concepts. Experience this state of thoughtlessness, of non-conceptuality, and then rest within this thoughtless state for a moment. If, during meditation, conceptual proliferation arises, then, to suspend further increase, utter a very forceful and short P'ET. In the wake of the P'ET, you are transported to the spiritual dimension of nothingness, free from conceptual proliferation. This dimension of nothingness is not a dull nothingness, it is a vivid, brilliant nothingness, and let yourself rest within that brilliant dimension that defies mental conceptions and vocal articulations. This is it.

It is good to repeat this meditation again and again. The main thing is not to pursue the objects of the discursive thoughts when we meditate. We should trust that the object of our perception will not influence our mind negatively. We just simply let it be, leaving the object of perception and the apprehending mind as it is, without any interaction. If we manage to suspend discursive thoughts and emotions in this manner, even for a moment, a few seconds or minutes, it is said that samsara has stopped as far as we are concerned, for that very brief moment.

The Dzogchen teachings talk about the difference between mind and awareness. For example, when we recognize our self-awareness, rigpa, the grosser aspects of mind disappear like bubbles on water. It is like the clouds or mist in the sky that merely evaporate and disappear within the expanse of space itself.

It is said that all phenomena have the dreamlike quality of illusions. The question of whether phenomena are real or not real becomes non-applicable. We cannot question whether a dream is true or false, or an illusion is real or unreal, the question is a wrong question. Look at the example of the barren woman. If somebody poses a question about the son of a barren woman, the issue will be invalid. Likewise, if we question the reality or unreality of the dreamlike quality, that question is invalid.

Rigpa self-awareness does not give birth to the discursive mind. Neither does it prevent the discursive mind. As far as the self-awareness of rigpa is concerned, it treats the discursive mind and non-discursive mind equally. Again, if we engage in a debate about the physical attractiveness of the child of a barren woman, these arguments will be invalid.

As another example, we are now staying here in the world, and if I say I will go to China and then come back to Norway, you will understand me, but if we had been on the moon, looking down at the world, traveling on Earth loses its meaning. Likewise, when we become awakened, there is no birth and no death.

When our spiritual being is rooted in the self-awareness of rigpa, we will, from that perspective, know no birth or death, no increase or decrease, no coming or going, and so forth. But if our being is rooted in dualistic consciousness, alaya consciousness, then our mind will know birth, death, increase, decrease, coming, and going, and so forth. It comes down to whether we have realized the view without references or not. There is a quotation that states, if we recognize the suchness of reality, then this itself is Buddhahood, but if we do not, this will be a deluded sentient being. In the same manner, if we recognize rigpa, this is the attainment of dharmakaya, whereas if we do not, that is samsara as alaya consciousness.

Questions and Answers

Question: We have the eight consciousnesses, just now you were talking about recognizing rigpa, but I struggle and find it difficult. At a previous teaching, you spoke about the foundation consciousness, the alaya consciousness, and the seeds. I struggle with the concept of foundation consciousness and how to realize rigpa. I wonder if you could clarify that?

Answer: There exists what is called the "alaya-vasana" and the "alaya-vijnana," fundamental consciousness and fundamental awareness. The fundamental awareness, alaya-vijnana, is intrinsic, it is primordial. It has existed since beginningless time, and it is uncreated. Therefore, it is non-composite. Whereas alaya-vasana, or fundamental consciousness, is influenced by our discursive thoughts and emotions because the propensity of our discursive thoughts and feelings are deposited into fundamental consciousness. But these propensities cannot be deposited into alaya-vijnana, fundamental awareness. For example, the empty sky can be said to be the basis for all appearances, as all appearances exist within space. But we can also talk about space being intrinsically empty. Likewise, alaya-vijnana is transcendental reality because it transcends proliferations, whereas alaya-vasana is not a transcendent reality. Therefore, alaya-vasana is fundamental consciousness from where conceptual proliferation can take place. Do you understand?

Questioner: That part is clear, but the part where we recognize rigpa is outside of what you explained. How should we understand it?

Answer: If we recognize fundamental consciousness, alaya-vasana, then this will naturally be transformed into fundamental wisdom. If alaya-vasana remains undetected, the potential to deposit further discursive thoughts and emotions, karma, will always be possible. Whereas if that alaya-vasana is transformed into fundamental wisdom, alaya-vijnana, then the base where we can deposit karmic propensities is not there anymore. So, there is nothing to store. Take the analogy of the rainbow appearing in the sky. The nature of the sky is intrinsically empty, whereas the rainbow appears very vividly and colorfully. When the rainbow disappears, where does it go? The rainbow is a product of many factors coming together, but when it fades into the expanse of space, where does it disappear? Some people teach that fundamental consciousness is the Buddha-nature, but this is not in line with the teaching of the Buddha. When a person becomes enlightened, fully spiritually awakened, it is debated whether alaya-vasana exists or not. If there are contributing causes and conditions, responsible for sustaining alaya consciousness, alaya-vasana consciousness will be there. But when these contributing factors are withdrawn, the alaya-vasana consciousness will collapse and disappear. Alaya-vasana consciousness is there because of the principle of interdependence. We can then pose questions like "Are the dharmakaya and alaya consciousness identical or not?" or "Are rigpa, self-awareness, and discursive mind identical or not?"

It is a difficult task to directly introduce the student to the ultimate spiritual view before enlightenment. For example, there is a quotation from a sutra, which says that when we claim that we have perceived the sky, we can question the way we have seen it. If we want to observe the space of the sky itself, our perception should be devoid of shapes, colors, and so forth, excluding these defining characteristics.

Accordingly, the Buddha tries to refute existence by establishing the non-existence of existence. Then he proceeds further to confirm this non-existence to be non-dualistic, or in other words, transcendental reality. And from this non-dualistic reality, he further refines it into non-elaboration. According to these teachings, it is stated that trekcho, or non-elaboration, is the actual suchness, or reality, of the nature of our mind. So, we need to understand the nature of existence and non-existence, and in a progressive order, understand the nature of non-dualistic reality, and the quality of non-elaboration.

If we pay attention to our mind, we will perceive that the mind is free from any defining characteristics, regarding colors, shapes, sizes, dimension, and so forth. This is to understand the emptiness of our mind. Since our mind has no characteristics, we have to perceive it subtly, because we cannot feel the texture of our mind, like touching a surface with a finger. The nature of the mind is beyond existence and non-existence. Still, it is capable of cognizing because the nature of this mind is clear-light and luminosity.

According to this teaching, our mind is the creator of samsara as well as the creator of nirvana. When we speak of introducing directly rigpa nature, this is what that means. The mind is created as the natural expression of rigpa. The mind and rigpa as such are entirely different, but this difference is only in aspects. Primarily, they can be regarded as being identical. For example, the ocean and its waves are different, but they are still the same. Likewise, with heat and fire. The wind is the leading cause for waves to arise on the surface of the ocean. Similarly, karmic winds will stir the mind, and the discursive mind will emerge from rigpa. It is not that the mind creates trouble, not even the conceptual mind and thoughts, or the negative emotions for that matter. That which creates the problem is when we fixate and cling onto the rambling thoughts and feelings as well as the mind itself. It is the clinging that creates the trouble.

We can for example experience clinging to and fixation on our conceptual thoughts or emotions, by viewing positive thoughts as something superior, and negative thoughts as something inferior. Then we try to cultivate positive thoughts and suppress or abandon negative thoughts. In these teachings, the very attempt to develop good thoughts, and to get rid of evil thoughts, is viewed as a sign of fixation on the idea of something being good or something being bad. There is a saying that goes: As long as there is a fixation, no matter what, we have not arrived at the right view.

Deciding upon one thing, and one thing only

We now proceed to the second point that strikes the vital point, "Deciding upon one thing and upon one thing only." This is connected to meditation. Initially, it is crucial to grasp the theoretical meaning of the view. Otherwise, it will be difficult to meditate.

The word for meditation in Tibetan is "gom," and it means to familiarize oneself. What we are supposed to familiarize ourselves with is the spiritual view. If we have not been adequately introduced to, or adequately grasped the meaning of this view, then our meditation will become ineffective.

Deciding upon "one thing and one thing only" means to do one thing, namely, to view whatever manifests, such as thoughts, concepts, ideas, feelings, and so forth, as the integral expression of the nature of our mind. Therefore, there is nothing to adopt and nothing to abandon. To be able to cut through the primary vein of samsara, it is essential to decide upon this one thing, and this one thing only.

The purpose of engaging in meditation is to pacify the discursive thoughts that are evoked by clinging to the dualistic perception of the viewer and something viewed. In this meditation, we should progressively come out of the dualistic fixation of there being a viewer and something viewed. We should transcend the confinement of the viewer, the action of viewing, and the object viewed into experiencing transcendental reality.

I think it is like when we watch a movie. There is the darkened theatre, the screen, the projector behind, and the film projected. If the screen or other contributing causes are lacking, then, even if there were a projector, it would not be possible to project the movie, and we would not be able to see it. In a working cinema, everything that is in the projector will get projected on the screen. The projector must be fed with movies beforehand to project. If we do not supply the projector with any material, there will be nothing to project.

The above example may illustrate how our karmic propensities are deposited into our fundamental consciousness. If these propensities remain within the fundamental consciousness, they are in a neutral form, neither positive nor negative. But once these neutral propensities get activated, they get activated into either a positive or negative projection, being like positive or negative seeds.

Our wandering in samsara begins with ignorance, which then gives rise to dualistic perception or fixation. Our dualistic perception further proliferates into complex discursive thoughts. These complex and rambling thoughts also proliferate into complex emotions. The emotions propagate into karma, and in this way, we go through the process of ignorance, dualistic fixation, thoughts, feelings and this creates karma. The karma begins with the mental state. Therefore, karma is qualified by mental action, termed volitional action. The voluntary mental action further induces physical and vocal responses. Thus, we create karma.

Due to this proliferating process, the five aggregates evolve. Based on these, we experience all the shortcomings and frustrations of samsara. The root of all this can be traced back to ignorance. Therefore, intrinsic awareness is vital to overcome fundamental ignorance. The term rigpa, translated into English as self-awareness or just awareness, also has a meaning of clarity as a cognitive ability.

The development of samsara and its frustrations is based on the principle of conditionality. Therefore, if we uproot the fundamental cause of samsara, which is ignorance, then all the remaining branches of ignorance will also get destroyed. This is the meaning of the statement "knowing one liberates all." Even if we know many things, but fail to understand this vital point, this is regarded as knowing nothing. According to this reasoning, we can say that all sentient beings before enlightenment know nothing. This was spoken by the Buddha.

Let us suppose that we are properly introduced to recognizing the view, but when we try to enter meditation to sustain this view, discursive thoughts and emotions arise. Whether our mind now proliferates, causing us to experience anger, attachment, even happiness or misery, or continues to rest calmly on the object of meditation, it is important to recognize dharmakaya.

If we experience that our mind is resting calmly, abiding in the view as the object of meditation, we should recognize this as the nature of mind. Also, if thoughts and concepts arise, we should not feel that we have moved away from meditation. We should view thoughts and concepts as the natural expression of mind itself. These expressions are an integral part of mind. Even when we are experiencing ideas and concepts, we are not removed from meditation, if we recognize that these are just the natural expressions of our mind.

Metaphorically, it is like the flight of a bird in the sky; no matter how far it travels, it cannot fly beyond space. Similarly, all thoughts and concepts are contained within the fundamental nature of mind. The essential nature of our mind cannot be harmed whatsoever, even if negative ideas, thoughts, and emotions arise, because the mind is fundamentally empty. It is like nothing can damage space itself, even bombs.

Since beginningless time, we have been caught up in the

wheel of samsara, wandering around, experiencing all kinds of frustrations. But none of these samsaric experiences can create a dent in the fundamental nature of our mind. They cannot disprove the fundamental purity or emptiness of the nature of our mind. Whatever we experience regarding the first noble truth of frustration and misery, or whatever we experience concerning the second noble truth of emotional complexes and karma, as long as we view these things as expressions of the nature of our mind, the nature of mind will not be harmed. This is looking directly at the face of dharmakaya.

Up to this point, the instructions mainly reveal how to identify the original view, and how to combine it with meditation, and this primarily helps us to minimize or pacify our latent grasping onto dualistic perception. So, when we meditate in this manner, dualistic fixation will begin to loosen up, lessen its intensity, and accordingly we will experience meditative signs, for example, meditative experiences of blissfulness, clarity, and non-conceptuality. When we have these meditative experiences, we have to exercise further caution. If we fixate on these wonderful meditative experiences, we can also be bound by clinging to these.

At this juncture, we experience what is known as the meeting of the mother and child clear-light of luminosity. The mother luminosity is the primordial abiding clear-light, the clear-light of dharmakaya. The child luminosity is the clear-light that we cultivate through meditative discipline. To allow the mother and child clear-light to meet, the lama needs to introduce the student to the child clear-light. When the child clear-light is brought up through repeated meditation, the child clear-light will recognize the fundamentally abiding mother clear-light, enabling the meeting of the mother and child clear-light. When there is a unity of the mother and child clear-light, this is called the experience of the indivisible unity of the mother and child clear-light.

In short, while we are meditating, whatever thoughts and emotions proliferate in our mind, we should not try to reject specific ideas and cultivate others, we should let them be as they are. We just let them go.

So, it is vital for us to decide upon one thing and one thing only. If our mind is abiding peacefully, we see its nature as dharmakaya, the absolute fundamental nature of the Buddha. If the mind stirs, we do not try to reject thoughts but recognize them as the natural expression of the nature of emptiness of our mind. When we meditate in this manner, if gross thoughts and concepts arise that disturb our meditation, we can also suspend these thoughts and emotions by uttering a brief yet powerful P'ET, as explained earlier.

When we meditate upon the view of Dzogchen meditation, there is no demarcation between the meditation session and post-meditation period. Ideally, we should be meditating regardless of whether we are in a formal meditation session or in post-meditation. In other words, we should sustain the view of rigpa both during meditation as well as during post-meditation. However, in the beginning this will not happen by itself. Therefore, we need to focus on meditating in the meditation sessions as well as during the post-meditation period. In the beginning, we need to meditate by taking refuge in an environment that is devoid of commotions and distractions.

The root text reads "Abide by the flow of what is only dharmakaya, decide with absolute conviction that there is nothing other than this." This refers to whether resting or agitated with thoughts, concepts, and emotions, the nature of the mind is dharmakaya in both cases. It is essential to arrive at certainty of this and merely sustain that in meditation.

I think that this practice is vital for both you and me. Sometimes, when we get a lot of stress, we can look at it and shout P'ET. Or sometimes, if we feel lonely, look at the loneliness, this feeling, and go P'ET. It will help. And sometimes, if we are getting angry, we can shout P'ET as well. Sometimes if we feel a powerful attachment, say P'ET. Sometimes this is incredibly good, but do not do it outside, because this could lead to some problems.

When discursive thoughts and emotions arise, such as aversion or anger, the first instant of rage will not bind us to the wheel of samsara. It is when the irritation is prolonged in the second and third instants, that fundamental fixation arises. This is what binds us to the wheel of samsara.

As good meditators, we need to recognize the occurrence of discursive thoughts like anger and so on at the second instant. When we recognize it, we are not bound by it. When we see it in the second instance, the power of the discursive thought of anger weakens. In Dzogchen terminology, this is called self-liberation. The discursive thought of anger liberates on its own, without needing to be freed. It releases itself due to the mindfulness of the second instant.

We cannot block the occurrence of discursive thoughts and emotions. They will undoubtedly arise, but we can pay closer attention to them when they do appear, and not allow them to proliferate and evolve into dualistic fixation. This is a particularly important Dzogchen key-instruction. It is a bit like whether the sun is blocked by a dark cloud or a white cloud. As far as the blocking of the rays of the sun is concerned, they are the same.

Similarly, if there are positive or negative thoughts in our mind, both will block the natural radiance of the nature of our mind. It is something like when we are riding a horse; it does not matter if we fall from the right side or the left side of the horse. As far as the discomfort that comes from hitting the ground is concerned, the pain is the same. This is just a rough example. No example is precise.

So, while we are experiencing frustration, we can learn to look at the nature of this frustration. When we experience peace or happiness, we try to look at the quality of that peace and joy. If we do that, we are meditating, and we will also realize that the polarity of happiness and misery is the natural expression of the nature of our mind.

In brief, whatever arises within the expanse of our mind

needs to be carefully looked at, especially its nature. We do not even need to meditate in this case. We only need to realize that whatever arises within our mind is nothing other than what emerges as the nature of our mind. We can be somewhat like a hermit mediator in the wilderness of Tibet. He or she meditates on the peak of the mountain, isolated entirely from the rest of the world. He or she knows nothing about the world's economy, whether it is going up or down. Therefore, they do not have any fixation concerning the economy of the world.

If we find we are having a lot of rambling thoughts and conflicting emotions but look at the nature of these as the natural expression of the nature of our mind, this would be perfect. And if we are experiencing a lot of joy and happiness, we should look in the same way. In this way, we convert whatever we feel into the heart of meditation so that we are not separated from the object of meditation whatsoever.

Patrul Rinpoche, who wrote this text, was once asked a question by a certain meditator, who said he did not know how to meditate. Patrul Rinpoche responded by saying that the mind that thinks, "I am not able to mediate, and I know nothing about meditation," is meditating by looking at itself in this manner. For example, if the thought, "I am hungry, I need to eat something" arises, and we look at the nature of this thought, the thought will be converted into meditation. In short, meditation is not exclusively confined to sitting meditation. Meditation can be extended while we are standing, walking, lying down, in all kinds of different physical positions. From this point of view, there is nothing that we cannot meditate on. In fact, from this point of view, we are always meditating, if we bring attention to the nature of what we are thinking and doing. The most important thing is that we develop further into what is known as the state of non-meditation.

As far as an ordinary person is concerned, sometimes the mind experiences rest in meditation. But during meditation, the mind can also become agitated. This is how it is. It will happen for both good and bad meditators. So, what qualifies a good meditator if both good and bad meditators experience rest and agitation of mind? A good meditator can recognize the nature of the resting mind as being the dharmakaya, as well as recognizing that agitation and distraction also are expressions of the nature of mind itself.

In this kind of meditation, we just let the body be as it is, the speech as it is, and the mind as it is. This means that we should not try to fabricate movements of our body speech and mind, just let them be in their natural place, while continually sustaining the thread of being aware of the nature of mind.

If we do not interfere too much, the body, speech, and mind can take care of themselves. When we walk, we do not have to think about which leg to move forward. As soon as a thought to go somewhere arises, our legs start to walk steadily. But if we were to fixate on which leg it is best to place before the other, this would interfere with our stride. This also applies to breathing. We breathe naturally in and out. We do not have to draw our breath consciously. If we let our mind start to interfere with our breath by controlling it, then we will quickly have a problem with our breathing.

Our meditation should be like an eagle soaring in the sky. When an eagle is rising high into the heavens, it casts no shadow and does not leave any trace of where it has flown. In our case, we can say that we leave a mark, traced by our karmic footprints, but when our disturbing thoughts and emotions are liberated by themselves, there are no traces left, and we will fly high in the sky, as free as the eagle.

It is also said that liberation should be like writing a letter on the surface of running water. While we are writing on the surface of running water, the running water erases it without leaving an imprint. These are all examples on how we can be liberated instantaneously from disturbing thoughts and emotions on the spot, without leaving any mark. Sometimes, this is also termed "the natural pacification of disturbing thoughts and feelings, letting them be liberated by themselves."

To summarize, this is what is meant by "deciding upon one thing, and upon one thing only," regarding meditation. In brief, when we encounter appearances and sound and become aware of them in our mind, this meeting should be viewed as the natural expression of the nature of our mind. In general Vajrayana teachings, it is stated that appearance, sound, and awareness should be transformed into the threefold form, mantra and wisdom mind of the deity, but in this teaching, the threefold appearance, sound, and awareness should be viewed as the natural expression of the nature of the empty mind.

It is a bit like this: Whatever different physical postures we assume, these postures are not separate from the body itself. They are rooted in the body. The different body positions are just various aspects of the body. Likewise, whatever discursive thoughts and emotions arise within our mind cannot transcend beyond the nature of the empty mind. We need to comprehend this fact, that in this kind of meditation, neither negative nor positive thoughts and emotions deteriorate our nature of mind. The nature of mind is beyond declining or improving. We should also comprehend that in this meditation, it is not a question of whether we attain enlightenment or not.

As you can see, the vital point is quite simple, but to make it understandable, we are given many examples and analogies so that we can communicate something about this subject. We resort to all these modes of expression and explanations mainly as an aim to introduce the students to the empty nature of their mind.

Question: When I meditate on something, and I experience disruptive thoughts, I think that my mind produces these. Maybe things get better, but the next day the same thoughts come again, and the next day, for a long time. Do you still think a self-liberation method is something I should continue to do, or are there other methods, perhaps more in the direction of transformation?

Answer: In this meditation, we are not trying to block the rambling thoughts and emotions. We are taught to give liberty to our mind so that if thoughts and feelings arise, we let them appear. What is being shown here is that we allow our thoughts and emotions to take their course, by giving them full liberty. It is taught not to fixate on them, not to dwell on them. The important thing is to cut the fixation, not to cut the thoughts and emotions. The problems come as soon as we fixate on those thoughts and emotions, not because there are thoughts and emotions.

Questioner: But these thoughts come anyway, you can call this fixation or not fixation, they just come. Then I abide in them, and after some time I feel better, perhaps they disappear. But then they come the next day again and last for a long period. This can be about some disturbing things that happened previously.

Answer: I think it is like this, you know, something like day and night. Somebody may try to stop the night, because the night is dark, and they do not like the dark, wanting only sunshine every day. But this will never happen. Do you understand? The day is like the good thought; the night is like the bad thought. Like the night follows the day, the bad thoughts follow the good.

In this kind of meditation, we should not anticipate "no thought" or only "good thought." This is unrealistic. If "good thoughts" arise, also "bad thoughts" will arise. It is like day and night, or misery and happiness. They are dependent on each other. The crucial point is, despite either one of these arising, not to dwell on them with fixation, because fixation is what binds us to these thoughts.

So, in this meditation, as it is taught, all thoughts and emotions, good and bad, and everything in between, are the natural expression of the nature of mind. Therefore, they are an integral part of the nature of mind. So, there are no good thoughts to be adopted and cultivated, and no bad thoughts to be abandoned and eliminated. Because if all thoughts are the natural expression of the mind, then that is how it is.

For example, daytime and nighttime cannot transcend beyond space, daytime and nighttime happen within space. Likewise, good and bad thoughts, or good emotions and bad emotions, none of them can transcend beyond the mind. They occur within the expanse of the mind, and then they dissolve within the expanse of mind.

Therefore, if we want to reduce, or temporarily pacify disruptive thoughts and emotions, we should create an ideal circumstance, as is taught in the text. We should make ourselves an ideal environment, with little commotion or distracting factors. When we surrender to such a perfect setting and meditate, we will be less prone to disruptive thoughts and emotions. Therefore, taking refuge in an ideal environment for the sake of meditation is essential in the early stage.

The Buddha looked hard into finding an ideal example for the realization of the view. He said he could not find a better model than the outer sky. There is a meditation in which we merge our consciousness with external space. External space knows no direction, center or circumference. Space is free from all defining characteristics. So, we mingle our consciousness with the sky and remain in this state of sustained meditation. This will influence our mind positively.

Discursive thoughts and emotions that arise in our minds are like apparitions of the mind itself. These are the projections of the nature of our mind. They are the natural expression of the nature of our mind. The example of the ocean and its waves mentioned above is excellent.

Question: Yes, so the simple answer would be to practice more in a right way with the same method, and not to combine with other methods?

Answer: Your question can be answered by the third vital point, "Gain confidence directly in the liberation of rising thoughts." When we know the art of liberating a single thought or emotion, then that same art can be applied to all other thoughts and emotions. This means that the more thoughts and feelings we are bombarded with, the more we can meditate in the same way, because now we have the correct tool to liberate every one of them. As we recognize the arising of more thoughts and emotions, and they self-liberate as the natural expression of mind, the natural brilliance of the nature of mind is further enhanced.

If we do not perform the art of liberating instantaneously every occurrence of thought and emotion, it will be like the following analogy. There once was a thief in China, and one day he went out to steal. When people noticed that he was about to take something, everybody started to alert each other by ringing a bell. Since the thief knew he was a thief, and not an innocent person, he immediately blocked his ears with his two fingers, to prevent himself hearing the alarming sound of the bell. He thought that this would protect him from being recognized and caught.

In this kind of meditation, we are not trying to block the natural expressivity of the nature of our mind, our thoughts, and emotions. Because, even if we succeed in preventing our thoughts and feelings temporarily, sooner or later, they will resurface, and then we will have to block them again. Therefore, this would be a very exhausting technique. Whereas if we learn the art of liberating the arising of each thought and emotion spontaneously on the spot by itself, then this method will not be very exhausting.

A direct understanding of the view is to see that the nature of our mind is the fully awakened Buddha-mind. If we view ourselves as ordinary, unenlightened sentient beings, it will be like seeing ourselves as thieves. This is not being innocent. This is to feel guilty. Not comprehending the view is like identifying ourselves with the unenlightened state of mind. Whereas, having the vision of the view is understanding that fundamentally, our nature is Buddha-nature.

Think of it as if our Buddha-nature is presently buried

355

deeply underground. There can be gold hidden in the earth, as well as gold that has been dug up. As far as the quality and value of the gold are concerned, it is the same whether the gold is buried or extracted from the earth. Likewise, the gold of the Buddha-nature is buried deep within our psyche, but whether it is manifest, extracted or not, as far as its value and quality are concerned, this does not matter. The quality and value are the same. There is a text called *Uttaratantrashastra* by Maitreya, which is one of five treatises where the subject matter exclusively is about Buddha-nature. I have taught on this treatise before, here in Norway.

Question: This is just a quick question. I live in an apartment, and I wonder if I do this P'ET, and my neighbors hear it. Is that a big deal, or is that okay?

Answer: If it is okay for your neighbors then it is okay. If you are okay, then everything is okay, but if it is not okay for your neighbors, then it will be a problem. But perhaps it is okay, I think. In Tibet, a lot of people are very afraid to shout P'ET like that. They misunderstand. When the great lamas teach chö practice, people think it is very serious, imagining there being a lot of ghosts that can catch them, or something like that. It is like the demons were sleeping, and that the P'ET wakes them up. It is amusing. In chö practice, there is a lot of shouting P'ET, but in this practice, we only do it occasionally while meditating.

Also, during our meditative practice, if we encounter certain obstacles, like dullness, a lethargic state of mind, then we can sound a brief and powerful P'ET. This will help us to scatter the dullness. If we experience the opposite of dullness, excitement or agitation, then we can also shout P'ET to suspend the continuity of that agitation for a moment.

Sometimes, if I am exhausted, or I have a little headache, or don't feel good, I do phowa practice, sounding a strong "HIK!" This is helpful for me, using the HIK and P'ET like that. The HI should come from the naval area while visualizing the central channel. The P'ET should come more from the upper part of the chest. It is beneficial to learn to do this. Like it is stated here in this root text, "First relax, and release your mind, neither scattered nor concentrated, without thoughts, and while resting in this even state, at ease, suddenly let out a mind-shattering P'ET!"

We should not only shout P'ET when we experience dullness or excitement. We can also voluntarily disrupt our meditation by uttering the shattering P'ET. This will refresh our meditation. Like it is said in the second point, "Rest in the aspect of awareness, beyond all description. Stillness, bliss and clarity: disrupt them, again and again." If we do not interrupt the meditation, we might become fixated on a beautiful experience like blissfulness, clarity, or non-conceptuality. So, to suspend the fixation, we must disrupt our meditation with a shattering P'ET. If we deviate from actual meditation because of clinging to beautiful experiences, we will deviate into the four formless samadhis. Our meditation will become a cause to experience birth within the plane of existence known as the four formless realms. For example, clinging to meditative experiences or non-conceptuality may be mistaken for infinite space, causing rebirth is one of the samadhis of the four formless divine beings. Likewise, we might become mistaken with regard to blissfulness and clarity.

We should understand the beautiful meditative experiences that we encounter along this meditative path, such as blissfulness, clarity, and non-conceptuality, to be merely milestones. We should not get stuck by these milestones, thinking that they are the final destination. If we do, we will deviate and go astray from the actual path. Making this mistake is like taking a sculpture for a person.

Someone who is pursuing the higher spiritual path should aspire to attain supreme enlightenment, not merely to experience blissfulness, clarity, and non-conceptuality. When we yearn for supreme awakened enlightenment, we must advance past these milestones.

Gain confidence directly in the liberation of rising thoughts

Whether we are engaging in the process of listening, reflection, or meditation, it is essential to generate the motivation for supreme enlightenment, bodhicitta, for the benefit of all living beings. We are now going to talk about the view, meditation, and action of the great perfection, Dzogchen. When practicing the Dzogchen view, it is vital to connect with the Dzogchen teachings on trekcho. We should remember that the Dzogchen view is presented by introducing rigpa directly to the mind.

What is meant by directly introducing the nature of rigpa? It does not mean that we will lose rigpa if we do not meditate, or that we will attain rigpa if we meditate. The main thing to understand is that the origin of our mind is nothing else than the absolute fundamental nature of the Buddha, dharmakaya.

So, during meditation, whether the mind is dwelling, peacefully abiding or is distracted and agitated, in either case, both the quiet mind and the troubled mind should be identified as the nature of dharmakaya. When the view is put into actual meditational practice, the key instruction for this is to "Decide upon one thing, and one thing only." It means that our experiences of different appearances, as well as the internal thoughts and emotions, should all be viewed as different expressions of the nature of the empty mind, dharmakaya. This is the view of the trekcho teaching.

So, having been introduced to the view of Dzogchen, recognized it to a certain extent, and combined it with meditation practice, we arrive at the action part of "view, meditation, and action." The action is concerned with fruition. This is the third part of the root text, "Gain confidence directly in the liberation of rising thoughts." If we are not confident in the manner thoughts and emotions are liberated, our liberation will not be very decisive.

Dzogchen and Madhyamika

If we want to comprehend the view of trekcho of the Dzogchen teachings fully, it is imperative to study the philosophical view of Madhyamika. In Madhyamika, the Middle Way school of the sutra vehicle, we use the four reasonings to establish the unborn nature of reality and so realize the non-arising nature of all phenomena as dharmakaya. The Dzogchen approach differs from Madhyamika in that we are taught to apprehend the face of rigpa, or mind itself, directly. In brief, when we undertake the practices connected with view, meditation, action, and fruition, whatever discursive thoughts and feelings we experience, these rambling thoughts and feelings can be brought onto the path of the Dharma. If we can incorporate whatever appearances we experience or encounter, particularly adverse circumstances, onto the path of Dharma, then our practice will be beneficial. For example, like prescribed medicine acting as a remedy against a specific disease, the prescription of Dharma, working like medicine, is needed to bring benefit to our mind.

Ordinarily, we end up creating karma based on mistaken view or mistaken perception. The technical term for this is afflicted or polluted wisdom. No one is exempt from being conditioned by afflicted wisdom. Based on the presence of this afflicted wisdom in our mindstream, we experience various kinds of frustrations, difficulties, or fears. A mistaken view arises if we do not understand the reality of interdependent origination, the principle of emptiness and karmic causation, and so forth. Knowing that an erroneous view is responsible for creating many of our difficulties, we can be motivated to learn what is the correct view.

In the Madhyamika philosophical teachings, the view is sometimes referred to as the union of appearance and emptiness. In the Dzogchen teaching it is referred to as the union of awareness and emptiness, or sometimes it is also referred to as the union of clarity and emptiness. In Vajrayana, tantric Buddhism, the technical terminology is the union of bliss and emptiness. All these views can be regarded as unmistaken views or perceptions. The important thing is to cultivate an unmistaken view about karmic causality.

Examining the Guru

To be able to recognize the correct view, it is essential to encounter an excellent spiritual guide. Padmasambhava has said that surrendering to a spiritual guru without examining that guru, is like jumping off a cliff. Perhaps because the guru is jumping off the cliff himself, and the students are merely following in their footsteps. Such a guru may harbor spiritual complacency or conceitedness, mistakenly believing that he or she has attained a proper realization of the view of emptiness. This can result in all kinds of crazy actions, and the students, who out of blind faith did not check the guru out properly, follow in their footsteps. Such a relationship between student and guru can be disastrous for both.

But the student-guru relationship is not one-sided, it is not only the student that is encouraged to examine the guru, but the guru is also encouraged to review the suitability of the student. Padmasambhava said that if the guru fails to verify the capability of the student, it is like the guru is drinking poison. Such an inappropriate student-guru relationship can also prove to be disastrous for both the student and the teacher, especially for the teacher, because it will plant more stumbling blocks on the path of the Dharma, creating obstacles and hindrances, and so forth.

Ngöndro Practice

The actual realization of such a view does not necessarily come from being very learned and articulate or powerful in terms of worldly powers. We may also say that the recognition of such a view will not necessarily occur exclusively from meditation. It says in the Vajrayana texts that the realization occurs from purifying obscurations and developing the emotional positivity of devotion towards our spiritual ideal, our spiritual guide. Other than these two means, there is no way of realizing the view.

The purification of obscurations, gathering of the accumulations, and the development of devotional positivity towards our guru comes from the spiritual practice of "ngöndro," which are the preliminaries. Ngöndro practice is very exhausting, as we are asked to repeat the preliminary exercises of ngöndro five hundred thousand times. I have many Asian students, thousands of them in fact, but among them perhaps only ten have completed the whole set of ngöndro practices.

Even if the practice of Dzogchen meditation is straightforward, we must lay a rock-solid foundation through the preliminary practices. So, it would be good to review these methods and to undertake these practices to a certain extent. We can also lay the foundation by hearing, listening and contemplating these teachings.

Vajrayana Buddhism is, in general, very meticulous when it comes to guiding the student on the path of Dharma. On each level, or step of the path, it presents specific methods. The problem with this lies on the part of the student, because they often will not be able to follow the gradual path while fulfilling the required preliminary practices. The amount of work also indicates the need to exert what is called joyous effort in Dharma practices.

We will now go through the third part of *Hitting the Essence in Three Words,* termed "Gain confidence directly in the liberation of rising thoughts." After going through the third part, I would like to sum up the whole of the root text by presenting some key instructions, so that you can practice this Dharma in combination with your daily life.

The text says, "At that point, whether attachment or aversion, happiness or sorrow—all momentary thoughts, each and every one..." "At that point" refers to when we are trying to meditate on the view, whether emotions, attachment or aversion, or feelings of happiness, arise during formal or informal meditation, each of these experiences should be understood as the dynamic expression of the nature of the empty mind, dharmakaya.

When we are meditating and have succeeded in resting our mind on the nature of rigpa, without any thoughts or feelings, we will experience that thoughts and emotions spring up temporarily from this very expanse of stillness. When we recognize the arising of thoughts and emotions from the silence of the empty mind, that mere recognition of arising thoughts and feelings will not be enough to sever the root of the delusion. We also must recognize that the nature of those thoughts and emotions is non-dual, that the arising thoughts and feelings are nothing but the expression of the dynamic energy of the empty mind. If we recognize in this manner, the root of the delusion will be cut. When we see thoughts and emotions as the empty dharmakaya mind, the delusional thoughts and feelings will not perpetuate, because their continuity will be interrupted.

To recognize arising thoughts and emotions as the expression of the nature of the empty mind, the text states that "Upon recognition, leave not a trace behind. To recognize the dharmakaya in which they are freed." To recognize the dharmakaya in which they are freed, we are given the example of writing vanishing on water. If we write something on the surface of the water, the characters will disappear as soon as they are written. Similarly, the self-arising of the illusionary thoughts and emotions self-liberates as soon as they arise.

At this stage, thoughts and emotions become liberated as an experience of the unity of clarity and emptiness. This is because the nature of thoughts and emotions are clarity. Like all small rivers flow towards the ocean, all arising thoughts and feelings dissolve back into their source, the infinite, boundless empty mind.

These thoughts and emotions come about because of the dynamic energy of the dharmakaya mind. If we do not indulge in them or identify with them, then, through merely letting them be as they are, they will dissolve back into the ground of the empty dharmakaya. As far as the arising of thoughts, concepts, and emotions are concerned, they cannot be blocked. Instead, it is skillful not to block them, but let them arise, and then let them continually liberate on their own.

Here, the text says, "And just as writing vanishes on water, arising and liberation become natural and continuous. And whatever arises is food for bare rigpa emptiness." So, whatever arises as thoughts, feelings, and concepts become sustenance for bare rigpa emptiness. They will not be obstacles for bare rigpa emptiness. Instead, they become food for sustained rigpa. Therefore, the text says, "Whatever stirs in mind is the inner power of the dharmakaya king." Because the mind is dynamic, stirring thoughts and emotions are the expressions of this active mind.

Familiarizing ourselves with this kind of meditational approach is essential. Over time, due to the power of meditation, or familiarization, we will be able to convert the arising of discursive thoughts and emotions into meditation. Instead of the arising thoughts and emotions removing us from meditation, they will bring us into meditation. Not only that, we will be able to bring powerful mental poisons onto the path of the Dharma.

The yogi, who practices this kind of meditation on the view, employs the five sense faculties of seeing, hearing, smelling, touching and tasting like any other ordinary living being. Indeed, their sense faculties operate like the senses of any other living creature. Also, the yogi of this practice perceives form like any other. There is no difference in seeing a form whether we are an ordinary person or someone who is practicing the Dzogchen view. Likewise, there is no difference in experiencing the sensation of pain or comfort and happiness. The difference is that the perception of a sound or form by an ordinary being, who is not familiar with this kind of meditation on the view, will be followed by rejection or acceptance. This gives rise to an emotional complex, like craving and aversion, and so forth. But a good meditator, who meditates on the view, perceiving forms, sounds, and so forth, will not follow their perception of a form or sound with the notions of rejection or acceptance. These thoughts and emotions will be liberated on their own simultaneously with perceiving them.

The Three Modes of Liberation

Dzogchen highlights that the way thoughts and emotions are liberated is crucial. Therefore, the Dzogchen master, Vimalamitra, stated three methods how thoughts and feelings can be freed on the spot. These are three levels of liberation. The first mode of liberation happens through recognition and acceptance. The second mode of liberation is self-liberation, where rambling thoughts liberate by themselves, without any interaction. The third mode of liberation is termed liberation that is neither beneficial nor harmful.

These three levels to liberate arising thoughts and emotions can be explained with three examples. Thoughts being liberated upon recognition is like meeting a person we have met before. Self-liberation of discursive thoughts by themselves is like a snake uncoiling from a knot. The liberation of thoughts and emotions without any benefit or harm is like the example of the burglar entering an empty house.

With the attainment of the first mode of liberation, there will remain a small trace of dualistic fixation, because even if we attain liberation of thoughts and emotions, there will be a concept of a recognizer and something that has been recognized. There is a small fixation on the duality. During the second mode of liberation, there remains a subtle obscuration known as cognitive obscuration. The final and third mode of liberation is the ultimate mode of liberation. It is the perfect model of freedom.

If we do not understand the difference between these three modes of liberating thoughts and emotions, then our meditation on the view can become a contributing cause to experience the samadhi of the formless realm. For example, if we were to identify the first level of the mode of liberation to be the ultimate mode of liberation, this conclusion will become an obstacle. We will get stuck there and not make any effort to move onto the second and third mode.

Gaining Certainty of the View

To progress, we must develop certainty. Let us look at the first example, the first mode of liberation, which was like meeting someone we have met before. When we encounter somebody, we are familiar with, we have gained certainty. Likewise, when we meditate on the view, we need to attain certainty on the view, as if we have met somebody familiar. In this way, we will gain confidence that our mind is like the Buddha. We also attain certainty by regarding arising thoughts and emotions as the natural expression of the empty dharmakaya mind.

When we seek liberation, it is important to separate the worldly samadhis of the higher formless realms from actual Dzogchen Samadhi meditation. There are four progressively higher planes of such higher formless realms of existence: the "Sphere of Infinite Space," the "Sphere of Infinite Consciousness," the "Sphere of Nothingness," and the "Sphere of Neither Perception nor Non-Perception."

When we enter Samadhi, the deep meditative practice on the view, our sense faculties are interrupted, so we are not conscious of external objects. But instead of doing this, we may experience the mundane samadhi of the formless realm termed "Sphere of Infinite Space." When all objects dissolve from the sense faculties, what is left behind is the background, which is space. We can identify this as infinite space, but if we fixate on resting in this endless space, thinking this is the ultimate meditation, it will become a contributing cause to experience the plane of existence in the formless realm.

By identifying consciousness with the infinite space, we may meditate on the consciousness as being infinitely pervasive. This may limit us to the "Sphere of Infinite Consciousness."

Further meditation can cause sensations to terminate temporarily. This temporary cessation of feelings can turn into the third worldly Samadhi of the formless realms, the "Sphere of Nothingness."

The other meditative experience that can arise is termed "Neither Perception nor Non-Perception." In this meditation, objective appearances have been wiped out, and the consciousness becomes very bright and luminous. But this is still not the ultimate intent of Dzogchen meditation. It is just another meditative experience along the path of meditation.

Now, going back to the first mode of liberation, according to the great meditators, liberation upon recognizing thoughts and emotions is the ordinary liberation of the common meditator. In this meditation, we can experience an immense clarity of mind, because no appearances are being perceived through the sense faculties. Therefore, consciousness becomes increasingly clear and bright. But attachment to this meditative experience belongs to the worldly meditative Samadhis of the formless realms.

It is essential to recognize the way we liberate thoughts. Of the first, second and third modes of liberation, the first mode of liberation is the lowest. An ordinary meditator can achieve this, but it can easily be mistaken with the ordinary samadhis of the formless realm. In the second mode of liberation, we do not need to bring about external remedies to liberate our thoughts and emotions. They are freed on their own, on the spot. There is a quotation from Padmasambhava which says, "With meditation, enlightenment is there for everyone, without meditation, enlightenment is there only for me." "With meditation" refers to fabricated, deliberate meditation, "without meditation" refers to spontaneous meditation, without any deliberate effort.

We have created the wheel of samsara with our mind, but to abandon it, we do not need to recreate the wheel of nirvana, or, in other words, something that is opposed to samsara. Because, if we create such a nirvana with the same mind, that nirvana would be quite like samsara. We have succeeded in creating samara with our discursive mind, but now that we are not fond of samsara any longer, we want to get rid of it by creating nirvana. But if the creator of nirvana is the same discursive mind, that nirvana is not much more than samsara.

In this kind of meditation, it is essential to recognize the self-arising and self-liberation of thoughts and emotions, without the need to use an external remedy to liberate them, so that they can be freed on their own. As an example, when a snake uncoils, we do not need to help the snake uncoil, the snake is both able to coil and uncoil its knot. When it uncoils, we can ask ourselves, where does the knot go?

It is critical to recognize the mode of self-liberation, how thoughts and emotions liberate by themselves. During meditation on the view, no matter what kind of discursive thoughts and emotions arise, whether they are subtle or coarse, every one of them will get liberated on their own. They vanish. It is like when snow falls on seawater. There is no need to help the seawater get rid of the snow, the snow dissolves and vanishes by itself. Also, a strong wind can create big waves on the ocean, but we do not need to bring the waves down. The waves will come down naturally. This is how it is.

The third mode of liberation is termed "Liberation without there being any benefit or harm." An example of this is the burglar who enters the empty house. The burglar is not benefited, because there is nothing to steal. The house is not harmed, because there is nothing to lose. This liberation is accomplished by developing this kind of lofty view. Here, we do not entertain any notion of hope and fear, particularly not any concerns over having something to lose, that somebody might harm us, or fearing that our discursive thoughts and emotions will hurt us.

Ordinarily, we hope that right thoughts and emotions will do us good. We fear misery and hope to experience happiness. So, hope and fear are always there. In other words, we have strong fixations and grasping. But when we realize the Dzogchen view accurately, such strong, powerful grasping becomes increasingly weaker. It is like the example of a corpse at a cemetery. Even if hundreds of murderers surround a corpse at a cemetery, the body fears nothing. Because it is a corpse, it merely lies there. It has no conceptual thoughts like "I will be burned in a fire" or "I will be eaten by wild animals." All hopes and fears become liberated into the body of the dharmakaya.

Speech is said to echo mind. When a Dzogchen meditator passes out of this life, his or her body disintegrates into atomic particles, and their mind is liberated into the expanse of dharmakaya. As far as speech is concerned, he or she usually does not leave any testament behind. Patrul Rinpoche was skeptical of testaments left by certain Dzogchen masters. He believed that when a realized Dzogchen master dies, his body disintegrates into atomic particles, which means disappearing into the rainbow body, and the mind gets liberated into the expanse of dharmakaya, without the need for leaving any spoken testament. However, the Three Words that Strikes the Vital Point is said to be the testament of the Dzogchen master Garab Dorje. The difference, in this case, is that it was not left behind for any personal benefit. It was left behind to benefit others.

"Without this meditation, there will be delusion," means that if we do not grasp the meaning of the different ways in which liberation of thoughts occur, and persist in meditation, it is no guarantee that our meditation will liberate our mind.

Instead, our meditation will become part of the delusion. If we comprehend this instruction, and clearly remember the different levels of how liberation of thoughts occurs, then we are in the state of non-meditation, which is the dharmakaya. The text says, "When you have it, there is no meditation."

Question: This is not exactly related to what you were talking about, but I am unsure of the difference between terms like "rigpa's display," "the expression of rigpa," and "rigpa's adornment". Can you explain the differences?

Answer: I think these are English synonyms used by different translators. To understand these expressions, it is essential to realize the Buddha-nature, sugatagarbha, because the Buddha-nature is the root of everything. Rigpa is also a synonym for the Buddha-nature. The Buddha-nature has three distinctive attributes. It is essentially empty, its nature is clarity, and it is unobstructed. These three unique attributes are not dualistic, they are different aspects of the same reality, like the two sides of the same coin.

The term Buddha-nature is used to talk about it as an object. The term rigpa is used as a subjective experience. Rigpa means knowledge, and it also means to cognize. Rigpa cognizes Buddha-nature. In this way, rigpa becomes subjective, and Buddha-nature becomes objective. But there is no subject or object. Just for the sake of communicating the reality, we must resort to conceptual, dualistic language. Rigpa means aware, like being aware of specific objects. The object, in this case, is Buddha-nature. Buddha-nature is not an object, and rigpa is not a subject, but for the sake of communication, we must resort to language limitations. Rigpa can also become dualistic because when we say rigpa, it simultaneously implies "ma-rigpa." Ma-rigpa means negating rigpa, which means not knowing. If we know Buddha-nature, that is enlightenment. If we do not know Buddha-nature, that is un-enlightenment. Buddha-nature is also sometimes termed dharmakaya. Dharmakaya is another synonym for Buddha-nature.

The wisdoms which correspond to each of the five Buddhas are all different aspects of the single Buddha. We could also say different aspects of Buddha-nature. Buddha-nature, as described earlier, is emptiness, clarity, and unobstructed compassion. But these three are not separate features. They are dependent on each other. They are integral. The combined term for this is svabhavikakaya. In our case, when we are unenlightened, these three bodies of the Buddha, the three kayas, are correlated with our body, speech, and mind. Our three-fold body, speech, and mind are not separable. They are different aspects of one person. Likewise, the three kayas of a Buddha are not separable. They are various aspects of an enlightened being.

The Tibetan word for the synonymous terms "adornment" of rigpa, "expression" of rigpa, and "display" of rigpa is "tsal." It means that thoughts and emotions represent the dynamic playfulness of the mind, as the expressions of the empty mind. The nature of mind is not stale, it is entirely dynamic, and this dynamism expresses the energy of mind as all kinds of thoughts and emotions. Perhaps we could say that the ordinary mind can be both like a god and a devil. Maybe it would be easier to understand the mind in this way. If we claim the original purity of the mind, then we end up becoming a god ourselves. But if we get stuck with any secondary impurity, then we end up becoming a devil.

Sometimes it is difficult to understand physical things, but the mind is even more baffling. The mind has no color or shape, so it is difficult to describe. When we meditate, we look at our mind without reference to any subjects or objects. If we separate our experience into subject and object, meditation will be difficult. Sometimes I do meditation because the practice is important. We may visualize that we are Padmasambhava. But if we do this kind of meditation, we cannot be Padmasambhava in reality. We can meditate for a hundred years without improvement. Because when we arise from meditation, we are still ourselves. This means that if we meditate instead on the paramitas, wisdom or rigpa, we will understand more of the practice. We should think that the mind is Buddha and that the Buddha is mind, and then use our wisdom to look, check and experiment. This is a better way.

Hashang was a Chinese monk who came to Tibet and propounded a specific Buddhist view. There was not much difference between his view and the Dzogchen view, apart one crucial thing: In the Dzogchen view there is room for experimentation, but in Hashang's view, we are discouraged from experimenting with the mind or the view itself.

I remember, when I was twelve or thirteen years old, while I was in Dzogchen monastery, on the top of the mountain there was a famous cave. I was young when I went there for retreat. In the daytime, everything was beautiful and friendly, but at night I was feeling a little afraid. Strong wind blew, there was a lot of noise, and black shadows looking like animals or ghosts seemed to move about. So, I went inside the cave and shut the door. But being afraid, it was challenging to meditate, thinking there was something outside. At the time, I did not have any light. It was difficult. After about two hours, I became more and more afraid. But then I thought I should go outside to see what was happening. So, I took with me a stick, thinking there was a wild animal or something that wanted to catch me. But when I checked, I found that this shadow was a rock, and that shadow was some bushes. When I saw that everything was okay, that there were no ghosts, no animals, and that everything was safe, I went back into the cave and meditation was much better.

It is crucial that we understand emptiness and are sure about the view. If sometimes we have lots of thoughts arising while meditating, we may think we have lousy meditation, but the next day, if we experience no thoughts with everything very peaceful, we may think we are doing high-quality meditation. But, if we keep on in this way, then our whole life will be like good and bad, bad and good. It will never end, like day and night continually following each other. It is the same with feelings: feeling happy, unhappy, happy, unhappy. Sometimes I think that human beings are a little dull because sometimes we experience happiness, sometimes we experience suffering. It is like a continual changing answer to something; yes, no, yes, no.

It is challenging to overcome dualistic fixation and transcend beyond it. We are familiar with perceiving reality in a setting with subject and object, existence and non-existence, real and unreal, but we have a hard time transcending beyond this kind of dualistic thinking. If we were to introduce transcendental reality, it becomes difficult to both speak about it and understand it. It is a little bit like a small baby, who knows only two people, its parents. Similarly, we perceive reality, polarized into the duality of "this and that," but we do not know anything about the unelaborated, transcendental reality beyond that.

The realization of arhats and those on the shravakayana is said to be like the water contained in the footprint of an elephant. The spiritual realization of the Buddha is said to be like the whole ocean. If we compare our spiritual realization with that of the arhats, theirs will be huge, but the Buddha's realization becomes incomparable. The spiritual realization that we have is only a fraction of that. For example, we entertain all kinds of discursive thoughts and emotions, for instance, rambling thoughts about what is clean and what is unclean. There is also an intense fixation on what is happiness and what is unhappiness. We also fixate on what is impermanent and what is permanent, and on the difference between self and others. Of course, there is also strong fixation on the self.

When we work on the Buddhist path, it is good to follow the gradual path. We live in a modern era, in big cities, especially in Asia and Europe. People here are terribly busy, and it is difficult to find the spare time to complete ngöndro practice. Therefore, some lamas give exclusive permission to their students, so that they do not have to finish the preliminary practices but can delve directly into Dzogchen practice. But as far as Dzogchen practice itself is concerned, no-one is exempt from completing the preliminary foundational practices. It is also important to gather the necessary theoretical knowledge of what we are meditating on, and then try this out in our mind, reflect on it and contemplate. When we gain certainty, we combine this with meditation. The Dzogchen teaching is not like food served in a restaurant. We must be the chef ourselves, cook it, and eat it as well. Even a lama cannot be a chef and prepare the Dzogchen view to spoon-feed us. We must feed ourselves. The lama can only help us, but he cannot force-feed us.

The Buddha himself said that the Buddha does not wash away our sins or remove our suffering with his hands. The Buddha also does not transfer his spiritual realization directly to the student in a literal manner. But how can he help us, if he cannot clean our sins or remove our suffering with his bare hands? The Buddha can help us by revealing to us the methods of the Dharma. If we work at these methods, we will be able to help ourselves. This does not mean that the Buddha lacks loving-kindness and compassion. He has tremendous love and compassion, but in the final analysis, we must help ourselves.

For example, a dirty mirror cannot reflect an object placed in front of it properly. Likewise, if there are a lot of blockages and conditioning in our minds, we will not be able to reflect reality as it is. Therefore, it is essential to purify these blockages and conditioning by accumulating merit by using conventional Dharma practices. No doubt we would like to experience the clear-light of the mind, and of course, we would like to have the vision of "thigles," light spheres, in the expanse of the dharmata. But if different levels of obscurations block our energy, it will be challenging to have togal visions if we do not purify obscurations through conventional Dharma practice.

Purifying obscurations through accumulating merit should be done regularly throughout our daily activities. Conventional Buddhist practice is to go for refuge to the Three

Jewels and engender the will to become enlightened to benefit all living beings. Early in the morning, when we get up from our bed, we can form the altruistic attitude "Today, may I be able to deploy my threefold body, speech, and mind for the benefit of others." Our aspiration can be to help somebody mentally, physically, or vocally, as well as to help them to create merit, because a person with merit will achieve a higher vision of the absolute truth. For a person without merit, it is tough to create a view of absolute reality.

These conventional practices should not be overlooked because they help us to bring forth the deeply buried Buddha-nature. At the end of the day, when we are about to fall asleep, instead of feeling guilty about what we have done in the past, or anxiety about the future, we can mentally review what kind of good and bad deeds we have done during the day. If we have done good deeds, we can take delight in them and dedicate the merit for the benefit of all beings. If we discover that we have done wrong deeds, we can respond by feeling regret, and pledge that we are not going to repeat the same mistakes. In this way, we purify sinful acts and ensure that we can fall asleep without their adverse effects, so that we do not have to carry negative karma into our sleep and the next day. In this way, formal practice of bodhicitta comes down to developing an altruistic mindset "May I be able to use my body, speech, and mind to be of service to others."

Epilogue

It is crucial that we apply the three words that strike the vital points of view, meditation, and action. Other essential aspects of the Dharma will also serve to lay a foundation for us to actualize the view. When we realize the view, we will meet the original face of dharmakaya. This will give us a compassionate heart towards all. This is the meaning of the following statement in the root text, "For the view which has the three vital points, meditation, the union of wisdom and love..." From our insight into the view springs the union of wisdom and love. Wisdom is the knowledge aspect that sees the view. Love is the emotional aspect that radiates outwardly towards other living beings. These two, the wisdom aspect of the cognitive mind and the loving aspect of the emotional mind, are inseparable.

The final fruition of this meditation on the view is to attain what is known as non-localized nirvana, sometimes referred to as non-abiding nirvana. The radiance of loving-kindness and compassion will prevent enlightened beings to enjoy the one-sided extreme of the peace of nirvana for themselves. The realization of wisdom by gaining insight into the view will prevent such enlightened beings from falling into extreme peace of nirvana. In this way, the fruition of the practice at the highest level dawns as what is known as non-localized nirvana. When the root text continues, "...is accompanied by the action common to all the bodhisattvas," it refers to the actions of the bodhisattvas. These actions are the six transcendental virtues, the paramitas. Practicing the paramitas enables such a person to gather merit and wisdom that will further enhance the realization of the view.

This text is very brief, but the content is very profound and extensive. Patrul Rinpoche says that this theme is the heart essence of the lineage. He regards this pith instruction to be a revealed treasure. This treasure is brought forth from the depth of transcendental insight by the treasure revealer (Tib. tertön) of dharmakaya, the inner power of rigpa.

A treasure revealer needs to have a quality of profound insight. Not just any treasure revealer can reveal such a concealed treasure and realize the ultimate Dzogchen view. What Patrul Rinpoche is saying is that such a treasure does not compare to an ordinary treasure, dug out from earth or rock. Ordinary treasures revealed by average minds can only give temporary relief from the difficulties and pain of living beings. However, this treasure will relieve the frustration of samsara entirely. The richness of this transmission will help us to meet directly the original nature of primordial purity and realize the view. This treasure will help us to strip bare the original purity of rigpa.

Patrul Rinpoche says that the genesis of this treasure comes from the great Dzogchen teacher Garab Dorje and that this treasure was his final testament when he entered parinirvana, in other words, when he departed from this life. From a cloud of rainbows in the expanse of the sky, a voice bestowed this teaching on his immediate student Manjushrimitra. Then the transmission of this testament came down to another great Dzogchen master, the Great Longchen Rabjam. He further transmitted it to one of his distant students, Jigme Lingpa, while appearing as an emanated body. Finally, the transmission of the lineage came all the way to the direct guru of Patrul Rinpoche, and then to Patrul Rinpoche himself. Therefore, the transmission of this lineage has the blessing of the three lineages that came down from these three great masters. In this manner, the original transmission of this lineage has been passed down until now. Therefore, as we have had the chance to come across it, expound on it, and listen to it, we should think about it and put it into practice.

Patrul Rinpoche was one of the lamas that came from Dzogchen Monastery in Kham in Tibet. I have studied, reflected and meditated at the seat of Dzogchen Monastery for many years. Therefore, this instruction possesses, as the root text says, "The essence of the wisdom mind of the three transmissions. It is entrusted to my heart students, sealed to be secret." We may want to be his heart students or not. If we do, we should do so by studying, meditating and reflecting upon these instructions. The text says, "to my heart students, sealed to be secret," This means it should be kept secret from those who are only curious about the Dharma, but not from those who want to put it into practice. Even when we expound on these instructions, it is rather difficult to understand the meaning. In some way, the content is self-secret, even when it is explained. The Buddha summarizes the ultimate meaning of emptiness in the Heart Sutra. Many of us chant the Heart Sutra, but very few of us understand its profound meaning, let alone realize it. In that respect, even the Heart Sutra is self-secret. We do not need to keep it secret, because the content is not revealed very easily.

He concludes with the following few lines, "It is profound in meaning, my heart's words. It is the words of my heart, the crucial key point. This crucial point: Treasure it. Never let this instruction slip away from you." If we adhere to this advice, we will become suitable vessels, and we will become heart students of this great master. The reason behind such a statement is to show that this instruction is tremendously valuable. We should not just stop at theoretical knowledge, but think about the view, meditate on it, and bring it into our daily activities.

For example, in China, parents take quite good care of their children, not only when they are small. The parents will bring up their child and pay all their expenses. But by giving their child too many material gifts, the child becomes spoiled and takes the things it gets from its parents for granted. They do not see the value of the help they are getting. Likewise, Patrul Rinpoche has spent many years in solitude, meditating, contemplating, and attained the realization of such a view. His spiritual realization is transmitted by composing these instructions to us. We should treasure them as invaluable, behold them with utter care, and put them into practice.

This concludes the elucidation of Patrul Rinpoche's commentary to the root text *Hitting the Essence in Three Words* that strikes the three vital points of view, meditation, and action. I hope that you will be able to understand and meditate on the threefold view, meditation, and action as it is presented here. Perhaps you can read the root text as a prayer for some time. You can combine it in your regular sitting meditation and read it with the prayers until it sinks into your mind.

Patrul Rinpoche said that if the buddhas of the three times were to have a meeting and discuss what would be the most effective instructions to impart for the benefit for all living beings, they would not be able to find an instruction that is more practical and beneficial than the instructions presented in this text.

Guru Yoga

Since we now have received these instructions, and established a spiritual connection to the transmission, we should put effort into actualizing the clear-light mind of rigpa. How can we meditate on these instructions in formal sessions? We can begin formal meditation sessions with the usual practice of going for refuge to our spiritual ideals, the Buddha, Dharma, and Sangha, and then cultivate the will for supreme enlightenment, bodhicitta. We can then practice the cultivation of immeasurable loving kindness, compassion, joy, peace, and equanimity. After that, we can do a short guru yoga, which can be summarized in one simple line, in Tibetan, "lama chenno," which in English means "The lama knows." You can recite it three, six or nine times.

Earlier, we talked about the causal conditions that give rise to the realization of the view. It has been stated that other than the methods of accumulating merit and purify obscurations, plus devotion towards our spiritual ideal, the guru, there is no other method for realizing the view of primordial purity. Therefore, our meditation practice on the view should be preceded by taking refuge, bodhicitta, and guru devotion by reciting Lama Chenno.

Invoking the compassionate wisdom mind of the guru with this mantra can be viewed as a supplication towards our spiritual guide. Whether we manage to attract the blessings of the guru or not, depends very much on the devotion we cultivate in the supplication. The supplication, the guru mantra, can be sung melodiously. We do not only try to invoke the guru from the outside, but we also try to invoke the deep confidence within ourselves towards our spiritual guide. There are a few different melodies, depending on the various schools and traditions.

The Nine Cycles of Breathing Exercises

Following the invocation of the guru, it is a good idea to purify the stale air with the nine cycles of breathing. The instructions in the text tell us first to relax our body, speech, and mind. Purifying the stale air through the nine cycles of breathing will help us to render our body, speech, and mind at ease, in a state of relaxation.

Within our grosser nervous system, there is a structure of a subtle nervous system. It consists of the central channel, and the right and left channels. We will do the nine cycles of breathing as follows. We will alternate the nostril through which we breathe in and out by using our index finger. First three times in through the left nostril and out of the right nostril. Then three times in through the right nostril and out of the left nostril. We close the appropriate nostril by using our index finger, with the other fingers clenched in a fist. For the last three in and out breaths, we place the tip of our thumb on the base of the ring finger of our right hand and close the remaining four fingers over it, making a vajra fist. The back of this hand is then placed at the base of the thigh, and the arm and upper body are straightened. Some teachers teach the positioning of the hands in a very elaborate manner, but we do not have to go through that. We can do it like this.

When we breathe in, we close our eyes and mouth and then take a deep in-breath through the nose. Breathing out will push out all the stale air within our nervous system. Then we breathe in again, going through the same cycle.

To recapitulate, we start the deep in-breath through our left nostril, by blocking the right nostril with the index finger. Then the out-breath is pushed out through the right nostril. This also has the practical benefit of clearing our nose. It is a good idea to have a tissue at hand, just in case. We ventilate the stale air three times by breathing in through the left nostril and out through the right nostril. Then we reverse the order, and to do this, we must shift the position of the index finger. Repeat in the same manner, altogether, six times. During the third round, we do not block either of the nostrils, just breath in and out through both nostrils. During the third set, we place the back of both hands on the bases of the thighs and straighten the body as before. We repeat the whole procedure three times.

While we breathe, we do the following visualization. The tips of the right and left channels start from the right and left nostrils. The air energy that is inhaled passes through the left and right channels, all the way down into their bottom, where the ends of the side channels go into the central channel. The air that is brought in now moves up through the central channel, all the way to the top of the head. When the air moves, we should place close attention to the ascending and descending winds within the subtle nervous system in our visualization.

Having finished the whole procedure, we allow our body, speech, and mind to relax, and then sit at ease. This method will, to a certain extent, pacify the grosser or coarser aspects of rambling thoughts and emotions. The physical posture can be a little different from the usual meditation posture, by placing both palms on the knees. Unless the grosser aspects of the discursive thoughts are pacified, it is difficult to meet the original face of rigpa. This is because the grosser emotions obstruct us from seeing it.

When meditating, we will either experience stillness or some disturbance. As said previously, both the silence and movement of the mind should be viewed as the face of rigpa, as a natural expression of dharmakaya.

We can occasionally shout P'ET to disrupt deliberately our meditative experiences of clarity and non-conceptuality. Shouting P'ET helps us to interrupt any conceptually fabricated meditation, which is not a spontaneous meditation. The sound of the mantric syllable P'ET also has the practical benefit of separating the husk from the grain, meaning it will separate the obscuring factors from the original face of rigpa.

In this manner, we can try to sustain the original view of the rigpa that is being introduced and recognize it as much as we can. In the beginning, it is important to distance ourselves from all commotions and things that distract our mind. It also helps to simplify our lifestyle and activities as much as we can.

We can, for example, perform a one-week solitary retreat doing this, or even a one- or two-year retreat, where we do not have to engage in other activities, devoting all our time to this practice. To do so we need to distance ourselves and abandon all forms of commotion and distractions until we attain stability in this meditation. Once this is attained, we will not be affected by disturbances.

When we attain stability in this meditation, the dividing line between formal meditation and post-meditation collapses. Whether we are meditating or not, we will always be in a continuous state of meditation. We also must take into consideration how we conduct our body, speech, and mind in our daily life because activities in post-meditation serve as support for developing the view. At the end of a formal meditation session, we go through the practice of dedication. We distribute the merit and wisdom that we have gathered through our efforts to attain supreme enlightenment for the benefit of all living beings. We can also do aspirational prayers.

In brief, our realization of the view should not be divorced from the three vital points. Our meditation should not be divorced from wisdom, compassion, and love, and our actions, especially during the post-meditation period, should not be divorced from the six transcendental virtues of the bodhisattvas, the paramitas.

Taking a break, we can stand up in a relaxed posture, then merely throw our arms from side to side around our body to loosen up, while we mentally let go of every concern, worry, and fixation. To do this, we first stand up with our feet firmly on the ground, with a bit of space between them. Then, we straighten the whole body. We now tell the mind to loosen the body, to relax and be at ease with itself. This relaxation is also good for general health. There has been done a scientific study on this exercise, and they discovered that this reversed the aging of the arteries. When you do this exercise, be careful not to tense the upper part of the body, like the shoulders and neck—just let them completely loose. Let your body be so free that you are almost not able to hold it upright. Many people experience muscular tension, especially in the upper part of the chest, around the neck, or around the shoulders due to too much thinking and worries. Now, swing your arms loosely from side to side, letting them fold naturally around your body. Close your eyes while you do it. Do it for five minutes.

Taking the Refuge Vow

The nature of the refuge vow is the commitment to the Buddha, Dharma, and Sangha. We decide to rely on the Buddha, and we aspire to become a Buddha ourselves. We choose the Dharma as the path. We see the Sangha as the fellow travelers on this path. When we go for refuge to the Sangha, we commit to communicating skillfully with our fellow travelers, seeing them as friends. Not as ordinary friends, but as Dharma friends on the path to enlightenment.

Early in the morning as soon as you get out of bed, recite the short refuge prayer, "namo Buddha, namo Dharma, namo Sangha," at least three times while you join your hands at your heart. The refuge prayer can also be combined with offering physical prostrations on the bed or in the room. Prostrations involve touching our hands at three regions of our body, forehead, throat, and heart, or the three chakras, crown chakra, throat chakra, and heart chakra. This symbolizes the enlightened body, speech, and mind. When we place our folded hands on the crown of our head, this symbolizes the crown chakra, touching the throat symbolizes the opening of the throat chakra, touching the heart symbolizes the opening of the heart chakra. Whereas if we touch our hands at the forehead, throat, and heart, this symbolizes the surrendering and purification of the body, speech, and mind. We can perform full-length prostrations, stretching out our whole body on the floor, or we can offer half-prostrations.

Towards the end of the day, when we have gone to bed, just before we fall into slumber, we can do the practice of going for refuge by reciting the short or medium length refuge prayer, possibly also combining it with three prostrations. Those of us who have gone for refuge should adhere to this minimum practice each day, reciting the refuge prayer three times in the morning and three times before going to bed. The recitation of the refuge prayer reminds us of the enlightened attributes of the enlightened beings, who are our spiritual ideals. It also helps us to develop devotion to relate to them from the heart.

When students perform the refuge ceremony, they repeat three times: namo Buddha ya, namo Dharma ya, namo Sangha ya. And then three times: namo Guru dev, namo Deva dev, namo Dakini dev. And then "lek-so." At the very instant the students say lek-so, they receive the transmission of the refuge vow. We should try to preserve the transmission of the refuge vow that we have received throughout our life. We have committed to the three spiritual jewels, Buddha, Dharma, and Sangha. The Buddha as the teacher, the Dharma as the path, and the Sangha as the spiritual fellowship. As part of the refuge ceremony, you will get a few strands of your hair cut off. You will be asked in Tibetan, "Are you happy that I am cutting off a few strands of your hair?" and you can answer "I am delighted." Cutting a few strands of hair is symbolic. It symbolizes cutting through the obscuration from seeing the primordial purity of the mind. There are three levels of obscurations, emotional obscurations, cognitive obscurations, and the deeply hidden dispositional obscurations. Then you will be given a refuge name. You should remember it. The refuge name is your Dharma name, and you may want to be able to tell somebody it later.

I think that taking the refuge vow is to orient ourselves towards the safe direction of the Buddha, Dharma, and Sangha. Ordinarily, when we talk about going for refuge, it is understood as converting to Buddhism, but it means orienting ourselves toward the safe direction of the Buddha, Dharma, and Sangha. That said, it also involves committing to becoming a Buddha ourselves. To commit to becoming a Buddha, we determine to work on the path of Dharma. Usually, we are not able to work on the path effectively just by ourselves. Most practitioners need to work in fellowship with like-minded people and talk to someone who has more experience than themselves, like our teachers. This is the meaning for going for refuge to the Sangha. When we say, "going for refuge to the Buddha, Dharma, and Sangha," what we are saying is, "I commit to becoming a Buddha myself and work on the path of the Dharma, in fellowship with other like-minded people."

Conclusion

I am delighted to have come to Norway, to see Lama Changchub, Karma Tashi Ling and the Sangha group. I want to say thank you to Lama Changchub who invited me to come here, to Karma Tashi Ling Sangha, and to you, who came here to listen to the Dharma teaching.

I think Norway is an excellent country. You have a good government and a good environment. Everything is perfect. You also have a very compassionate lama, Lama Changchub. There is also a significant change here; you now have a magnificent temple. So, I hope a lot of people will come here in the future to practice and learn the Dharma, and that the

Sangha group will develop in the future.

Life is short, and we should learn how to practice, not only from teachings, but also remember to learn from the compassion of our teacher. If our teacher is very compassionate, we can learn it too. When we rely on the spiritual guide, or lama or guru, even if the lama happens to be very articulate and well versed in the Dharma, our priority should not be to learn about the theoretical aspect of the Dharma that the lama embodies. We should concern ourselves with learning the spiritual qualities of loving-kindness and compassion, as well as the wisdom that the lama represents.

The main thing is to put Dharma into practice. The criteria for being a good practitioner is not whether we are well versed in Dharma or not. The criteria for whether we are a good practitioner or not, is whether we can integrate our knowledge of Dharma into our daily life and practice it or not.

I am delighted with you all, and I hope that in the future I will be able to learn more English so that I can teach without translation. I have wanted to do this for the last eighteen years, but still, my English is not that good. But I know, when I start to learn, I can learn quite fast. When I now teach in Mandarin, it is the same as teaching in Tibetan. It is straightforward. But English is more difficult for me. During these four days of teaching with a translator, I understand about eighty percent of what is being translated. When Boyce was here, I could determine the quality of his translation, and I could detect if something were left out. Also, Lama Changchub is an excellent translator, but sometimes he forgets what I have said. Translation is a complicated process. Many of the teachers that come here speak English very well, and it is only me that he must help. Lama Changchub also teaches on his own and speaks English very well. So, I hope that in the future, I too will be able to speak English well. Thank you, everybody!

Made in the USA
Middletown, DE
10 February 2023